This is a volume in the
Arno Press collection

HISTORY OF MANAGEMENT THOUGHT

Advisory Editors
Kenneth E. Carpenter
Alfred D. Chandler

Consulting Editor
Stuart Bruchey

See last pages of this volume
for a complete list of titles

THE PHILOSOPHY
OF MANAGEMENT

THE PHILOSOPHY
OF MANAGEMENT

OLIVER SHELDON

ARNO PRESS
A New York Times Company
New York • 1979

58331

Publisher's Note: This book has been reproduced from the best available copy.

Editorial Supervision: BRIAN QUINN
Reprint Edition 1979 by Arno Press Inc.

Copyright 1923, by Prentice-Hall, Inc.

Reprinted by permission of Pitman Publishing Limited

Reprinted from a copy in the Library of the University of Illinois

HISTORY OF MANAGEMENT THOUGHT
   AND PRACTICE
ISBN for complete set: 0-405-12306-X
See last pages of this volume for titles.

Manufactured in the United States of America

———————

Library of Congress Cataloging in Publication Data

Sheldon, Oliver.
   The philosophy of management.

   (History of management thought)
   Reprint of the ed. published by Prentice-Hall, New York.
   Includes bibliographical references.
   1. Industrial management. I. Title. II. Series.
[HD31.S44 1979]   658'.001   79-7555
ISBN 0-405-12341-8

THE PHILOSOPHY
OF MANAGEMENT

THE PHILOSOPHY
OF MANAGEMENT

BY

OLIVER SHELDON, B.A. (Oxon.)

LONDON
SIR ISAAC PITMAN & SONS, LTD.
PARKER STREET, KINGSWAY, W.C.2
BATH, MELBOURNE, TORONTO, NEW YORK
1924

To

MY FATHER

FOREWORD

" Less is known, comparatively, of management than any other division of business activity. Judged purely by results, management, in the average understanding of the term, is a failure the world over. Mechanical wonders, scientific wonders, chemical marvels there are galore, but the science of management has yet to rise to the technique of an approach to scientific method. It is in its infancy.

" Business organization has not only had to deal with far greater aggregations of workers than ever before, but it also has had to deal with personalities far more intricate and self-willed than ever before. There being no longer possible a refined species of enslavement and exploitation of workers, management becomes more and more a study of personality, humanities, spirit, organization, leadership, development, reward, etc."

These words taken from J. G. Frederick's book on *Business Research and Statistics*[1] are profoundly true.

Industrial management is only just coming to be regarded as a science, and moreover one which no employer can afford any longer to neglect. The present economic condition of the world, and the urgent demand of the workers that they shall not be obliged to return to pre-war industrial conditions, both render a study of management methods particularly urgent at the present time.

It is imperative to eliminate all waste from industry. At present there is a vast amount of it due to bad managerial methods. Employers are too prone to devote all their attention to casting the mote out of the worker's eye, when really it would pay them much better to work at removing the beam from their own.

We need all the enthusiasm and effort which the workers

[1] The Library Press Ltd., London.

vii

can give—we need the most cordial co-operation between all who are engaged in industry, but we shall fail to secure these essential things if the framework within which industry functions is ill constructed.

Mr. Sheldon's book is a valuable contribution to the development of a better managerial practice.

No one who reads it can fail to grasp the principles which underlie good management. And the author recognizes that business has a soul ; that it is not a sordid mechanical thing, but a living and worthy part of the social organism.   It is not an end in itself but a means to an end, and that end is the well-being of the whole community. Any mechanical efficiency which takes no account of the personality and well-being of every person involved, stands self-condemned.

I wish every industrial administrator in the country could read this book.   It would vastly increase his sense of the dignity and the responsibility of his work, and open up to him great fields which it would amply repay him to explore.

                          B. SEEBOHM ROWNTREE.

AUTHOR'S PREFACE

MANAGEMENT in industry at the present time has the blood of a new youth coursing through its veins. It is full of a new vigour and a new enthusiasm. Its practice is being overhauled, both from the scientific and from the ethical points of view. Its performances are being weighed against, on the one hand, the standards set up as a result of scientific analysis; on the other, the standards established by a reinvigorated social conscience. Both as a productive enterprise and as a social trust, it is discovering fresh peaks to scale, and, with the energy born of new objectives, is branching out in this direction and in that, in pursuit of this theory and that principle, in the hope of finding some pathway to follow. Its personnel is also rapidly changing. It is absorbing some of our best brains ; it is marshalling in its ranks both scientists and artists, teachers and theorists, educationists and engineers. It is offering wider responsibilities and requiring more expert practitioners. As the barque of industry grows daily more heavily freighted, and ploughs through seas of increasing storminess and danger, the task of steering that barque is proportionately increased in complexity and responsibility. Perhaps even more significant than the imperial march of Labour in our day is the bugle-call which has wakened the camp of Management to the prodigious activity of an advance.

The danger for Management is a lack, not of activity, but of a plan of action. In the process of development, there is the danger lest the trees should blind us to the forest. Management is elaborating planning systems, employment departments, welfare schemes, time studies, foremen's development courses, costing systems, research bodies, and a thousand and one other branches of activity. With such an outlay of energy, it is essential that there should be an accompanying direction of that energy to some definite goal, and the development of a sense of the underlying causes which render these phenomena ultimately explicable. It is for this reason that the term " philosophy " has been introduced into the title of this book. Philosophy is the postulation of a vast query, which dwarfs into comparative nothingness the problems of day-to-day things. It demands of us whether we are conducting our practice according to any principles or laws, or merely snatching at the floating straws which pass. Whilst busying ourselves with the details of this expansion of Management, it would be fatal were none to query its purpose and inwardness. Have we linked all our new developments to some fundamental conviction and reviewed them in the light of some ultimate purpose ? Or, are we mere opportunists of a day—content that enough for the day is the good thereof that we can attract to ourselves—content that, if a new tree be planted and fostered into growth, it matters nought of the forest ?

It is in the belief that the direction of industry by that function broadly termed Management is a matter primarily of principles, both scientific and ethical, and only secondarily of the detail consequent upon the application of those principles that this book has come to be written. What follows, therefore, is not to be regarded as an exposition of any particular branch of Management, but rather as an attempt to define the purpose, the lines of growth, and the principles which shall govern the practice of Management as a whole.

In Chapter I, I have attempted to present a panoramic survey of the development of industry, noting those features in particular which appear to indicate the lines of progress in the future. In Chapter II, I review the fundamentals of Management itself, as one of the major partners in industry, tracing its gradual emergence from synonymy with Capital, and noting the effect upon its growth of the development of organized Labour. Management is a generic term, embracing many parts. I have, therefore, indicated the functions which it comprises, and the various human faculties necessary for the execution of those functions. The stability of Management is a point to be specially borne in mind. No matter what form industry may eventually assume, the guidance of industry must always belong to its management. In Chapter III, therefore, I have endeavoured to portray my conception of the responsibility of Management, both to the community which it serves and to the workers of all grades who constitute the human element in industry. A leadership, which is unaware of its responsibilities to the society of which it necessarily forms a part, cannot truly be said to contribute its full quota of efficient service. It is important, therefore, early in our consideration of Management in industry to insist that however scientific Management may become, and however much the full development of its powers may depend upon the use of the scientific method, its primary responsibility is social and communal. Its efficiency is to be judged, in fact, not only by scientific standards but also by the supreme standard of communal well-being. In Chapter IV, I consider the actual organization of the factory, based upon the divisions of Management advanced in Chapter II. It is contended that the organizing of the factory is not to be founded upon one principle alone, but on the union of several complementary principles. The functional form of organization must be tempered by certain features of the " Line and Staff," the " Departmental " and the " Committee " forms of organization. I have thought it worth while, at the end of this chapter, to point out certain analogies between the organization of the factory and the machinery of Government, with special reference to the Report of the Committee on the Machinery of Government, under the chairmanship of Lord Haldane (Cd. 9230, 1918).

Chapters V and VI are devoted to a broad consideration of the two main divisions of Management—the " Personal " and the "Impersonal" sides. Industry may broadly be said to consist of two comprehensive elements—the "personnel" of production and the "things" of production. Chapter V, accordingly, deals with Management in so far as it is called upon to manage men. Chapter VI deals with Management in so far as it is called upon to manage things. The former treats, therefore, of wages, employment work, economic security, welfare work, training and education, Trade Unions, and that basic principle of co-operation. The latter is concerned with research, costing, standardization, planning, and the co-ordination of all for the purpose of manufacture.

In Chapter VII, it is submitted that, for the proper execution of the duties of Management, as indicated in the preceding chapters, special training is indispensable. As Management becomes more complex and as its responsibilities increase, the practice of the profession becomes more difficult. A science of industrial management is developing before our eyes. Higher qualifications are accordingly requisite in those who apply the science and help in its development. This applies both to higl.er managerial officers, such as Works and Departmental Managers, and to junior managerial officers, such as foremen. I have, therefore, attempted to outline the mode of training and the subjects for study of both these groups. I have thought it desirable, moreover, to comment upon the new position of clerical work in industry, as a result of the new status of Management.

Finally, in Chapter VIII, I have emphasized the importance of recognizing that, in Management, we have the one stable element in the process of industrial evolution, and the consequent necessity of elaborating that which one may call its philosophy. I conclude, therefore, by stating as concisely as possible a suggested creed, as it were, by which the practice of Management in the future shall be governed.

In a survey of this kind, covering so wide a field, it has

not been possible to go into detail, or to support every contention by an array of facts. Indeed, to have done so would have obscured the main purpose. The detail is available in a hundred and one volumes. Here, my purpose has been to withdraw from the valleys, the towns, the roads and the fields, and, viewing the landscape from some delectable mountain, to muse awhile upon the answer to the deathless question which one generation hands on to another—Whither ?

In conclusion, my best thanks are due to Mr. B. Seebohm Rowntree for his kindly criticisms and invaluable advice, and to the members of his personal staff for many helpful suggestions.

OLIVER SHELDON.

CONTENTS

ILLUSTRATIONS

APPENDIX

THE PHILOSOPHY OF
MANAGEMENT

CHAPTER I

THE SOCIAL AND INDUSTRIAL BACKGROUND

SUMMARY

(a) The continuity of historical progress ; need for comprehension of the historical perspective. The general influences of social life upon industry—publicity, self-development, association, science.

(b) Development of general public knowledge of industrial affairs, preceded by the development of public intelligence, and emphasized by the war ; effect upon management.

(c) The new conception of work ; work for interest rather than profit ; recognition of the social value of recreation ; effect upon management.

(d) The spirit of association ; present disintegrating forces; the unrepresentative character of official Trade Unionism ; the opportunity of management to make the factory the basis of association.

(e) The growth of the scientific spirit, in both labour and management ; the possibility of a science of management.

(f) Need to survey the mentalities of Labour and Capital ; mentality of Labour cannot be judged either from the individual worker or from the Labour publicist. Distinction between " ferment " and the " mass." The character of the revolutionary spirit ; the effect of increased education. The ethical nature of Labour mentality. The change to industrial action. The power of Labour mentality ; its attitude to status and working conditions. The lesson for management.

(g) Capital as such has no mentality ; effect of joint-stock ownership ; need for making Capital human. The position of the director ; union of Capital and administration in the salaried director ; possibility of Capital becoming humanized.

(h) Essential humanity of industry ; the uneven development of material and human sides of industry ; need for a motive, leadership, and co-operation. The onus on management to set up the right ideal. Necessity for a renascence of public thought before industry can follow such an ideal.

LIKE the Napoleonic wars, which bridged the transition from the eighteenth to the nineteenth century, the war of 1914–1918, though it has introduced new elements into the factors determining our national progress, has not by any means swept away the problems which marked the beginning and dogged the steps of the preceding century. It has given us new viewpoints ; it has defined hitherto obscured peaks in the social landscape ; but the broad features of that landscape, for the most part, remain the same.

We have travelled fast ; in a few years, as in the era of the so-called Industrial Revolution, we have covered the normal advance of fifty, but at any point in that advance we can easily see how comparatively slight have been the changes effected, and how much of what existed still remains. However ardently we may search for a new world, we are ultimately compelled to look for its foundations in the debris of the past. Now, as throughout history, we cannot escape from the great evolutionary law of continuity.

I take up at random a collection of papers on the industrial situation in 1914. [1]   What are the subjects with which the writer deals ?   The causes of industrial discontent ; a national minimum wage ;   co-operation and profit-sharing ;   the problem of the unfit ;   the problem of unemployment ;   efficiency in production—the very subjects which are topics of discussion to-day.   The seven years from 1914 to 1921, even though they cover the crowded epoch of the war, represent but a short span in the life of industry.   Many of the prevalent writings, achievements and aspirations of our own day may be compared, for instance, on the political side, with the efforts of the Chartists of eighty years ago, and on the industrial side, with the theories and experiments of Robert Owen of a century ago.   Theories have grown into certainties, small beginnings have swollen into vast movements ; tentative experiments have become accomplished facts.   Changes have been effected rather by the ebb and flow of public opinion, sympathy and effort than by any new factors

[1] *The Way to Industrial Peace.*   By B. S. Rowntree.   (Fisher Unwin, 1914.)

which have definitely redirected the flow of progress. Certainly new factors have been introduced—electrical power, motor traction, new methods of production, fresh programmes of Labour emancipation, great advances in the framework of factory life—but these have only become fully operative through the growing adaptability of public opinion to new conditions. Without the growth of public opinion, economic and political progress is slow. Indeed, such progress is only as fast as public opinion can run.

We cannot hope, then, to grasp the significance of the modern conditions of industry unless we have at any rate a rough idea of the evolution of its main features. " A review of the process of historical evolution," says G. M. Trevelyan,[1] " teaches a man to see his own age, with its peculiar ideals and interests, in proper perspective as one among other ages." Before we plunge into the paths and by-paths of to-day we should gain that perspective, for the raw materials of yesterday are indeed the finished products of to-morrow. It is not enough to look at the one without the other. Nor indeed is it enough to survey one aspect of industrial life without viewing all. Before we can attempt to inquire into the philosophy of management, we must take a bird's-eye view of industry as a whole. Moreover, it is only the stern limit of space which forbids us to contemplate the entire panorama of the social life of which industry is an inherent part. In the past industry has suffered from too narrow a vision of itself. The worker has been regarded as a worker rather than a citizen. The vital relation of industrial production to the ordinary social life of the community has been obscured by years of comfortable complacency and moral respectability. Industry has been treated as incidental to rather than fundamental in the life of the community. This point is considered in a later chapter (*vide* Chapter III). For the moment we must endeavour to abstract from the

[1] *Clio—a Muse, and other Essays.* By G. M. Trevelyan. (Longman, Green & Co., 1913).

present welter of events and tendencies which affect industry .those positive features which appear the most significant, then view them in the light of their past development, and finally consider how far war conditions have altered them or how far public feeling has altered towards them.

In considering the present characteristics and tendencies of social life, though indeed its every murmur reacts upon the sensitive drum of the industrial ear, we can only hope to pick out the more direct of its influences on industrial life. We should also remember that those influences which now appear the most striking may not, from an industrial standpoint, be peculiarly significant. Events may appear great whose effects are truly negligible. " Compare, for example," says Mr. Townsend Warner, " the importance of the Great Fire of London in 1666 with the foundation of the Bank of England about thirty years later. The first left the trade of London paralysed, but only for a very short time , the second, intended to be nothing more than a temporary financial expedient, has ended by influencing profoundly the whole commercial system of the country, because its effects have been cumulative."[1]

What, then, are the features of the general life of our modern community, directly or indirectly affecting industry, which we may select as of enduring significance in relation to both the past from which they have developed and the future which they seem to predict ? We may summarize them under four headings—

(a) Publicity.   (b) Self-development.
(c) Association.   (d) Science.

By publicity, we mean a widespread public intimacy with the internal workings of industry. By self-development, we mean that spirit which is creating a new philosophy of work. By association, we mean the development of that spirit which is making in different groups for different

---

[1] *Landmarks in English Industrial History.* By G. Townsend Warner, M.A. (Blackie & Son, 1920, 11th edition.)

kinds of combination. By science, we mean not only the development of research in special fields, but also of a more widely diffused critical and analytical spirit.

It will be seen that in the above enumeration we take no account of those more immediate factors of our social life, such as the present financial situation, the growing responsibility of women, the challenging of our industrial supremacy in the world—factors which indeed will modify the structure of industry, but which for our present purpose may be regarded as subsidiary.

The remarkable development of general knowledge of industrial affairs during the past half-century is one of those significant facts, which, by its very ubiquity, fails to challenge attention. It is so intimate that we are inclined to overlook it ; yet it is fundamental. Not only is the worker in industry better informed on industrial affairs, but so is all that heterogeneous mass of the people outside industry. Some 30 per cent, at least, of the modern newspaper is devoted to industrial matters—arbitrations, conferences, strikes, inventions, legislation and theories. A far larger proportion of the population than ever before are shareholders in industrial concerns, in the affairs of which they naturally take an interest. As taxpayers, the general bulk of the people are increasingly constrained to look to industry for that trade revival which it is hoped will relieve their burden. As consumers, again, they turn to industry for that reduction in prices which it is anticipated will restore the social equilibrium.

The war emphasized this tendency. The general public became, as it were, shareholders in that vast enterprise which was co-ordinated under the Ministry of Munitions. It came to watch the work of the Control Boards as it watched the deeds of armies. With a strange sense of novelty, the nation realized, more vividly than ever before, its dependence upon the mills of the North, the foundries and shops of the Midlands, and the shipyards of the coast. It watched with eagerness the volume of industrial production, the doings of Labour and the efforts of Management. It became as familiar with works councils, industrial research, and bonus payments as with trench warfare, poison gas, and Cox's bank.

A long course of development of public intelligence, however, had preceded this intensification of public interest in industrial affairs. Popular elementary and adult education, the latter with a strong economic and social bias, had been sowing their seeds throughout the preceding century.[1] The growing tendency of the Universities to offer greater facilities for social and industrial students had contributed to the harvest, while the publicity afforded to Parliamentary papers and the Reports of Royal Commissions had brought the facts of industrial life within the reach of the general reader. The expansion and increasing urgency of industrial legislation swelled the movement, as did the activities of a Press increasingly alive to the pregnant significance of industrial affairs. To these influences must be added the effects of the spread of municipal enterprise since the 1835 Act,[2] the linking of industry and politics by the interworking of Trade Unions and the Labour Party, and the growth in numbers, organization and power of Trade Unions, Co-operative Societies, and Friendly Societies.

The confluence of all these educative forces, combined with many another less apparent factor, and emphasized by the peculiar conditions of the war, has finally resulted in a singular intimacy between industrial life and the general life of the nation, which is a phenomenon of our own age alone. This intimacy has reacted both upon industry and upon society generally. It has affected the individual both as a worker in industry and as a social unit. Again, not only is industry increasingly subject to the informed criticism of the community it serves, but

[1] The reader is referred to the first 29 pages of the Final Report of the Adult Education Committee of the Ministry of Reconstruction (1919). Cmd. 321.

[2] Municipal Corporations Act (1835).

the directors of industry are subject to the continual and searching criticism of those whom they direct.

The conduct of industry to-day is no longer to be regarded as a " trade secret " of directors and managers. The public, in its Parliament, its municipal bodies, its press, and its self-educative associations, is presenting a running fire of pertinent inquiries. The wage-earners are similarly questioning the policies, the ethics, the methods, and the organization of those who control the application of their labour. The social demand for publicity in all these matters is one of the most striking features of our time, a factor destined to change the whole face of industry. Business, once regarded as the mysterious occupation of a singularly prosperous body of individuals, is now coming to be judged by the efficiency of its service in production, and not by the prosperity of its owners.

The converse of this is also true. If industry may now and still more in the future be regarded as conducting its activities under the glare of the public searchlight, the awakening of public interest in industry, which first kindled the searchlight, also imposes new responsibilities upon the community. If the public demands more of industry, industry demands more from the public, since its efficiency depends to an increasing extent upon the general comprehension of industrial needs. If the public plays the searchlight upon industry, industry asks that what the searchlight reveals shall be impartially judged. In other words, if the relation of industry to the community is to be recognized as primarily one of service, industry stipulates that the community shall be a fair master. Hysterics about prices, profiteering, sweating, " ca canny," and Unionism are hardly proper to a community claiming the responsibility for the service which industry renders.

The increase of public interest in and consequent responsibility for industry has therefore profoundly ← influenced the practice of the art of industrial management, by establishing a relationship between the community and industry which must inevitably and increasingly modify the whole conduct of industrial enterprises.

The second general feature of modern society, immediately affecting industry, is the augmented sense of the desirability and instinctive need for self-development under incentives other than those governing daily work. We are witnessing a profound change in the conception of work. It is not that the members of society are less eager to exercise their faculties, but that they wish to do so without their livelihood depending upon it. Our allegiance is being transferred from the conception of work under the impulse of gain alone to that of work under the impulse of interest.

Wartime conditions materially aided in fostering this new conception of the motives which should govern the application of human effort. The majority of the nation turned their hands to tasks in which the motive of pecuniary profit, though often still operative, was shot through with the finer threads of a high incentive. The reversion after the war to conditions where personal gain once more becomes the dominant motive of work, has revealed a great lack in the general scheme of industry which the wartime motive had temporarily supplied. Mr. Bevin, national organizer of the Dockers' Union speaking at the Dockers' Inquiry (1920), said : " Labour has growing aspirations, and cultural development means as much to it as to the middle and upper classes." [1]

[1] The report in *The Times* of 7th Feb., 1920, reads as follows—
" Labour had growing aspirations, and cultural development meant as much to it as to the middle and upper classes. They were building for the workers houses with one living-room. That was an insult to them. The old parlour might have been disused, but it would be the workman's library of the future. If the Court refused this claim, it had one alternative. It must go to the Prime Minister and the Minister of Education and tell them to close the schools, that industry could only be run by reducing Labour to the pure fodder and animal basis. Teach the people nothing and let them learn nothing, for to create in their minds aspirations and the love of the beautiful, and at the same time to deny them the wherewithal to satisfy them, was a false policy and a wrong method, and it would be better to keep them in dark ignorance."

The remark is as true as it is significant. The worker in industry, in common with workers generally, is not content with earning his wages alone. He needs leisure in which to devote himself to other occupations whither his interests lead him. This need is in tune with the general tendency of our time to regard work for gain as but a subsidiary part of human activity. Recently, General Booth, after a tour of the world, commented upon the almost universal lack of a will to work.[1] What is indeed lacking is a reasonable incentive to work. Increased leisure has allowed the worker to become absorbed in tasks in which he can express himself far better than in the routine of the factory. He is beginning to see that, while he must earn a livelihood, work for the sake of his interest in it is a far more enthralling pursuit. Industry is therefore faced with the necessity either of capturing the interest of the workers, or of so functioning that they are allowed an increasing amount of leisure in which to pursue those activities where their interests lie. Either alternative lays upon industrial management an onus which it will tax its utmost capacity to bear.

The modern demand for that leisure which makes self-development possible, springs, moreover, not alone from the failure of the motive of gain, but also from the recognition of the social value of recreation. The modern philosophy of work suggests a fair allowance of time for recreation. This is a more recent development than is generally supposed. The Industrial Revolution made a clean sweep of the sports and pastimes of the bulk of the nation. A witness before the Commons' Committee on The Health of Large Towns in 1840,[2] in reply to a question regarding the amusements of Manchester, said :

[1] " I find in nearly every country there is emerging a kind of antipathy to work. It is a very serious danger, especially for the next generation, if we are going to cultivate the idea that there is something inimical to human life and happiness in work *per se*." —General Booth, as reported in *The Times*, 3rd Aug., 1920.

[2] *Vide, Life and Labour in the Nineteenth Century.* By C. R. Fay. Cambridge University Press, 1920.)

" None athletic, except when a number of the more disorderly stole off to the borders of Cheshire and Yorkshire—to have a ' mill ' as they called it." It is indeed only within the last fifty years that recreation has been regarded as a necessary complement of work. It has taken us a century, since 1819, to reduce the average working day by four hours ; and only within the last ten years have the more progressive industrial leaders realized that a portion of even so-called " working hours " must necessarily be regarded as recreational. In this respect, again, industrial management is faced with a developing situation, which is governed by factors which spread their roots far beyond the domain of industry. When the whole tendency of our age is to explore the place of recreation in the life of the individual, industry can no longer cling to such shibboleths as an " eight hour day " or " a forty-eight hour week." There is no divinity in a number, and it is useless for industry to fabricate a divinity to which the spirit of the community refuses to pay homage. Industrial management will be compelled to recognize that for its wage-earners, as for the community generally, adequate leisure for the pursuit both of non-remunerative work and of recreation must ultimately be assured.

The third general feature of our age, profoundly affecting industry, is the widespread spirit of association—not that association which is a natural human impulse, but that conscious and deliberate combination of individuals, having wide differences upon general matters amongst themselves, but possessing one or two views in common, for the purpose of furthering and strengthening those views through the augmented power derived from the bare fact of their association.

The nineteenth century witnessed the flowering of this spirit in every sphere of social activity. Trade unions, co-operative societies, friendly societies, political clubs, athletic clubs, charity organizations and religious associations sprang into being during the last century. Little could be done without forming a society to do it.   To-day the spirit of association is somewhat obscured by the fact that it has, as it were, over-reached itself, and is threatened by serious disintegrating forces.   The formation of societies and associations has, in the first place, resulted in diversity rather than unity.   The reasons for which associations have been formed have become so numerous and so detached from one another that an individual may belong to several forms of association.   Instead of uniting large masses of men, therefore, the spirit of association has often tended to divide society into a multitude of small groups based upon differences of opinion, locality, and interests.

In industry, the reverse of this may appear to be the case, in view of the amalgamations and agreements between unions on the one hand, and on the other between groups of employers.   Such amalgamations, however, are largely the tactical moves of the executive officers of associations, and do not truly represent popular tendencies.   When an association for any purpose is first formed it is normally carried forward by the impetus of its supporters.   As it develops, however, it is compelled to fashion a constitution and build up an organization according to the objects it has in view, until the point is reached where its supporters find themselves divorced from governance through the inevitable intervention of the very organization which they have created.   Increasing subdivision necessarily takes place, and everywhere elected executive bodies or appointed officials come between them and the objects for which they stood.   We find, therefore, that this spirit of association tends to be increasingly circumscribed by the organization which it calls into being, with the result that, on the one hand, there is a tendency towards subdivision, and, on the other, a tendency towards the usurping of authority by the executive officers of the association.   Amalgamations of industrial associations, consequently, whether of Labour or of Capital, are generally carried out on account of the tactical gains to be secured rather than because of a natural and spontaneous impulse on the part of the members.

This is particularly the case as regards the Trade Unions. The tendency towards amalgamations and agreements between unions [1] is the result of organization deliberately planned by the heads of the unions concerned, and does not to any perceptible degree arise from the spontaneous desire of the members. It is, in fact, not truly the outcome of the spirit of association, but an administrative change for tactical reasons, rendered possible largely by the apathy of the members. In consequence, there has been a reaction against skeleton organizations which do not represent the pith and marrow of the membership—a reaction which is evidenced by such recent developments as the Shop Stewards movement, the constant bickering between unions, unauthorized strikes, secessions of union branches, antagonism to union leaders, and the collapse of the Triple Alliance. [2]

[1] *Cf.* (a) Amalgamation of Co-operative Emplòyees' Union, the Shop Assistants Union, and Warehouse Workers' Union. (1920.)
(b) Amalgamation of Amalgamated Society of Carpenters and Joiners and General Union of Carpenters and Joiners into the General Union of Carpenters and Joiners. (June, 1920.)
(c) Amalgamation of Amalgamated Society of Engineers and ten smaller engineering societies into the Amalgamated Engineering Union. (July, 1920.)
(d) The new constitution of the Trade Union Congress, under which is appointed a General Council of Labour. (1921.)
(e) Amalgamation of National Federation of Women Workers with the National Union of General Workers. (Feb., 1921.)
And many other similar amalgamations and agreements.

[2] *Cf.* (a) Opposition of Port Sunlight co-partners to National Association of Carpenters and Joiners. (Nov., 1919.)
(b) Secession of the Welsh Branch of the National Union of Clerks. (July, 1920.)
(c) Unauthorized strike of Manchester compositors. (Aug., 1920.)
(d) Unauthorized strike of N.A.U. of Engineers and Firemen, at Sheffield. (June, 1920.)
(e) Dispute between National Union of Railwaymen and Amalgamated Engineering Union. (Feb., 1921.)
(f) Repudiation of agreement by operative spinners at Oldham. (Sept., 1920.)
(g) Break-up of the amalgamation of the Boiler-makers' Society with the Sheet and Iron Workers' and Light Platers' Society, formed in Sept., 1919. (Dec., 1921.)
And many other similar disruptive indications.

To-day, then, we are witnessing an intensification of the original spirit of association. The common interests upon which any association is based are being drawn within a smaller circumference. The tendency is to resent the imposition of organizations which either do not represent the movements among the mass of the adherents or are too remote from the personal feelings and opinions of individuals. There is a growing feeling that the officers of a large association may come to represent an outlook remote from that of its membership. It is significant that in 1918 the Labour Party permitted individual membership as distinct from membership through trade associations, thereby giving official recognition to the fact that the Trade Unions, affiliated socialist societies, and co-operative societies did not wholly represent the opinions of those supporting the cause of Labour.

This recent development of the spirit of association in industry, reflecting as it does a similar development outside industry, places the problem of the Trade Union and the Employers' Federation in a new light, especially for those engaged in industrial administration. An association, to be vigorous and effective, must faithfully reflect the will of its adherents and form an intimate part of each adherent's interests. Mankind, as a whole, is instinctively communally-minded. Industrial management is thereby presented with the opportunity of making the factory rather than the class the basis of association. Where large-scale association in Unions and Federations appears to be failing, the association which every factory can offer may fill the gap. For specific purposes, large-scale association may be necessary, but it is seldom spontaneous. The life of the factory, however, is more compact and less remote ; it may well, under judicious management, provide the true basis for spontaneous association. The most natural bond between individuals is that of co-operation in a common enterprise. Co-operation within factories is more natural than co-operation between classes, irrespective of factories. The bond which unites groups of workers in different factories, while it may be necessary, cannot provide the same simple and natural co-operation as the bond of common factory life. Industrial management should realize that there is nothing incompatible between the association of the workers in the communal life of the factory and their association, in a more remote and impersonal way, for the achievement of specific objects affecting their class.

The fourth general feature of modern social developments which has a definite effect upon industry is the growth of that analytical and critical spirit usually termed " scientific." There is no need to stress the patent fact that we live in a scientific age—an age which bases its beliefs and actions rather upon ascertained and proven facts, than upon faith, tradition, or habit. The present age, indeed, cannot pretend that all its beliefs and actions are actually as yet thus based ; its attitude may be described as inquisitive rather than synthetical. Its mark in history will be a large question-mark—the mark of a generation determined that the beliefs and life of the future shall rest upon a sounder foundation of truth.

This spirit of inquiry—the same spirit as is dispassionately reviewing and analysing Church and State—is rapidly permeating industry. Labour is querying the ethical justification of the present industrial structure. It has established its research wing in order that its claims may be founded upon irrefutable facts. It is questioning the methods of management. Management, too, is querying its own methods. It is setting up new branches to test and analyse the facts of industry, both human and material. It is tending to base its policies upon definite information, to build its organizations in accordance with a scientific analysis of the work that they are called upon to perform, to control its manufacture by standards which are the outcome of precise inquiry and accurate measurement.

It is tending to adopt the scientific method of analysis and synthesis in all branches of management, and to make continuous provision for the observation and recording of facts. It is marshalling, comparing, and weighing its facts before formulating and applying its principles.

The application of this movement of the social mind in the business of industrial management is one of the main justifications of this book. As a community, we are beginning to formulate a science for each branch of our communal activities. We are developing an engineering science, a theological science, a domestic science, and a social science. A science of management in industry is a natural outcome of our age. In the following chapters the idea of management as a science—a developing science —underlies every paragraph.

Before our review of management begins, however, it will be well to survey in brief the mentalities of the partners of management—Labour and Capital. Management, as a function of industry, is easily distinguishable from either ; it remains the stable element in the interplay of both. It is not tied to Capital, since normally it has little or no financial interest in the business it directs. It is not attached to Labour, since its function is the direction and control of Labour. It stands dispassionately free, equally critical of both its partners. In its work, however, it must constantly be guided, not only by the facts of the situation, but also by its comprehension of the general as well as local mentality of its partners. Particularly in the case of Labour administration, no factory stands alone. There is a Labour problem, which transcends the boundaries of individual businesses—a problem which lies behind the minor problems of day-to-day management—the problem of the mental attitude of Labour as a body. Industrial management needs to clarify its mind on this subject before it can successfully carry out a practical Labour policy in individual industries and factories.

The general method of assessing the attitude of Labour is either to select an individual who may be supposed to typify Labour, or to quote the words of Labour theorists and publicists, and saddle the mass of Labour with responsibility for them. Apart from these two methods, it is usual to deny that there is any group-mind which can properly be called " Labour." It is very necessary to define exactly the significance of the term " Labour " when used as a generic title. Dr. Shadwell draws a useful distinction between the " ferment " of the theorists and extremists, and the " material or mass " of the general body of organized Labour. " There is a massive movement in progress," he says, " and gathering way towards a transformation of the industrial order ; but it does not contemplate the use of violent means, nor is its goal any of the Utopias sketched by theorists."[1] The " ferment " represents the versatility of progressive thought, the haste, extravagance and violence of extremists, and the internally disruptive element of agitation. The " mass " stands for a more bulky and unwieldy movement, proceeding by slow and experimental stages, based upon commonplace and widely accepted facts. It is this " mass " which is truly " Labour." We may call it " organized Labour " in so far as it is almost wholly attached to the Trade Union organization, but its mentality is far from being organized. The bare fact of its technical organization is no warrant for ascribing to it an acceptance of the " Labourism " of its publicists. The difficulty of the mass of Labour is that it is largely inarticulate. We have to guess the words which it strives to utter.

It would be idle to deny, however, that the mass of Labour is mainly revolutionary, if, by revolution, we mean that relatively slow and painful concentration of tendencies, acts and feelings which are directed broadly, apart from the minor difficulties of daily working conditions, towards

[1] " The Revolutionary Movement." A series of articles contributed to *The Times* by Dr. A. Shadwell (1921).

an emendation of the social system.[1]   An indication of
this lies in the tendency of Labour to devote itself increasingly to education—largely of an economic and social
character.   " The working man," says Mr. J. H. Thomas,[2]
" more than at any other time in the history of the country,
is reading that type of book which brings him knowledge
and improvement, the works of the scientist, the philosopher, the historian, the publicist, the technical expert."
He is increasingly to be found at colleges, evening classes,
adult schools, summer schools, settlements, university
extension courses and public lectures.[3]   He reads his
newspapers and journals.   He may even be found reading
Taylor and others who have developed and expanded
Taylor's philosophy.   The desire for a larger mental life
is particularly noticeable among the younger men.

Where education is increasingly sought, the spirit of
violent revolution perishes.   The true revolution goes
steadily on.   What we are witnessing is the slow pressure
of the social shoulder to the wheel of change.   The clamour
of the extremist is but the creaking of the wheel as with
difficulty it turns.   The pressure comes from the mass of

[1] *Cf.* Report of Trade Union representatives of the National
Industrial Conference, held 27th Feb., 1919, on Industrial Unrest—
" The fundamental causes of labour unrest are to be found rather
n the growing determination of Labour to challenge the whole
existing structure of capitalistic industry than in any of the more
special and smaller grievances which come to the surface at any
particular time."

[2] *When Labour Rules.* By the Rt. Hon. J. H. Thomas, M.P.
(W. Collins, Sons & Co., Ltd., 1920.)

[3] Membership of the London Working Men's College in 1920
was approximately 1,500.   Ruskin College, Oxford, trains an average
of thirty-five students a year, while thousands take its correspondence
courses.   The Labour College in London has about thirty students
and some thousands attending its evening classes through all its
branches.   The Workers' Educational Association at the close of
the year 1916–17, registered 10,750 members and 2,336 affiliated
organizations.   During that year, ninety-nine tutorial classes were
carried on, 154 one-year classes, seventy study circles, and 526
public lectures.   For the year ending 31st May, 1921, this Association enrolled 19,294 students in classes, 1,038 in residential summer
schools, and over 1,000 in study circles.   It is a federation of 2,986
working-class and educational institutions and organizations.

Labour, and its strength lies in Labour's deliberate practice of " self-help " as a means to progress.

The significance of this progressive mentality of the mass of Labour, however, lies not only in the self-educational methods its more earnest exponents adopt, but in the spirit which informs it, and the field in which it chooses to operate. Its spirit in the main is neither political, philosophical, nor scientific, but ethical. It has been described by its enemies as the spirit of class warfare, of the dictatorship of the proletariat, of the battle against Capitalism, of a world upheaval, of Bolshevism and Communism. It is impossible to find among the general body of working men any substantial justification for such a description. The mass movement of Labour, in so far as one can frame words to express it, is directed chiefly against the mal-distribution of the advantages and opportunities which wealth makes possible, and is grounded in the belief that there is no ethical justification for it. It is not a class-war, for wealth is not distributed according to social classes. It is not a political movement, for the body of Labour is still dismembered between the old political parties, and shares much of the general political apathy common to all grades of the community. It is not a philosophical movement, for the philosophy of the movement is seriously divorced from the feeling of the general mass of Labour, and indeed the rank and file worker has no clear and conscious philosophy. Galsworthy comes closer to its heart when he divides society into those who give orders and those who receive them. It is a distribution of power, advantages, and opportunities, based upon no acceptable code of ethics, to which the spirit of the mass of Labour is opposed. It asserts that the present distribution of power amongst individuals is—not entirely ineffective for good, not wholly unrepresentative, not unprogressive, not unworkable—but ethically unjustifiable. It queries the whole moral basis of human values, as assessed under the present social and economic *régime*.

Equally significant is the shifting, during the last fifty years, of the field in which this spirit operates. In 1838, the Chartists looked to the desired changes in the social order being effected by political action—especially by universal suffrage.[1] In the " eighties," John Burns and his followers anticipated progress by the action of municipal enterprise. To-day it is held that progress involves the recasting of the mould of industry. Labour is, perhaps unconsciously, realizing that advance comes not so much by legislation or philosophy, as by hammering out of the basic social necessity of industry that form of industrial commonwealth which shall provide, as Henry Ford says, " not only a living, but a life."

In general, it may be said that Labour in the mass desires a more equitable distribution of social opportunities, to be achieved by a remoulding of the wealth-creating and distributing agency of industry into a form in which the service rendered to the community shall be the ultimate criterion of the reward received, whether by an industry or an individual. Undoubtedly, Labour, in common with all classes of the community, has shared in the general post-war obsession that wealth is in itself an ultimate end. The " living " has obscured the " life." Fundamentally, however, the claim of the mass of Labour is not for material equality, not for wealth irrespective of the means whereby it is gained, but for its own moral right to be given an open road to self-realization.

Industrial management may go seriously astray if it should wrongly assess this mentality of Labour. It may, for instance, seriously delude itself if it should work on the assumption that high wages would settle the Labour

[1] " As the means by which alone the interests of the people can be effectually vindicated and secured, we demand that those interests be confided to the keeping of the people. . . . Therefore, we demand universal suffrage. . . . If the self-government of the people should not remove their distresses it will, at least, remove their repinings. Universal suffrage will, and it alone can, bring true and lasting peace to the nation ; we firmly believe that it will also bring prosperity."—Petition of the Chartists to the House of Commons, 1838.

problem.   The Labour problem is ethical rather than
material.   Were wages at a much higher standard and
the fabric of industry unaltered, the essence of the problem
would still remain.   Industrial management, again, may act
on wrong lines if it under-estimates the power of Labour.
That the mentality of Labour is largely inarticulate forms
no justification for supposing it to be inert.   That it
frequently fails to bear out the interpretations of its publicists forms no ground for the assumption that it is inchoate
and irresolute.   The power of Labour resides primarily
in the moral basis upon which its claims rest, in the development of its education, and in its weapon of Trade Unionism.
Trade Unionism is not Labour, but its instrument.   Trade
Unionism is an organization, not a spirit ; but in so far
as it advances the cause of Labour it may legitimately
be described as a lever which Labour uses.   Like every
organization, it may eventually crumble when the need
for which it was designed no longer exists.   The time
may come when Labour will speak for itself, and its
voice confound the words of those who claimed to speak
for it.   But in the education which it is now winning for
itself, and in its reliance on ethical assumptions, it is
developing itself apart from its official instruments.   It is,
therefore, this development on the part of Labour that the
industrial management of the future should primarily
consider, for it constitutes the more profound basis of
Labour power.   It is the development, moreover, which
is gaining for Labour the support of those who, though not
workers, are won over to the cause of Labour.   It is not
the fact that Labour has been organized into vast battalions
which should so much concern the management of industry
as that it is slowly but surely preparing to offer to industry
a contribution of greatly increased value, and at the same
time is pleading for a re-direction of the course of industry
on grounds which compel us to question the very
fundamentals of society.

The mentality of Labour reveals itself most clearly in its

attitude to its own status and working conditions.   Status is a question of relativity.   The problem of social status, whether of a class or of an individual, does not, therefore, require the determination of an absolute standard, but rather the determination of relative standards.   A community, as it grows, makes available material and spiritual advantages through the activities rendered possible by the fact of association.   Certain advantages are thus socially created, as distinct from those created apart from the community.   Different grades of the society contribute different faculties to the creation of those advantages. It thus becomes possible to make an assessment of human values according to the contribution made to the communal advantages, which we may call social ethics. Labour claims that status should be founded on such values. Wide discrepancies in status, it claims, arise from a mal-assessment of the values contributed to the communal good.   Its claim for a higher status is in essence, consequently, an ethical claim.   It is a claim for a re-assessment on purely ethical principles of the social value of a person or a group.   Such problems, therefore, as the allocation to Labour of some portion of industrial control, the provision of representative machinery for Labour, and the sharing of profits with Labour are to be regarded as problems in social ethics.   The question is not what is desirable, not even what is possible, but what is right.   What ought Labour to have ?   It is a new attitude for industrial management to adopt, but it is the only attitude which holds out any hope of a satisfactory settlement of the difficulties confronting us.   " All industrial problems," says Mr. W. L. Hichens, " resolve themselves into moral problems, and how far we succeed in solving those questions depends on the degree of moral consciousness to which the community has attained.   Failure, therefore, to solve our industrial problems implies a moral failure on our part." [1]

[1] " The Wage Problem in Industry "—an address to the Royal Society of Arts, by Mr. W. L. Hichens, 1921.

Again, the mentality of Labour is revealed in its claim for better working conditions. That claim has been developed in the blast of oppression and the darkness of hardship. The beginnings of the factory system were accompanied by conditions which to-day seem incredible— the herding of orphan children into factories, the twelve to fourteen hours of work per day, the bestial conditions for women, the preposterous Poor Law system, and the iron repression of agitation. These things gave birth to revolt which still persists, since conditions in spite of great improvements are not yet satisfactory. The claims of Labour are still concerned with wages, hours, working environment, and economic security against unemployment, illness and old age.

These claims, however, are based not upon might, but right. It is a question of ethical justification. Higher wages are claimed, for instance, not because it is supposed that a given industry can afford them, but because it is held that industry as a whole ought to be so conducted as to be able to afford them. It is not wages which should conform to industry, but industry which should conform to wages. Labour claims that the service which it renders to the community receives no just reward, and that industry must address itself to the end of remedying that dereliction in social ethics. The mass of Labour knows nothing of economics, but there is firmly implanted in its heart a sense of social morality. Industrial management must meet Labour on the same basis. There can be no battle between economic arguments and moral convictions. The two are on different planes. Management must justify itself morally before it can satisfy Labour.

In conclusion, it should be pointed out that the mentality of Labour has been profoundly affected by the war and by post-war conditions. The situation is perhaps too recent to admit of precise analysis, but we shall find on surveying it that those conditions which particularly affront the moral sense are those to which Labour emphatically takes exception. Of these, " profiteering " and extravagance have been the most blatantly immoral. Organized Labour, indeed, has been very largely concerned with nationalization, the employment of women, industrial control and wage systems, but the minds of the mass of the workers have been more profoundly affected by the sins against the social conscience which profiteering and extravagance represent. The unrest of Labour is attributable in a far greater degree to these items than to any more academic considerations such as concern its leaders.

Management in industry is in a large measure the management of men, and unless it understands the mentality of its men it must be ineffective. The mass of Labour is not to be judged by standards which cannot apply to it, but by its mass-mentality. The interpretation of that mentality is the preliminary task of management. I have suggested that it is inherently ethical, and that only by dealing with the human problems involved as primarily questions of social right can management hope to steer the bark of industry into peaceable waters.

So long as industry remains the shuttlecock of demand and supply, so long as it continues to be regarded as an economic necessity rather than a social responsibility, so long as it is conducted with but the barest relation to the dictates of our social conscience, just so long will progress be uniform with that of the menacing past. We need a revolution of method to meet a revolution of thought, a renascence in earnestness to combat a renascence of revolt, a restoration of faith to overcome a recrudescence of doubt. In our conception of the industry of the future we must assure its oneness with what our social morality demands. Our conduct of industry must be such that the assumption that what is ethically highest is most beneficial to all receives practical expression and ample proof.

The structure of industry, however, is not composed only of Management and Labour. That which gives its name to the present system of industry—Capital—is the third partner. Capital as a whole has not as yet arrived at anything which can be called a mentality. In its present form it is of too recent origin. The early capitalist, who was not directly either an employer or a factory owner, only foreshadowed the modern capitalist. At some period between the breakdown of the Guild system and the beginning of the factory system, the capitalist began his chequered career. " Long before 1776, by far the greater part of English industry had become dependent on capitalistic enterprise in the two important respects that a commercial capitalist provided the actual workmen with their materials and found a market for the finished goods."[1] The capitalist was a factor and a merchant. He controlled materials and markets, but the worker largely owned his own instruments of production and settled his own working conditions. Gradually, however, even before the application of power to machinery, the capitalist began to encroach on these spheres. He began to own the looms and other instruments necessary for manufacture, and lend them out to domestic workers. Later, he began to group these instruments in single buildings, and bring workpeople together to operate them. When steam power came, these tendencies became general practices, and the factory system began. The capitalist became not only a buyer of material and a seller of products, but also a direct employer and owner of plant.

Even then, however, Capital had not begun its modern existence. Though the Industrial Revolution meant a vast extension of capitalistic enterprise, the modern form of Capital was not determined until the introduction of the limited liability joint-stock company in 1862. This meant the separation of the capitalist from the employer, the division between Capital and Management. The owners of a business may be thousands of shareholders ;

[1] *The Economic Organization of England."* By Sir William Ashley (1919). (Longmans, Green & Co.)

the immediate employers may be salaried officials owning little or no capital. Capital in its modern form is only sixty years old, and its place in industry to-day is impersonal. As a rule, it is divorced from industry as a human force, and enters in only as a matter of ledgers and cheques. Before it can be said to have a mentality, at least as regards industry, it must become human. A link of human relationship must be forged between the owners of capital and the workers. If Capital is to be a permanent partner in industry it cannot remain impersonal. It is not enough that it should raise the money and take the dividends; it must breathe the industrial air and throb with the industrial heart. It must take its responsibility as well as its dividends. It must become a human as well as a financial agent in production. To hold an industrial share must be regarded as a pledge of loyalty to the great body of industry.

Meanwhile, however, Capital, in any human sense, is becoming more scattered and more remote. It has been estimated that the number of persons owning capital in joint-stock companies is in the vicinity of 1,000,000; and the number is being daily augmented. At the same time, the "family business," in which Capital and Management are united, is dying out. On the other hand, there is a great increase in the number of employees holding shares in their own concerns. Ownership of capital, in fact, is no longer the prerogative of any class, nor is it, except in an indirect and often remote way, concerned in the conduct of industry. There is nothing impossible, however, in the suggestion that the ownership of industrial capital may one day belong mainly to the workers in industry. The £469,000,000 which the banks and investing public lent to industry in 1920 is £700,000 less than the drink bill of this country for the year ending March, 1921. The money involved is well within the capacity of Labour and Management to supply. It may be that when the capitalist is merged in the practical worker, Capital will be humanized.

We have said that, speaking generally, Capital as yet has no mentality. But that statement hardly holds good of Capital as it affects industry through its appointed representatives, the directors of individual concerns. These are often far more competent and enlightened men than has been the case in the past. Many of our chairmen of companies are among the leading industrialists and political thinkers of our day. The modern director, very frequently, is no longer completely obsessed with the idea of what the concern can give him, but is interested rather in the contribution which it makes to the good of the community. Thus, he employs capital, not only for purposes of bearing dividends but also for purposes of industrial policy. The mentality of such a director has approximated somewhat to that of the statesman, who, whilst bound to maintain the solvency of his country, is guided by considerations other than those of finance alone. This, further, often holds good of large groups of directors, such as are concerned in the amalgamations and agreements between groups of Capital, which are outstanding modern features.

The fact is that the science of business administration, the size of many modern concerns, and the intricate organization of business have shown the need for a marked degree of training and ability in the heads of modern concerns. Such positions cannot be left wholly to the whim of shareholders. Democratization of ownership has led to specialization in administration. The tendency has, therefore, grown for the representation of Capital in industry to be entrusted to Management. The older idea of an industrial trinity—Labour, Management, and Capital—is passing. Capital is only an industrial partner in so far as it is absorbed in Management. Otherwise, it remains an impersonal factor in the form of money, machines, and buildings. As a human element in industry, it is only expressible in terms of Management and Labour. It has, therefore, as a whole, developed no tangible mentality, nor can it do so till the whole body of shareholders realize that they, no less than the workers, form an integral part of industry ; that their partnership in it compels them to bear their proportion of responsibility for its methods and objects ; and that the income they derive from industry is only justified by the service they themselves render. The time when industry could be regarded as a " penny-in-the-slot " machine for shareholders is passing. Either Capital must accept a direct burden of industrial service, or it must be content to be shouldered out of industry, except as a wholly impersonal factor—possibly, later on, to be re-humanized by coming under the joint ownership of Labour and Management.

Industry is not a machine ; it is a complex form of human association. The true reading of its past and present is in terms of human beings—their thoughts, aims and ideals—not in terms of systems or of machinery. The true understanding of industry is to understand the thoughts of those engaged in it. The advance of science and the cult of efficiency have tended to obscure the fundamental humanity of industry. We have paid in largely to our account of applied industrial science, but we are almost bankrupt of human understanding. The material side of industry has its place, but it is a subordinate one. Indeed, if the fundamental problem of industry can be reduced to the limits of a single question, that question would be : How best can we achieve and maintain a fair balance between the *things* of production—the machines, the buildings, the materials, the systems—and the *humanity* of production—the workers, the foremen, the managers, the shareholders ?

This is the problem which is at the root of all the problems facing industrial management. Industry cannot be rendered efficient while the basic fact remains unrecognized that it is primarily human. It is not a mass of machines and technical processes ; it is a body of men. It is not a complex of matter, but a complex of humanity. It fulfils its function, not by virtue of some impersonal force, but by human energy. Its body is not an intricate maze of mechanical devices, but a magnified nervous system.

The present industrial " impasse " is due to the subordination of the human to the material element. Whilst our industries have grown increasingly scientific, we are denied the fruits of our efforts, because we have failed to keep pace in the art of human leadership, understanding and co-operation. Pursuing things, we have neglected men. Winning efficiency from our machines, we have forfeited efficiency in our workers. The need of industry is a stronger electrical thrill of common human understanding. " It would be a curious ending to our industrial leadership of the world if the successful conversion of our industries to the needs of the Great War proved to be our last great triumph. At present, it looks as if the reconversion of our industry to the needs of our life might prove to be beyond our powers." [1]

An industry designed to meet the needs of our life—physical, mental, and moral—must be living. The aim of management must be to render industry more effectively human—more truly a corporate effort of human beings, united for a common object and moved by a common motive. To achieve that end we need, firstly, a motive and an ideal ; secondly, leadership and co-ordination ; thirdly, work and co-operation. All these factors are interdependent.

In the course of the succeeding chapters, it will appear that the ultimate motive of industry should be that of

---

[1] *Manchester Guardian.* 6th June, 1921.

Cf. also the address of Hon. James J. Davis, Secretary of Labour, U.S.A., to a convention of the National Hardwood Lumber Association at Philadelphia, 1921.

" This great volume of wealth, this rapid advance, we have been able to achieve in fifty short years by intense application of a genius for the *mechanics* of industry. Now I believe we are to work a new era in the world's progress by applying our national genius to the *humanics*, the human side of industry. . . . Greatly as we have been building, our material resources have still been only partly uncovered. Our *human* resources have hardly been touched at all."

service to the community ; that the art of leadership will develop with the growth of the science and the realization of the social responsibility of management, and that co-operation will come when the motive, or the ideal, is real and when the leadership is compelling.   Only efficient management can justly demand greater efficiency from Labour—and efficiency cannot grow if the partners in industry are trying to realize different ideals.   On the other hand, the bond of a great ideal has ever led to the strongest forms of association and the finest achievements.   But since to management is entrusted the guidance of industry, it must take the initiative in defining and pursuing that ideal. Management in itself has no axe to grind.   Whether the motive of industry be primarily profit or service, and under whatever form it is conducted, management must persist. It is therefore the body from which the setting up of a new ideal may most naturally come.   The future of industry rests in its hands.

The background of industry, however, is composed, not only of the thoughts and interests of those engaged in it, but also of the entire mentality of the community to which it stands related.   The progress of any section of a community is governed by the progress of the whole. It is impossible to carry out a great scheme of industrial development, founded upon the common humanity of those engaged in industry, unless it is supported by a vivid public feeling, an informed public opinion, and a resolute public will.   " It is not consistent with equity or wisdom," said Burke, " to set at defiance the general feelings of great communities and of all the orders which compose them."   The converse is equally true.   It is impossible to carry through great social changes unless the general feeling of the community provides the impulse.   The re-direction of industry demands what Wells has finely described as " a renascence of thought about political and social things " —" a great deliberate renascence of will and understanding."   Nothing short of this can ensure that the turmoil and oscillation of the present will develop into an ordered progress in the future. Without the application of concentrated thought, the unwavering pursuit of a common purpose, and the rigour of infinite and patient effort on the part of all grades and classes of the community, there seems little hope of lasting recon-struction. We may build our Jerusalem or create our Babel. We may discover our Utopia, or yield to Nemesis. The choice between progress and chaos lies before us. We shall achieve the one or fall into the other, according as the intellectual and moral capacities of the people are either brought to bear upon the great task of building a worthy industrial and social future or are allowed to be squandered in the nothingness of little things.

The background of industry is a medley of thought. Springing from a past across which the winds of divers philosophies have blown, and swept hither and thither by the stormy blasts of war, this thought is left scattered and purposeless. The task of this generation, and of industrial management in particular, is to consolidate and redirect it, so that industry may set out upon the highway to a new era.

CHAPTER II

THE FUNDAMENTALS OF MANAGEMENT

SUMMARY

(a) Definitions of Administration, Organization, and Management; Management is the outcome of human association for an object. The distinction between the art and science of management. The science of management cannot be final since it includes the human element.

(b) Management began as synonymous with Capital; divorce between the two brought about by inventions, wider markets, and consequent expansion. The effect of joint-stock ownership was finally to separate ownership and management. This was facilitated by improvement in general standard of public probity, by rise of factory *esprit de corps*, and by factory legislation. Rise of Trade Unionism gave a new direction to management.

(c) Management has become a profession. Impetus given to this tendency by certain effects of the war. This depends upon the stability of management in industry.

(d) Management is being actuated by spirit of analysis; it is the science of applying other sciences. It is a group of interdependent functions. The fundamental divisions into Finance, Administration, Preparation, Production, Facilitation, and Distribution. Division of Preparation into the functions of Design and Equipment; of Production into the function of Manufacture; of Facilitation into the functions of Transport, Planning, Comparison, and Labour. The distinction between Distribution and Production; division of Distribution into the functions of Sales Planning and Sales Execution.

(e) The faculties requisite for execution of functions. Misconception with regard to clerical work. The division of faculties into Determinative, Administrative, Executive, Service, and Operative.

(f) Assurance of three fundamental principles; that there exists a scientific basis of management; that management can function by scientific means; that graduation in the science must come to be the main qualification of the manager.

THERE are three terms, constantly recurrent in any treatment of the structure of industry, which it is important to define with some exactitude—Administration, Management, and Organization. Though frequently treated as almost synonymous, the three terms, if not easily separable, at any rate should convey quite distinct impressions.

For the purpose of this book, they may be defined thus—

Administration is the function in industry concerned in the determination of the corporate policy, the co-ordination of finance, production and distribution, the settlement of the compass of the organization, and the ultimate control of the executive. [1]

Management proper is the function in industry concerned in the execution of policy, within the limits set up by administration, and the employment of the organization for the particular objects set before it.

Organization is the process of so combining the work which individuals or groups have to perform with the faculties necessary for its execution that the duties, so formed, provide the best channels for the efficient, systematic, positive, and co-ordinated application of the available effort. [2]

Organization is the formation of an effective machine; management, of an effective executive; administration, of an effective direction. Administration determines the organization; management uses it. Administration defines the goal; management strives towards it. Organization is the machine of management in its achievement of the ends determined by administration.

[1] *Cf.* The functions of the Cabinet, as described in the Haldane Report on the Machinery of Government (Cd. 9230, 1918), and quoted in Appendix to Chapter IV.

[2] *Cf.* Definitions by Mr. J. N. Schulze in a paper read to the Taylor Society, and published in the Bulletin of that Society for August, 1919.

" An organization is the combination of the necessary human beings, materials, tools, equipment, working space and appurtenances, brought together in systematic and effective correlation, to accomplish some desired object."

" Management is the force which leads, guides and directs an organization in the accomplishment of a pre-determined object."

" Administration is the force which lays down the object for which an organization and its management are to strive and the broad policies under which they are to operate."

Similar definitions are given by the same writer in a paper presented to the Taylor Society, published in the Bulletin of June, 1920. In the latter, however, it is made clearer that it is the business of management to " keep within the governing policies imposed upon it by the administrative officials."

This book concerns all three.. The title is selected because it is the popular mode of describing the combination of the three. The term " Management " is so commonly used to cover the formation of policy, its execution, the designing of the organization and its employment that it would be somewhat too academic to insist in a title upon distinctions which popular thought fails to recognize.

Management, in this general sense, including both Administration and Organization, is the natural outcome of human association, whether in industry, household, or State. Wherever persons are grouped together for a common purpose, the need arises for a leadership which shall determine policy, settle spheres of authority, and organize and control the application of effort.   In this respect, industry shares a need common to every social enterprise from church to guild, municipality to empire, war to university. Just as an orchestra requires a conductor, so a social enterprise, furthered by the combined efforts of human agents, requires direction, regulation, and co-ordination.

The exercise of human faculties in combination makes essential the exercise of the human faculty of management.[1] Management is to be regarded, therefore, not as an imposition upon industry, but as an inevitable development from the expansion of industry.   It is not external to, but inherent in, industry.

Being the exercise of a special human faculty, moreover, management is an art.   The present emphasis is laid upon the science of management. Undoubtedly there is a science of management, but it is to be sharply distinguished from the art which employs that science. A profound knowledge of the ascertained and codified facts of management does not necessarily entail a capacity for management. Scientific knowledge is an essential preliminary to the practice of an art, but it is not the art itself.   The science of management has not as yet been reduced to an acceptable

[1] *Cf.* the opening remarks in *Factory Organization and Administration*.   By   Hugo Diemer.   (McGraw Hill Book Co.   2nd Edition, 1914.)

form. Our knowledge is fragmentary and, since it concerns the actions of human beings as well as of material things, must necessarily remain so to a certain degree. In practising the art of management, we are working upon a partially scientific and partially unscientific basis. The efforts of those who are furthering the cause of " Scientific Management " are directed, therefore, to rendering that basis increasingly scientific, so that the exercise of management may be based upon a wider span of knowledge. The danger lies in the assumption that every extension of knowledge must circumscribe the art. Were the science of management as detailed as the science of medicine, there would still remain the necessity for the art of the manager as for the art of the doctor. The practice of management is, therefore, in this sense, not a science but the human application of a science. Indeed, were management a science alone, it could have no human philosophy. The science of painting teaches that by the mixing of certain colours of a certain composition, and by their application in a certain way to a certain canvas, a painter may produce a picture. But not every person who knows these facts is an artist. Similarly, not every person who knows that planning in a certain way will produce certain productive results, that costing carried out in a certain manner will reveal certain facts, is a manager. Other things being equal, the greater the knowledge of these facts the better the manager, but knowledge is not the only qualification. There is needed, in addition, the human faculty of managing—the faculty which not only knows that certain methods will produce certain results, but also is able to apply them to particular circumstances. We may legitimately look forward to the elaboration of a science of management which will lay down certain principles, founded upon indisputable premises, but it would be a fatal error to imagine that such a determination of principles would obviate the need for the human faculty whereby those principles may be applied. The modern effort to discover principles of management will result, not in making the task of the manager more simple, but infinitely more complex. This is a fact which is often overlooked. The application of Taylorian " Scientific Management " has been regarded in many quarters as a quick short-cut to success. No system, however scientifically founded, can' lead to success, unless the human faculty of applying that system is sound. The principles of Taylorism have helped vastly in the task of formulating a science of management. They have indeed revealed the hitherto unrealized fact that a large part of the business of management can be reduced to a science. But they have not in the smallest degree detracted from, and, rather, have enhanced, the value of the pre-eminently human capacity of the manager to manage.

Neither should it be supposed that any science of management can embrace all the factors entering into the practice of management. Into every branch of industry the human factor enters, and where that factor exists, there must always remain a field outside the province of science. No amount of scientifically determined facts and principles can materially affect the problem of labour, except by indirect means. Science may elaborate, for instance, principles for the planning of work which are capable of universal application, but it must inevitably make the reservation that such principles are subject to the vagaries of the human factor. In other words, in so far as management deals with things, its methods can be reduced to terms of scientific principle ; but in so far as it deals with men and women, it can only use scientific principles to the extent that the men and women are willing to subject themselves to them. The science of management may arrive at definite conclusions for each element of a man's work, but it is the art of the manager alone which will induce the man to put those conclusions into practice. There may be a science of costing, of planning, of manu-facturing, and of dispatching, but there can be no science of co-operation.

This reservation is important, for there is a tendency, in the modern cult of efficiency, to imagine that, given a basis of scientific principles, the art of the manager consists only in applying those principles. This is far wide of experience. Where human beings are concerned, scientific principles may be so much waste paper. Certainly there are scientific ways of engaging and discharging, of paying, and of stimulating employees. But we have to recognize that such scientific methods are as likely to fail as to succeed, unless there is more in the manager than the knowledge of a set of working principles which he tries to twist around to meet the situation. A science of management can only affect the circumstances surrounding the relations of management and workers ; it cannot touch the immediate human relations. That must remain a problem of mentality, of spirit, of ideals. The accumulated experience of the whole world would not ensure the wise application of one single principle to the relations of one man with another. The development of management as an industrial art, therefore, must come, not only by the construction of scientific principles governing the methods by which management may achieve certain ends, but also by the growth of a spirit in industry, governing the relations between all the various grades engaged in the conduct of industry.

At present, our science of management is in the most infantile stage. The practice of management is accordingly a matter of habit and chance. The true spirit of management is almost equally undeveloped. Our ideals are confused, our human attitude is guided by no fundamental belief in the purpose of industry. Our human relations are accordingly chaotic and jagged. Management, however, is in its youth ; it has only recently come to be a distinguishable entity in industry. It has only lately emerged from the chrysalis of capital ; its wings of science and spirit are not yet spread for flight.

The early story of the art of industrial management is

coincident with that of the early developments of capital in industry. Long before the so-called Industrial Revolution, industry had advanced from the stage of local production and marketing, and had become dependent upon the enterprise and organization of the capitalist agent. Management does not begin, in the general sense which we attach to it, until the beginning of the factory system. The capitalist, once a merchant and only indirectly an employer of labour, then became a direct employer. With the concentration of labour and machinery in factories came the necessity for industrial management. This still remained a capitalistic function. Factories were small, and were owned by single individuals, responsible alike for the provision of capital and the organization of production. Whereas the old main distinction between capitalist and worker had been that the former had good access to the markets whilst the latter performed the business of production, the distinction now vanished, in that the capitalist both undertook marketing and organized production in his own factory. Personal relations, however, remained much the same. The former merchant collected his workers under one roof, worked with them in the workshop, and ate his meals by their side. He shared hardships with them, and, rising from a generation which knew the deeps of poverty and the weariness of persistent toil, his inclination was to save any little surplus which fell to his lot. The early captains of industry were men of little or no education, gathering capital by the sternest thrift and the most determined simplicity of living, and achieving any success only by the exercise of a native wit inherited from many generations of sea-faring adventurers and by a gruelling, dogged perseverance at work. They combined the functions of capitalist, manager, and operative.

Progress gradually led to the division of these functions. The influx of new inventions, following upon those of Watt and Boulton, gave rise to a new class in industry—

that of the master mechanic. The capitalist manufacturer
found that, to take advantage of the benefits accruing
from the latest mechanical improvements, he required
specialists in mechanical work. He engaged, therefore,
mechanics to install and supervise the working of the new
machines. Simultaneously, he found his markets widening
beyond the range of his knowledge. Foreign markets
were brought nearer by means of steamship services,
and home markets developed consequent upon the provision
of railway facilities. Commercial management became a
business which he could no longer personally conduct,
and he engaged men qualified by a knowledge of markets
and means of transport to supervise the sale of his products.
These two developments inevitably led to increases in the
size of his factory. Inventions of all kinds and wider
markets occasioned increased production. The factory
grew ; the business of management became a big concern,
and the manager surrounded himself with a staff of
supervisory officials and clerks.

The period of this rapid development may be taken
roughly as the first half of the nineteenth century. The
Great Exhibition at the Crystal Palace in 1851 marks
the peak of this era of prosperity—the firm establishment
of the machinery age, and the development of management
in industry as an extension of ownership. After this
ensued a period of severe industrial depression beginning
in the portentous year of 1873—a wave of depression by
no means confined to England alone. Everywhere lack
of confidence paralysed trade. That wholehearted assurance which characterized the first half of the century
was singularly absent as the second half began. Two
significant factors contributed to this state of affairs ;
firstly, the development of industrial enterprise and technique abroad, especially in America and Germany ;
secondly, the philosophical reaction against the existing
industrial system, led by such prominent figures as Southey,
Carlyle, Kingsley, Maurice, Dickens and Ruskin. Each

of these in his own way seeking a motive and an ideal in industry and finding nothing but darkness, subjected the current conduct of industry to scathing criticism and scorn.   The need arose, in consequence of these two factors, for two new branches of the art of industrial management; firstly, the cultivation of a finer technique, of research, and of scientific methods of production, to enable British industry to compete with its foreign rivals ; secondly, the development of a new attitude to the human element in industry.

The momentum of these and other factors culminated in the recognition by legislation of the full privileges of limited liability in joint-stock ownership. This vast change was rendered inevitable by the change in the character of the owners of industrial undertakings.   The generation which had brought British industry from the Industrial Revolution to the middle of the century was followed naturally by a generation without the hard and rugged experience of its predecessor.   As wealth, luxury, and ease grew, the leadership of industry began to lack force and determination.   Ownership became inclined to rest upon its oars ; it became decreasingly a driving force.   Joint-stock ownership followed, and with it came management in the modern sense.

This change in the ownership of industry made possible three significant developments, each of which tended to distinguish the entity of industrial management.   Firstly, it made possible large scale production.   Increased capital spelt extension of activities.   Bigger plants, bigger staffs and wider ramifications called for a more continuous and expert application of administrative capacity.   Organizing became a scientific business, and the wielding of vast organizations an art.   Democratic ownership implied a definite divorce between ownership and management.   A new class sprang up to replace the old self-made capitalist of the 'fifties—men engaging in the direction and organizing of industrial concerns as a profession.   Distributed ownership was followed, therefore, by specialist management. Thirdly, amalgamations, agreements and understandings between corporations now became inevitable, which in turn required that each concern should be directed by a permanent and expert body of men, so that policy might be co-ordinated throughout a trade.

Management, at the beginning of the twentieth century, therefore, stood in a more clearly defined position than at any time previous. It had gradually drifted away from synonymy with Capital, and had assumed an entity of its own as a definite function in the industrial organism, distinguishable alike from Capital on the one hand and Labour on the other. Indeed, not only had it converted a duality into a trio, but it had also become the determining factor in the trio. Professor Marshall quotes Francis Walker, the American, writing in 1876, as follows[1]—The man who has the faculties required " to shape and direct production, and to organize and control the industrial machinery rises to be master of the situation. It is no longer true that a man becomes an employer because he is a capitalist. Men command capital because they have the qualifications to employ labour profitably. To these captains of industry, Capital and Labour resort for opportunity to perform their several functions." The modern claim of Labour that it should employ Capital instead of being employed by Capital is at any rate a stage nearer achievement, in so far as it is coming to be the case that management employs Capital. The faculty of business management now often attracts Capital to itself ; it no longer follows blindly where Capital leads.

Meanwhile, other factors were contributing to the establishment of management as a separate entity in industry. Firstly, there is the significant factor mentioned by Professor Marshall, when he writes " The wholesale transference of authority and responsibility from the

[1] *Industry and Trade*. By Professor A. Marshall, quoting from *The Wages Questions*, (Ch. XIV), by Francis Walker. (Macmillan & Co., Ltd., 1919.)

owners of each business to salaried managers and officials would have been impossible had there not been a great improvement in the morality and uprightness of the average man ; for even as late as the seventeenth and eighteenth centuries we find the great trading companies breaking down largely in consequence of the corruption and selfishness of their officials."[1] This rise of a professional morality in management clearly facilitated its development. Without it, one may well conceive that the position of management in industry would even now be hardly that which it has come to occupy in the industrial trinity. Secondly, there is the important development in industry of what one may term *esprit de corps*. As the association of Labour tended to grow on lines apart from individual factories, efforts were made to stimulate a corporate factory spirit, a devotion to factory rather than class. It was an effort, in spite of the inherent difficulties of large and growing businesses, to retain that personal devotion which the early captain of industry could command. In the fostering of this spirit, shareholders could give no lead. It depended wholly upon management. Thus began a realization that, under a system of distributed ownership, the actual leadership of the factory must depend upon the manager. The joint-stock system irrevocably separated Capital from any immediate influence upon the spirit and " tone " of the factory.

Thirdly, there is the growth of industrial legislation. The hours of labour were first limited by legislation in 1819, and were progressively limited in 1842, 1844, 1893 and 1908. Legislation with regard to safety began in 1844 in respect of dangerous machinery ; developed in 1864 with regard to various processes in scheduled dangerous trades, and has been considerably amplified subsequently. State inspection of individual undertakings began in 1850 with the inspection of coal-mines, and has grown until now every factory is subjected to an infinity of restrictive

[1] *Ibid*, p. 323.

regulations enforced by periodical inspections. The application of these rules made a competent and whole-time managerial staff essential, and gave to it an authority and responsibility which a body of shareholders could not possibly exercise.

Lastly, the emergence of the factor of organized Labour completed the triumph of management over Capital as the primary power in the industrial structure. The effect of the Labour movement and of the social activities connected with it upon the development of management may be traced in three distinct ways : (a) as a result of Trade Union organization ; (b) as a result of the assumption, either by the State or by voluntary bodies, of responsibility for the social conditions of the labouring classes ; (c) as a result of the recognition of bargaining in the determination of wages and conditions, and of the machinery instituted to carry out the bargaining on recognized and standard lines.

Each of these factors required the co-operation of management—the operation of a function which, while representing ownership, was yet intimate with industrial affairs locally and was replete with an expert knowledge of trade conditions. Joint-stock ownership possessed neither of these faculties ; the factory management was alone competent to fill the bill.

The growth of the Trade Union movement during the last century has been the main factor in bringing management into its inheritance. The change in the status of Labour has been the one great revolutionary force in industry since the beginning of the factory system. Growth of factories, the development of trade agreements and factory understandings, legislation, scientific methods and inventions, and foreign rivalry have contributed their quota to the emergence of the function of management, but by far the greatest influence has been exerted by the increasing solidarity and organization of labour. Factory administration might have continued to be the pastime of a few representatives of the shareholders had Labour remained as the factory system found it in 1800–1850. Signs were not wanting even then that Labour was no easy steed to be ridden. Strikes are by no means phenomena solely of the factory era. But, on the whole, despite Luddite riots and other violent ebullitions inevitable in a period of such radical change, Labour was comparatively quiescent, and, through close association with the small employers of the period, little inclined to aggressive movements. To-day, the situation is far otherwise. If the beginning of the nineteenth century is to be known as the Industrial Revolution in terms of machinery, transport and power, the latter half of it may with equal justice be named the second Industrial Revolution in terms of Labour. The growth of Trade Union organization has been by far the most formidable agent in the revolution. It has made the business of factory administration pre-eminently a problem in humanics, just as the revolution in mechanical methods made it to a great extent a problem in engineering, research, and material organization. The story of Trade Union development, in fact, if on the one hand it records the gradual emancipation of Labour, on the other hand provides the key to the gradual expansion of the field of management. The development, moreover, has not only made the expansion of the responsibility of management essential, but has also given the main direction to the work which management must perform, and determined a large proportion of the technique of the manager. Knowledge of factory and social legislation, intimacy with social conditions, and a capacity for the skilful use of bargaining and other machinery in dealing with Labour have come to be supremely necessary items in the technique of the industrial administrator. The growth of management has taken place in every field of industry, but more than in any other in the field of Labour administration.

Management has gradually become a profession. Its task has increased in difficulty, responsibility and complexity, until to-day it touches all the sciences, from chemistry and mechanics to psychology and medicine. It calls to its service, therefore, men and women with tact and ideals, with the highest scientific qualifications and with a strong capacity for organization and leadership. It is employing lawyers and doctors, accountants and artists, and, by directing their professions, is forming a supreme profession of its own, with all the implications consequent upon such a line of progress, of standards, qualifications, apprenticeship, and technique. It is no longer the "middle-man" between Capital and Labour ; no longer the wedge which takes all the strain. It stands rather in a co-ordinating position between the two, owing allegiance to neither, but acknowledging as master the public will of the community alone.

The position of management, however, requires consolidation. Its recognition as the controlling entity in industry has to be developed and strengthened. A tremendous impetus in this work was given by the war. The older methods of management were not adequate to bear the weight of war-time pressure. Weaknesses were revealed, which served to indicate the further expansion which management must undergo. The war-time factors conducing to this end may be stated as briefly as possible, without the elaboration they deserve, in the following terms.

(1) *The progress of industrial science*, stimulated into prodigious activity by war requirements, and furthered by the war-time researches of the more technical Universities. There is indeed little need to stress either the lack of facilities for or interest in industrial science previous to the war, or the urgency of its need since the war. Many large firms have now instituted research departments, for both applied and pure research. Smaller firms have united in the promotion of research associations and laboratories, under the stimulus of the Privy Council Committee on Scientific and Industrial Research. The Universities are co-operating ; as, for example, the valuable activities

of the Manchester University School of Industrial Technology. Science, moreover, deals with both the material and the human aspects of industry, with both products and mentality, the work and the worker.

(2) *The post-war economic situation*, with its sudden demand for the increased production of peace-time goods, and the increased costs of labour and material consequent upon the rise in prices. Indeed, the whole economic situation—fluctuating prices, inflated currency, demoralized exchange rates, excessive costs, unprincipled speculation, and intolerable taxation—has brought industry, and more particularly the management of industry, to such a pass that neither old standards nor old practices any longer are adequate.

(3) *The stirring of the social conscience*, slowly but implacably demanding, with no uncertain voice, that the old state of affairs in industry shall not return. Labour is in no mood to accept former standards as those of a " land fit for heroes." Employers are, in an increasing number of cases, convinced that the future must not be as history has been. The general public outside industry has almost unconsciously accepted new standards in its conception both of the position of industry in the national hegemony and of the position of those engaged in industry in the social commonwealth.

(4) *The electrifying impulse from America* towards efficiency in every sphere of industrial management. The war operated as a tremendous motive force there even more than in this country, and American industries started off at double speed, developing the while an almost fanatical cult of efficiency, which has culminated in the Prohibition law. European industry has been affected particularly as regards management. The teachings of F. W. Taylor and his successors have now become classical in the industrial literature of every leading productive country.

(5) *The urgent necessity for economical production*, in view of the incessant wage demands, the high cost of raw

3

materials and running expenses, and the need for producing cheap goods to cope with restricted demand and adverse exchanges. Generally speaking, the manufacturing " margin " has been reduced to the breadth of a cotton thread. The utmost accuracy in costing and the consideration of every detail in the process of production have accordingly become imperative.

(6) *The recognition of the importance of conferences*, both in industry and outside. Every industrial concern now has its system of conferences and committees of every kind. Conferences also, between firms, for a trade generally, and on a national scale are of daily occurrence. The Whitley Council scheme is only representative of a general tendency which the war stimulated.

(7) *The continued growth of inventions* for both manual and clerical operations. The war era has been almost as prolific in invention as was the era of the Industrial Revolution. The impulse of the war stimulated inventiveness ; the impulse of reconstruction has maintained it.

The sum of these influences has been to add to the complexity and responsibility of management, and, at the same time, to emphasize and define its position. Upon management has been cast the burden of reconstruction. The bearing of the burden has meant the wearing of the crown. It stands to-day in industry as a young man girding himself for a race. It is emerging as the directing agent in industry. That element which has always been inherent in industry is now assuming new attributes, and undertaking new functions as the recognition develops of its leadership.

The essential feature of the new management is that it is becoming a profession. In some directions it is already a profession, but only in those directions where the work performed is regarded as " professional " in pursuits other than industry. The new management is coming to be professional in itself, and professional in all its grades. A profession presupposes the existence of a science or

codified arrangement of truths, facts, and principles. It
also presupposes in the professional man a study of that
science and the attainment of some recognized standard
in his learning. The belief, therefore, that industrial
administration is tending to and must ultimately become
a recognized profession is founded upon a new conception
both of the task of management and of the personality of
the manager, using the words "management" and
"manager" as catholic terms for the whole body of those
engaged in the direction, organization, and facilitation of
industry. This science of management, that is the
elaboration of facts and principles into a codified statement
of knowledge which the would-be manager must acquire
to qualify for his profession, is now being gradually evolved.
The science is as yet in its experimental stage. Different
writers and theorists propound different codes. Vast
wells of experience still remain untapped. It has not yet
attained the rigidity of Law or the precision of Medicine.
But the work proceeds. It is possible now—a thing but
a few years ago unthought of—for a student to study the
subject, and with a modicum of practical knowledge of
any particular industry in a comparatively short time to
diagnose and suggest remedies for its diseases. "Modern
management," says Mr. A. P. M. Fleming, "has a technique
quite apart from the technology of the particular works
concerned." The time is indeed coming when it will be
possible to take up industrial management as a career as
a man now takes up law or enters the church. The
elaboration of a technique of management cannot but
render management definitely professional. Where there
exists a definable technique, certain precise standards can
be laid down, the attainment of which will qualify a man
to practise. It is not beyond the bounds of reasonable
anticipation to foresee the time when positions in industry
will be advertised like that of a Town Clerk or Borough
Surveyor ; when open examinations in standard subjects
will determine whether a candidate is fitted for the practice

of his profession ; when the technique of management will be found in the curricula of the Universities, and when associations of professional managers, like those already existing of electrical engineers, barristers and surveyors, will be formed for the promotion of the interests of the members and the furtherance of their profession. This time is close at hand. Already the science of management is being taught in the Universities ; already there are institutions devoted to its development and the association of those practising it ; already there are journals and societies engaged in determining and disseminating the facts of the science ; already there are necessary qualifications, perhaps only roughly discernible, but yet capable of being formulated into general terms, for many of the administrative posts in industry.

In America, even more than in this country, the movement has grown, and indeed perhaps has run riot. The " industrial engineer " in America is a professional man. He is the medical man of industry. This is a special development, or perhaps a premature one, for the future of the management specialist is not outside particular concerns but as an active agent in them. The " industrial engineer " at present acts as an advisor to the management ; the day is not far distant when he will *be* the management, no longer requiring outside assistance, but himself competent, trained and qualified to execute the duties of management.

The existence of such a science and profession clearly depends upon the stability of management. It is because management is the one inherent necessity in the conduct of any enterprise that it is possible to conceive of it as a profession. Whether capital be supplied by individuals or by the State, whether labour be by hand or by machine, whether the workers assume a wide control over industry or are subjected to the most autocratic power, the function of management remains constant. Not even the increasing employment of committees in the management of individual concerns affects this stability, since clearly committees must either be dependent upon or be composed of technical experts. Patients cannot be doctored nor sermons preached by committees. Where there is a technique to be applied, the technically trained man alone can carry out the work. If we elaborate a science of management in industry, the industrial manager of the future must inevitably become a student first, and a professional man afterwards.

As modern management develops, it is almost unconsciously becoming increasingly scientific. Though it may not deliberately be aiming at the elaboration of a science, its methods are conducing to that end, since it is growing in its everyday affairs more analytical. The management of a generation ago was synthetical without being analytical. It relied on chance or on initiative. It built on a foundation of faith. It did not pause to analyse, to dissect, to investigate ; seeing a chance, it took the risks and plunged. Modern management is inclined to build upon a surer foundation. The risks are greater ; the penalties of failure are heavier ; the competition is closer. Costs must be taken out, operations must be studied, the workers must be psychologically examined, the progress of work must be investigated. No problem in the business of manufacture is so insignificant that it can be settled without due consideration of the facts. Initiative without knowledge is risking too much.

Clearly, the more the spirit of analysis comes to actuate management, the closer are we drawing towards the formation of a science. We should be careful to note, however, the distinction between the science of management and those sciences which management employs. As the instruments which management uses become more scientific, the use of those instruments itself must become scientific. The co-ordination, organization and direction of sciences is itself a science. Though, for example, the science of medicine is employed in industry, it is not of itself a component part of the science of management. Management employs this and other sciences, but its own sc ence is distinct from them all. It is the science which analyses the task of industrial management and each branch of that task, and finally lays down a basis of knowledge upon which management may act in its use, organization, and co-ordination of other sciences, to the common end of production.[1]

Despite our preliminary definition of management, and despite our survey of its growth, the term must still convey only a blurred impression. It remains, therefore, to determine, firstly, the main divisions of the task of management ; secondly, the qualities requisite for the various grades into which management falls ; thirdly, the form of organization in which the divisions of the corporate task and the divisions of human faculty may be most efficiently combined. This last problem is treated in Chapter IV ; the first two problems we may consider at once.

The work of management may be described as a group of interdependent functions based upon fundamental divisions of the task of production. The knowledge of these fundamental divisions is the true basis for the development of an industrial enterprise. It is to the industrial administrator what biology is to the physician or mechanics to the engineer. It is his foundation, determining the lines of growth. The vast size of many industrial undertakings, and the fact that they have largely swollen to their present proportions without any reference to the basic divisions of production make a return to those bedrock facts a prime necessity. For, though concerns may grow by the sheer strength of a constructive brain, their

---

[1] *Cf.* the remarks of Mr. A. H. Church. " The *technical* efficiency of operation is not part of the science of administration. . . . The science of management does not teach, and does not pretend to teach, operative efficiency. If we do not know how to prevent a fabric from shrinking or how to temper steel springs, that is a defect in operative efficiency that no system of management can, by itself, overcome. . . . Management is the science of applying technology, but does not increase efficiency of technology."—*The Science and Practice of Management* (Chapter III), by A. Hamilton Church. Engineering Magazine Co., 1914.

maintenance at a high level or their further development is, under modern conditions, a problem, not only of personality but also of the application of scientific truth.

The heyday of empirical business administration is over. To-day is the day of scientifically regulated progress, based upon a rigorous analysis of the body industrial. Our problem, therefore, is to divide the task of production into scientific sections, on the basis, firstly, of the natural lines of industrial growth ; secondly, of the indissoluble connections between related activities. These are the two principles by which the main functions of management are to be determined. The first principle lays down that industry is an organic growth, and that its functions are the outcome of a process of devolution from the original state wherein all functions were combined in one individual. The second principle lays down that the division of the task of management shall be according to the relations existing between groups of activities, like being grouped with like. The first of these principles, although made much of by Mr. Hamilton Church, who remains the leading authority on this treatment of the subject, is clearly of only academic value if the same results can be obtained by the application of the second principle alone. [1]

It is of greater importance that our analysis should be scientifically based on the facts as they exist than that it should follow the lines of a process of devolution which is largely hypothetical. Moreover, since our analysis is being made with the object of determining the grouping of the general task of management, our division of that task must be such that each function is conceivable as capable of direction by a single individual. [2]

[1] *The Science and Practice of Management*, by A. H. Church. Engineering Magazine Co., New York, 1914. *Vide* Table IV, facing page 74.

[2] *Cf.* the following—" The science of organization can then be defined as the process of dividing a complex object into minor activities, each of which is well within the scope of individual effort."
" Laws of Industrial Organization," a series of articles contributed to *Industrial Management* by Mr. C. E. Knoeppel.

We have, therefore, to determine the functions of management in such a way that, firstly, each function forms a compact group of intimately associated activities ; secondly, each function is clearly distinguishable from other functions ; thirdly, each function is suitable for single control. Upon this basis it is suggested that the functions of management are as shown on the accompanying diagram (*vide* Fig. 1).

The function of Finance is to be sharply differentiated from other functions. It is the function primarily concerned with the provision and allocation of capital. As such, it is outside the province of management proper, and may be described as the sole function of capital in industry. In so far, however, as it requires a proportion of the management to watch its application and attend to such matters as rating, taxation, cash, insurance and investments, it cannot legitimately be omitted. The control of the finances of any business is a matter for the owners of the business, the shareholders, and their representatives. Management is concerned only in the use of capital, not in its provision. Finance, in fact, is a " business " function, not a " works " function. It is the function of capital, not of management. The Company Secretary, the Cashier, the Chief Accountant and the Auditors are not part of management proper. They are the officials of capital, and as such are to be distinguished from the officials of such management.

Following upon the function of Finance comes that main division called Administration, which is concerned in the co-ordination and organization of the corporate activities, the determination of business policy, and the ultimate control of the executive. This function stands mid-way between Finance and Management proper. It is the function of the " boss " ; the function which the active owner of a business retains to the last and cannot devolve. Clearly, however, this function is divisible into two main parts : firstly, that part which is concerned in policy-forming ; secondly, that part which is concerned in

(Figure 1.)

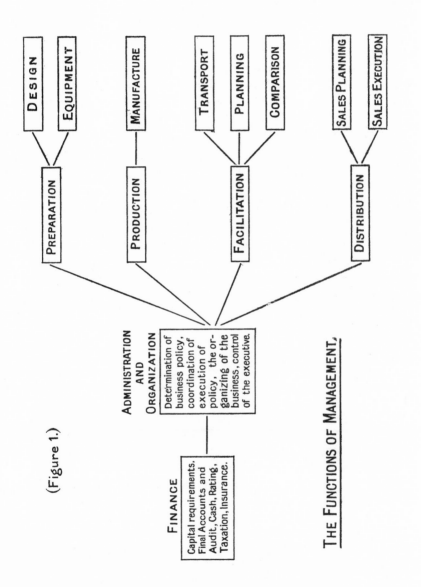

DESIGN	EQUIPMENT

PREPARATION

MANUFACTURE

PRODUCTION

| TRANSPORT | PLANNING | COMPARISON |

FACILITATION

| SALES PLANNING | SALES EXECUTION |

DISTRIBUTION

ADMINISTRATION
AND
ORGANIZATION

Determination of
business policy,
coordination of
execution of
policy, the or-
ganizing of the
business, control
of the executive.

FINANCE

Capital requirements.
Final Accounts and
Audit, Cash, Rating,
Taxation, Insurance.

THE FUNCTIONS OF MANAGEMENT.

organization and control.   The former may be called the
" determinative " element, the latter, the " co-ordinating "
element.   The former is more closely allied to Finance,
since the decisions taken upon broad business policy must
normally be based upon financial considerations.   The
latter is more closely allied to management, since its
business is the organization and control of management.
In the average concern, the determinative element is
represented by the Board of Directors, and the co-ordinating
element by a Managing Director or General Manager—
or, as in America, by a President.

Further, in so far as this co-ordinating element spreads
itself into the field of management, it covers the function
of control generally.   Under this function come all those
in a factory whose business it is to co-ordinate the activities
of others.   This includes what are generally known as
" departmental managers."   These form what one may
call the subordinate division of the function of Administration.   Their immediate business is the supervision of
actual manufacture, but such supervision necessarily
involves the co-ordination of all the other functions which
contribute to the efficiency of manufacture.   Their
primary function, therefore, is the co-ordination of other
functions.   This function in the average factory has
not yet been fully developed.   There are no clear dividing
lines between Administration, Control, Planning and
Manufacture.   What we have not yet fully determined
is the place of co-ordination in industry.   We recognize
it wholeheartedly at the head of an organization, but we
have yet to realize that the function which is necessary
at the head must also be continued down through the
various limbs of the organization.   At various points
in an organization there must be centres of co-ordination,
and where that is exercised the function of Administration
may be said to be in operation.   Such centres or points
are those at which the processes of manufacture can be
divided, i.e. at the head of each section of the function of

manufacture. Mr. Church has described this function—though he interprets it somewhat differently—as " the great Organ of Synthesis." It is the function which, both at the top of the organization and in the various divisions of the function of manufacture, controls and co-ordinates the activities of all contributory functions.

Following the function of Administration, which spreads out both into the province of Finance and into the legitimate field of Management, we come to the whole area of Management proper. The first main division of this area is into the four groups known as Preparation, Production, Facilitation and Distribution. This primary division is necessary to draw the distinction between the actual production of the goods and the contributory factors which, on the one hand, must precede production, and on the other hand, go to aid production. This distinction is fundamental in that it determines that which is basic and that which is auxiliary. In the gradual elaboration of the tasks of management, the basic character of the actual production of the goods is overlaid. The basis upon which the whole fabric of management is built is the making of the goods. All else is preliminary or contributory to that one fundamental fact. We may surround the actual making of the goods by what organization we will, but the basis of production remains perfectly distinct from any preparative, facilitative, or distributive activities which may appear necessary. Such activities, moreover, must necessarily be based upon production and relative to it. They can only operate in proportion to the operation of production.

Production may be described as the actual making of the products ; Preparation, as the activities necessarily preceding such manufacture ; Facilitation, as the activities contributory to production ; Distribution, as the business of disposing of the products.

The Preparative functions may be described as Design and Equipment—the two groups of activities preceding the application of effort to the actual materials of production. Design contributes the original idea of the product, specifies its appearance, size, shape, weight, etc., according to the nature of the product. Equipment contributes the necessary plant, machines, and tools to enable that idea to be put into operation. These are the two " originative " functions without which production cannot begin. Both, however, have facilitative aspects, in that Design is constantly correcting and checking, improving and altering the original purpose, and Equipment must continually repair and maintain the plant it provides. But, in the major sense, they are rather preparative, for the main reason that without them no production is possible, since, though labour may be available, it has no guidance as to the object of its effort nor plant wherewith to put its effort to effective purpose.

We cannot make until we have determined what we are going to make. Design, however, necessarily varies in character between trades. In engineering, Design is a question of the preparation of designs and drawings. In other concerns, the actual designing of the product—i.e. the determination of its specific characteristics—may be almost negligible once it has been decided to manufacture certain definable products. In the latter group, the " Design " is more a question of raw materials than of drawings. For instance, in a concern manufacturing a food product, the "Design" consists mainly in the purchasing of the necessary ingredients. It would be legitimate in such a case, therefore, to substitute the term " Purchasing " for the title of this function. Between these two extremes—the one, where design of the product is all-important, the other, where design is a comparatively minor affair, except in terms of raw materials—there will be every grade, including combinations of both. For instance, in some concerns the actual product may be mainly dependent upon the skill of the purchasing agent, but Design operates in the specification of the mixings of ingredients and in the determination of the shape, size and decoration of the boxes, wrappers or tins in which the product is to be put on the market. Generally speaking, however, where the manufacturing process consists in the assembly of various parts into a completed whole, the function should clearly be called Design, but where the process consists in the progressive treatment of specific raw ingredients, it would be clearer to call it Purchasing. In the latter case, the function may be described as covering all the activities previous to the arrival of the raw materials at the factory—the transport inwards, the insurance during transit, the research into methods of cultivation, and, if a concern grows or produces its own materials, the control of its premises and estates and methods of production.

The other function of Preparation is the provision of the necessary plant, tools and machines—the function of Equipment—the function concerned in the provision, erection, installation and maintenance of buildings, machinery, power, light, heat and fittings. This is clearly distinguishable from other functions. It is distinguishable from Manufacture in that Manufacture makes use of the plant but is not responsible for its provision. It is distinguishable, again, from Design in that it provides the necessary equipment for the execution of the design. As a part of such provision it will be responsible for space distribution, factory lay-out, the suitability of buildings and plant for the purposes for which they are erected, and the installation of labour-saving devices, such as cranes, railroads, conveyors, bogies, and lifts. After the installation of such equipment, the function is responsible for their upkeep, repair and cleanliness. It has, therefore, two main divisions—installation and maintenance. But the maintenance is wholly dependent upon the original installation, and, though such maintenance may be regarded as Facilitative rather than Preparative, its character is wholly different from those activities grouped under the heading of Facilitation. It is illogical, therefore, to regard Equipment as anything but a Preparative function.

The business of Production—the second main grouping of the activities of management—is single and clearcut. It is the actual manufacture of the goods—the employment of the various machines, processes, operations, faculties and methods involved in the making.

This function of Manufacture consists of the application of skill and effort to the transformation of the material. It is the actual " doing " of the work, apart from Design which says what shall be done, apart from Equipment which provides the means for doing it, and apart from Planning which lays down in what order and in what volume it shall be done. This function has been called " Operation " by Mr. Church, though probably " Manufacture " is a more self-explanatory term. He describes it as follows: " Operation comprises the actual technical processes of manufacture, the operation of the machine, the use of the tool, and the skill of the foreman and of the operative, as embodied in the way they apply the tools and machines to the material. Alteration in the status of material is the fundamental and distinguishing act of Operation." It is possible, however, to over-emphasize the rigid outline of this function. For practical purposes, the process of manufacture may include activities other than that of actual operation. For instance, it may include a certain proportion of inspection, the worker, as an integral part of his task, being responsible that no faulty product or material is passed. Logically, of course, this is clearly distinguishable from his activity purely in making, but for practical purposes it may be quite impossible to separate the two. It is suggested, therefore, that the term Manufacture admits of the inclusion of other activities, which may be regarded as essential to and inherent in the actual operation and yet distinct from it. Manufacture is the basic industrial function. It is the essence of industry ; the original activity from which all other activities, as a concern develops, take their rise. Every function is a devolution from the function of Manufacture. In that it is basic, it is the function which distinguishes one industry from another. Other functions have main characteristics in common, wholly apart from the nature of goods manufactured. In the actual manufacture, however, every industry and even every concern in the same industry stands alone.

The functions of Facilitation, on the other hand, are peculiar to no single industry or plant. They are common to the administration of every factory, irrespective of the nature of the products. Their general purpose is to facilitate the actual production—to take over those necessary activities which are not inherent in the immediate manufacture of the goods, so that the concentration of effort upon such manufacture may be unhampered by considerations of an alien character. The first facilitative function is that of Transport—the function responsible for the storage, transport outwards, and internal traffic of the factory. This function is to be distinguished carefully from Equipment on the one hand, and Planning on the other. Equipment provides and maintains the necessary machines and erections for transportation and storage—warehouses, store racks and bins, conveyors, bogies, railway stock and lifts—but is not concerned in their use. Planning, on the other hand, makes arrangement for the progress of work on the basis of the transport facilities, but does not actually control their use. The function of Transport is the function which makes the most efficient transportation dispositions and controls the use of transport facilities. It operates according to the schedule of the Planning function, and uses the equipment provided by the Equipment function, but is as distinct from both as is the function of Manufacture. It is equally distinct from the function of Distribution in its business of transporting finished products to depots, travellers, or customers.

The second facilitative function is that of Planning—

the function concerned in planning the progress of work from the reception of the customers' orders, through the various processes of manufacture, until ready for delivery. It is the function which draws up the arrangements according to which manufacture is carried on, issues the necessary instructions as to the volume and method of the work to be done, regulates the efficiency of the operations on work in progress, and directs the progress of work from process to process. There is a clear distinction between this and the control exercised by the co-ordinating element of Administration. Planning is not control ; it rather draws up the necessary regulations which control puts into practice. Planning determines that a certain volume of products shall be manufactured according to a certain schedule by a certain time. It bases such a plan upon the information provided by the function of Comparison. Administration then ensures that all the functions combine effectively for the execution of that plan. Planning is also distinct from Design. Design lays down the character of the product, and makes the necessary specifications. Planning makes the scheme for its production ; Administration controls the carrying out of the scheme.

The third facilitative function is that of Comparison— the function concerned in the observation and recording of the activities of all other functions, and the comparison of such records with definite standards. On the technical side it includes the analysis of and research into materials, processes, and methods ; on the administrative side it covers the recording and comparison of the facts and figures of time, quantity, and value. Clearly, Comparison is closely associated with Planning. It is upon the facts and deductions made by Comparison that Planning is able to base its schemes. The two sections of Comparison, however, must be clearly distinguished—the technical from the administrative. There is, indeed, much to be said for regarding them as separate functions, were it not that their respective attitudes to the other functions are identical.

They represent the same human faculty making inquiry and collating results in two separate spheres. In research of all kinds, statistics of cost, output, stocks, consumption, idle time, and the like are bound to be required. It would, therefore, be difficult to regard research as wholly separable from Comparison. Were Comparison purely the accumulation of data, irrespective of the deductions to be drawn from such data, the inclusion of research under Comparison might be unjustifiable. Since the function is concerned, however, not only with the compilation of statistics but also with their comparison to show certain facts, just as research is concerned with the compilation of technical data to reveal other facts, the two cannot properly be divided.

The fourth function of Facilitation is that of Labour— the function concerned in the proper treatment of the human element in industry. This must be distinguished alike from the function of Manufacture and the co-ordinating element of Administration. In one sense, the relation of Labour to Manufacture is comparable to that of Equipment to Manufacture, since it provides the necessary labour. Without both equipment and labour, Manufacture cannot function, though it is separable from both. Whereas, however, the major portion of Equipment is concerned in the provision of buildings and plant, and is therefore a Preparative function, the major portion of Labour is concerned in the maintenance of employees after engagement, and is therefore a Facilitative function. Moreover, where Equipment is a " creative " function, in that it erects its premises and plant prior to the application of effort in manufacturing, Labour, in the Preparative sense, is purely a " selective " function, in that it selects from a natural source of effort. The selection of employees is to be regarded, therefore, rather as a part of the process of facilitating the application of effort than as preparative to such application. The function of Labour is concerned, then, with the engagement, transference and dismissal of employees, the fixing and payment of wages, the control of the human conditions of work, the training of the workers, the fostering of co-operation and the well-being of all engaged in production. Administration, on the other hand, regards the worker, in a functional sense, purely as a contributory factor to manufacture. It is not concerned with his welfare, training or wages, but only with his work. The function of Labour treats the man as a man, apart from the activity in which he is engaged. Other functions regard him in terms of the work he performs; the Labour function regards him as a human entity.

The remaining functions are those of Distribution, which we may describe as the business of disposing of the manufactured product. The whole operation of Distribution forms a quite distinct branch of any business. It is not possible to regard it as inherently associated with the activities of Preparation, Production, or Facilitation. In so far as the determination of sales policy is concerned, Distribution must come under the general direction of Administration, but, as a matter of management, it is to be regarded rather as a self-supporting unit, with its own Planning, Comparison, and Labour divisions. Its area being more restricted, however, though it is certainly divisible into functions corresponding to those of Production and Facilitation, the two immediate divisions seem to be clearly those of, firstly, Sales Planning, secondly, Sales Execution—the former corresponding to the facilitative functions of Planning and Comparison, the latter corresponding to the productive function of Manufacture, with subsidiary elements corresponding to certain parts of the functions of Equipment, Transport, and Labour. Sales Planning may be described as covering the devising of sales plans, the study of market conditions and of products, and the provision of collated data on all the factors affecting the execution of a sales policy. Sales Execution may be described as the actual execution of sales plans, the recording of results both of sales and of advertising, and the taking of such immediate steps as are necessarily more closely allied to execution than to planning as, for example, the engagement of travellers and their training, the purchase and transport of advertising matter, etc. Incidentally, it is suggested that the transport of manufactured goods is a factory facilitative function, in that the business of Production and Facilitation is not completed until the finished products are delivered to those places from which the Distributive function takes them over for immediate distribution to customers. Should the goods be dispatched direct to customers from the factory, it seems clear that, in this respect, Distribution and Transport coincide, and it is a matter of convenience only as to which function covers such dispatch and transport. If more than one form of delivery is in use as, for example, both to depots and direct to customers, obviously, since the Transport function is responsible for delivery to distributing depots, it will be the more convenient that it should also be responsible for the direct delivery to customers.

The suggestion made here, therefore, is that Distribution management is a separate and isolated division of the business, and that its two main functions are Sales Planning and Sales Execution ; but that Distribution administration is inherent in the administration of the business as a whole. In so far as Distribution is governed by the dictates of a general business policy, it is concerned in factors which concern all other functions of the business, and must accordingly be covered by the general control of Administration. In so far as, after the determination of that policy, it is a wholly separate group of activities from those concerned with the manufacture of the goods, its execution of that policy, by the framing of its own plans and by its own means of carrying out such plans, cannot but be regarded as entirely divorced from the functions of Production and Facilitation.[1]

---

[1] These notes on the functions of Distribution are inserted here in order that the functions of a business as a whole may be fully displayed. In the remainder of this book, the business of Distribution is not further discussed.

Thus far, we have determined the basic functions of industry ; we have not referred in any way to the welding of these functions into a form of organization. If it be true, however, that they constitute scientifically determined divisions, on the grounds of natural development, of inherent association and of human faculty, then it must follow that the building of an organization must coincide with these lines of demarcation. Organization, however, is more than a problem of functions. It is rather the combination of work-functions with human faculties. Organization, in fact, not only determines the piece of ground upon which a man shall work, but also the faculty he is to exercise in that work. Thus, several men will be engaged in the work of one function, but each will contribute different faculties—advisory, supervisory, clerical, and so on. It is these various faculties which we should now proceed to determine.

Before this, however, there is one general misconception which should be cleared away—the idea that " office work " is a function. Logically, there is no common factor binding different sections of office work together. Different offices are performing different types of work under different functions. In theory, this is normally recognized ; but when it comes to the making of an organization the theory is overlooked, and all office sections irrespective of basic functions are herded together under one control. What we must recognize is that clerical work is not a work-function but the exercise of a specific human faculty employable in any function. Unless we recognize this primary distinction, the resulting confusion may be considerable.

We may now consider of what nature are the faculties necessary for the proper execution of each function. All the officers of a function are not necessarily executive. Some will be advisory, others investigational. Possibly one officer will combine several faculties. He may investigate, advise, and put into execution. It is important, however, to distinguish between the three. The division of faculties may be said to have come about in the same way as the division of functions. Each faculty may be regarded as a devolution from that hypothetical condition of the " one-man " industry, where the functional divisions of faculty are concentrated in one individual. The growth of the concern involves not only a devolution of work, but also a devolution of the faculties to be exercised in its performance. Thus, together with the delegation to engineers of the installation and maintenance of Equipment are delegated also the supervisory, executive, investigational, and other faculties necessary for the execution of that work. It comes, therefore, that the work to be done is divided according to the functions already enumerated, and the requisite faculties are divided according to the various responsibilities, qualifications, and techniques necessary for the execution of those functions. We arrive ultimately at the stage where definite grades of workers, determined according to the faculties necessary, contribute their respective quotas to the common end of the efficient execution of the function.

The suggested division of faculties is shown on the accompanying figure (*vide* Fig. 2). An attempt is also made to define the title normally given to the officer contributing each faculty. This is, of course, somewhat invidious, since there is no recognized interpretation given to any of these titles. It serves, however, to bring the suggested grades more into the perspective of everyday affairs.

In considering this figure, it is necessary to remind the reader that it does not represent a form of organization, but only the faculties to be applied to the task of management. It is only half the picture. The other half is the analysis of functions. The two together form the groundwork of an organization. The description opposite each faculty in the figure is an attempt to give the broad distinctions between the sub-divisions of these faculties ;

THE FACULTIES OF MANAGEMENT

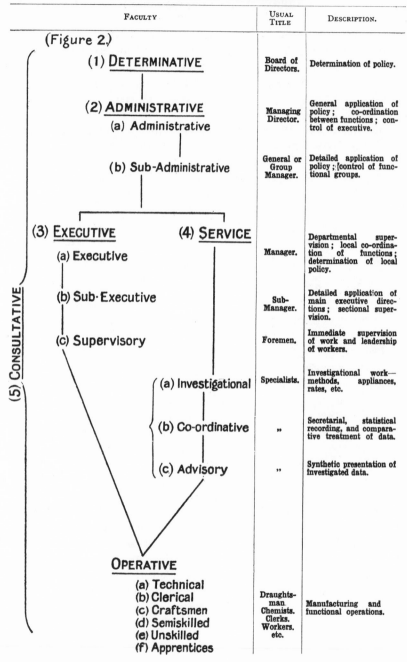

FACULTY	USUAL TITLE	DESCRIPTION.
(Figure 2.)		
(5) CONSULTATIVE		
(1) DETERMINATIVE	Board of Directors.	Determination of policy.
(2) ADMINISTRATIVE (a) Administrative	Managing Director.	General application of policy; co-ordination between functions; control of executive.
(b) Sub-Administrative	General or Group Manager.	Detailed application of policy; [control of functional groups.
(3) EXECUTIVE (a) Executive **(4) SERVICE**	Manager.	Departmental supervision; local co-ordination of functions; determination of local policy.
(b) Sub·Executive	Sub-Manager.	Detailed application of main executive directions; sectional supervision.
(c) Supervisory	Foremen.	Immediate supervision of work and leadership of workers.
(a) Investigational	Specialists.	Investigational work—methods, appliances, rates, etc.
(b) Co-ordinative	,,	Secretarial, statistical recording, and comparative treatment of data.
(c) Advisory	,,	Synthetic presentation of investigated data.
OPERATIVE (a) Technical (b) Clerical (c) Craftsmen (d) Semiskilled (e) Unskilled (f) Apprentices	Draughtsman. Chemists. Clerks. Workers. etc.	Manufacturing and functional operations.

it is equally possible that the individual may combine several faculties. It is submitted, however, that in the execution of the corporate task of production, the faculties as shown must be exercised in some form or other if that task is to be adequately performed.

The five main headings indicate the broad divisions. The first faculty at the head of the organization determines the policy of the concern. Without that faculty the business is at the mercy of every wind. The second faculty controls the general application of that policy, co-ordinates functions and the divisions into which individual functions may be split, and controls the executive faculties. The third faculty provides the local supervision and co-ordination in departments and sections of departments. The fourth faculty investigates and co-ordinates data and, upon those data, is able to act in an advisory capacity to functions. The last faculty is that which actually performs the task and applies the skill to actual operations. Running through these grades comes the faculty described as Consultative. This faculty may be provided by specially qualified individuals, whether of the staff or from outside, or by the combination of individuals in committees. It is the faculty provided by Boards of Directors, Works Councils, inter-functional or inter-departmental committees, and the manifold conferences and meetings which form so distinctive a feature of modern organizations. It is the special faculty, moreover, which is introducing the workers in industry to the business of management.[1]

Finally, the combination of these faculties with the various functions of management will provide the frame of the organization. This development from the fundamentals discussed in this chapter is considered in Chapter IV. It remains here to note three fundamental principles

[1] In connection with the faculties to be exercised in the execution of functions, the reader is referred to Chapter V of *Scientific Management* by A. D. Denning. (Nisbet & Co., 1919.)

which this chapter has revealed. Firstly, we are in a position to be convinced that there exists a scientific basis of management. Beneath all the haphazard developments of the past century, it is possible to trace general principles which a scientific investigation of facts would support. We can no longer doubt that the business of industrial management can be analysed into sections, and that upon an accumulation of facts it should be possible so to determine what those sections cover that they can ultimately be accepted as standard divisions of the work of management. We can also be sure that management is an entity in industry, clearly distinguishable alike from Capital and Labour. In the spirit of our age, moreover, we are in a position to see that habit and custom, founded upon an ignorance of basic truths, can no longer pretend to direct the developments of industry, and that foremost among the needs of those engaged in management is the capacity for scientific thinking. Custom has played its part. It has, as Professor Marshall writes, "rendered the supreme service of perpetuating any such change as found general approval"; it has "supplied a permanent body of general design on which each fresh mind might try to make some variation for the sake of economy of effort, of increased utility, or more pleasing effect." [1] But the sway of custom is being displaced by that of science. Where in the past we have neglected to analyse and to construct upon assured foundations, in the future we must plan our operations upon a carefully designed and calculated scheme, according to standards established by the closest investigation.

Secondly, if we have established the principle that management can be reduced to a science, we have simultaneously arrived at the conclusion that management can operate by scientific means rather than by the autocracy

[1] *Industry and Trade*, by Professor A. Marshall. (Macmillan & Co., Ltd., 1919.)

of the " boss." Management is no longer the wielding of the whip ; it is rather the delving into experience and the building upon facts. Its leadership is based upon knowledge rather than upon force. Its task is no longer solely that of " getting the job through." Rather, in many of its activities, it operates through the application of a capacity trained in the investigation and solution of problems. Management, in fact, instead of being a law unto itself, has found that there are laws which it must obey.

Finally, we must be convinced that the practice of management can no longer be entrusted to incompetent individuals. It is no sinecure for the eldest son ; no path of roses for the leisurely parasite. If management is founded upon a science, if its practice is a profession, then in the future we must expect its exponents to be men of high ability and the fullest knowledge—men who have graduated in their profession, and are qualified thereby to be entrusted with the responsibilities which its practice imposes.

CHAPTER III

THE SOCIAL RESPONSIBILITY OF MANAGEMENT

SUMMARY

(a) Management is primarily the art of directing human activities ; science is supplementary. This distinguishes management from technology and likens it to the professions. Two broad sections of social aspect of management—(a) relation to the community, (b) relation to those it directs.

(b) Production and distribution are relative to the needs of the community ; this forms the economic basis for the belief that industry exists for the service of the community ; service cannot be wholly economic ; it is ethical in motive. This motive becomes clearer as management takes up its new position. It is a motive acceptable to both management and labour. This motive or ideal subordinates wealth to well-being, it gives an ethical as well as an economic value to goods. It gives the community an interest in industrial methods and the industrial structure. Certain implications follow upon this motive, the achievement of which depends upon efficiency.

(c) The doctrine of service forms a new conception of relationship of management to labour. The worker is primarily an individual and a citizen ; factory life reacts upon social life. Management, therefore, has a communal responsibility. Necessity for a human side of management. Need for courtesy and fellowship, in which management must lead. Need for psychological research in industry. Need for industrial idealism. Need for an application of democracy in industry.

(d) The doctrine of service concerns the standard of living and hours of work. Standard of living is not only material, but dependent upon efficiency, as a basis for a high general standard. Effect of fatigue study on problem of leisure. Communal disadvantages of long hours and monotony ; a fruitful field for psychology.

(e) Certain indications given by the doctrine of service as regards unemployment, industrial control, and prosperity sharing. Rights involve obligations, privileges involve service. Need to resurrect the basic ethics of industry. Co-operation must replace competition. Material progress must be accompanied by moral progress. This begins with a realization of the basic purpose of industry.

IN the preceding chapter, industrial management was treated of as a necessary activity, developing with the progressive complexity of industry, covering certain well-defined areas, executed by certain general methods and involving particular faculties. The combination of these was the basis of organization. Organization, however, is not management, nor is the task of organizing a business the same task as managing a business. The organization of the factory is the design of the garden before management plants and nourishes the seeds which are to form the garden produce. Administration makes the design ; organization is the design ; management uses the design. Management, however, is not simply a function concerned with machines, layout, accounts and scientific methods. It is primarily an art—" the art of managing by direction or regulation." (*Century Dictionary.*) Above all it is a human art. Management is, indeed, above all, the art of directing and regulating the activities of human beings, during great portions of their waking hours, for the satisfaction of the material needs of their fellows, and for the satisfaction and development of their own material requirements and moral and mental faculties.

There is an immediate need to emphasize this point. Industrial management is primarily the management of men. The present wave of scientific study in management is often criticized on the grounds that it tends to make it careless of the human element. It cannot be denied that modern developments have added to the task of management many supplementary functions of a more or less technically scientific character. This, however, in no single respect, has robbed management of its first and foremost task of managing men. All the science which modern research and progress have brought to the methods of industrial administration is justifiable only if thereby the management of men is rendered more efficient. Applied factory science cannot produce without men, but men can produce without science. Men are fundamental, science is supplementary.

" The art of managing men," said Sir Lynden Macassey in a lecture to the Institute of Industrial Administration, "getting the best out of them, is usually regarded, in my experience, by Capital as a sort of customary by-product of technical ability." Before we come to the problem of organizing the factory, it is essential to make it quite clear that the pre-eminent task of management, through all the various channels of production and facilitation, is the direction of the activities of human beings. The exercise of management, therefore, requires human faculties. It is not the operation of a machine, but rather the direction of a complex and nervous organism. Obviously this demands more than scientific method, more than efficient machinery, more than technical skill. Permeating these, and greater than any one, is the necessary quality of human understanding. This is not inherent in any technique. Technique may be of the highest, but without the leaven of human understanding its contribution to production may be of little avail. The practice of management is therefore wholly distinct from its underlying technique. In this respect, management comes into line with the recognized professions. In none of them is knowledge of itself enough ; each one requires the qualities of human sympathy, understanding, and skill in its application.

In the building, therefore, of an organization through which management may efficiently carry out its duties, the human factor with which management must deal must be taken into reckoning. It is not enough that the administrator should erect his organization upon an analysis of the material divisions of his task, the methods of accomplishing it, and the faculties necessary for its execution. He must also analyse his aims, his ideals, the spirit which shall rule and inform his management, and his relations to the human element in the actual work of production. A scientific analysis of the various features of management is useless, if the fundamental fact be overlooked that management is not solely the scientific employment of a machine, which shall produce in rigid ratio to the care exercised in its construction, but rather the art of combining human and material factors into a single harmonious enterprise.

The responsibility of management is a human responsibility, occasioned rather by its control of men than its application of technique. The student of economics does not bear the same responsibility as the manager who applies his economics. Whether management knows much or little of its own science, its responsibility remains unaffected. The responsibility of management resides in the fact that the industry which it directs is composed of human as well as material elements. Furthermore, that responsibility is enhanced by the fact that industry exists for the satisfaction of human needs. Management has, therefore, a responsibility not only to the human element within industry, but also to the human element which industry serves.

Consequently, in considering the social aspect of management, there are two broad divisions : firstly, the relation of management, as an integral and directive force in industry, to the general body of the community ; secondly, the relation of management to the human element engaged in industry. In the one, management bears the responsibility of industry as a whole, since it holds the reins of industry ; in the other, it bears the responsibility of its own service to those whom it directs.

In its relation to the community, management is representative of industry as a whole. For management is, as it were, the helmsman of a giant schooner, which it steers, amid winds and waves, towards the harbour of its communal end. That is the fundamental purpose of management. During the last two centuries, industry has become increasingly complex, so that its fundamental purpose has been obscured in the maze of operations necessary for its accomplishment. Professor Sorley recently described industry as " the human processes by which material things are made subservient to the creation of values ; that is to say, the production of something which is, or which is supposed to be, of worth to men."[1] It is not industry, in fact, but the community which assesses the value of the products of industry. The object of

---

[1] " Some Ethical Aspects of Industry," by Prof. W. R. Sorley, Litt.D., F.B.A., LL.D., in *Lectures on Industrial Administration.* (Pitman, 1920.)

industry is not, therefore, pure production of goods, but the production of those goods which, in the eyes of a part or the whole of the community, have some value. In so far as management contròls such production, it must operate in some direct relation to the community. It is charged with the production of such goods as are socially requisite or for which a demand exists. Incidentally, it should be made clear that management is here used in a generic sense, and that in proportion as the workers are consulted, proffer suggestions and skill, or even knowingly and willingly assist in production, the workers themselves share with management that same responsibility.

The production of serviceable goods, however, is not all, since the community requires that those goods shall be made available at a price which it can reasonably afford to pay, and shall be of such a character as reasonably to satisfy the needs which they are designed to satisfy. This constitutes a demand from the community for efficient production, by means of efficient administration, management, and organization, skilled workmanship, fair profits, and legitimate wages.

It is clear, therefore, that fundamentally, whatever may be the obscurities which economic progress has introduced, industry, and more especially the management of industry, is subject at any rate in an economic sense to the community. This is the foundation of that theory which postulates " service to the community " as the primary motive and fundamental basis of industry. " Unless industry is really recognized as primarily a national service, in which each individual is fulfilling his function to the best of his ability for the sake of the community, in which private gain is subordinated to public good, in which, in a word, we carry out our duty towards our neighbour—unless we build on this foundation, there is no hope of creating the House Beautiful." [1]

[1] Mr. W. L. Hichens, in *Some Problems of Modern Industry.* (Nisbet & Co., 1918.)

In so far as the motive of industry is that of service, it cannot be wholly economic. Any service which places the good of the person or community served above the advantage gained by the servant cannot be wholly economic or material. It may be economic in character but must be ethical in motive. It is this motive which distinguishes the modern interpretation of the service rendered by industry. That industry renders an economic service to the community has never been doubted ; the new philosophy insists that the good of the community, furthered by such service, shall be the determining factor, rather than the monetary profit which is incidental to such service. The lack of this motive in industry prompted Ruskin to place the professions infinitely above it in the scale of social service, because, whilst the professions were actuated by the motive of " a good service," the motive of industry was self-seeking.

How far does the condemnation of Ruskin hold good in this generation ? With the changes in the times, the spirit of industry is undoubtedly changing. As ownership comes to lean more and more upon management, and the latter proceeds to fashion an entity of its own and carves out its own province and its own standards of accomplishment, it is beginning to find a new motive, more in harmony with its struggle towards a professional standard, driving through the direction of its efforts, a new philosophy informing its endeavours. Management is finding the light of a new spirit glinting from the pinnacles of its corporate task. That spirit is the spirit of service—the conception of industrial management as a social force directing industry to the service of the community. It is a motive in which both Management and Labour must share. Who knows that it may not be the motive which will ultimately link all the partners in production in a common enthusiasm for a mutually acceptable object ?

In a " Bill of Rights " of 119 labour unions which

assembled at Washington recently, the following significant words occur—

" The ideal of America should be the organization of industry for service, and not for profit alone. . . . Labour is anxious to work out better methods for industry, and demands that it be assured that increased productivity will be used for service and not alone for profit."

The same voice echoes on this side of the Atlantic in the famous opening phrase of the Foster Report of the Industrial Council of the Building industry—

" It sounds across the whole industrial arena, the trumpet call of a new idea—the conception of our industry as a great self-governing democracy of organized public service."

As capital recedes from actual participation in the day-to-day affairs of industry and management extends its sphere, the motive of profit alone becomes increasingly remote and archaic.   As the primary partners in production become increasingly untrammelled by the interference of capital in the conduct of industry, the need for a motive and an ideal, which will adequately interpret the fundamental purpose for which industry exists, becomes a common necessity. The profession of the manager is becoming a public one ; he is beginning to sense his obligation to the community. We are indeed witnessing the entry into the direction of industry of ethical considerations as a determining factor in policy, at least equal to considerations of profit or personal advancement. Such considerations assume rights held by the community, not only over the products of industry but over its methods. They assume industrial responsibilities with regard to the conditions which the community may impose. " Business will sooner or later have to justify its management. It will have to sustain its claim to social support."[1] That support will be afforded in proportion as management is

[1] Mr. S. Elmo Lewis.

actuated by motives generally acceptable to the conscience of the community.

If the motive of service is to determine the ideal towards which industry directed by management is to strive, there stand before industry three concrete objectives, summarized by Mr. Seebohm Rowntree in the following terms—[1]

(1) Industry should create goods or provide services of such kinds, and in such measure, as may be beneficial to the community.

(2) In the process of wealth production, industry should pay the greatest possible regard to the general welfare of the community, and pursue no policy detrimental to it.

(3) Industry should distribute the wealth produced in such a manner as will best serve the highest ends of the community.

The ideal of service, in fact, subordinates wealth, its creation and distribution, to the higher necessity of well-being—a well-being not of individuals but of all the component parts of the community. For the spirit of the leadership exercised by the directors of industry counts for not a little among national ideals. If industrial leadership is self-seeking, devoted only to material ends, national ideals tend to follow a similar course.

Moreover, in this connection it must always be remembered that a low material standard, consequent upon the under-production or mal-distribution of wealth, involves a low moral standard. "A higher standard of living is not merely physical enjoyment and capacity to spend ; it involves, in a higher degree, honour, character, sense of responsibility, and thrift." [2]

The value of the products of industry, therefore, is not wholly, as the economists declare, their value in exchange.

[1] *The Human Factor in Business.* (Longmans, Green & Co. 1921.)

[2] The late Sir H. B. Rowell, K.C.B., in *The Glasgow Herald*, 30th Dec., 1920.

It is conceivable that goods may possess an ethical value which is assessable in no ratio whatever to their economic value. The ethical value of goods produced under " sweated " conditions, or of goods deleterious to the well-being of the community, may indeed be in inverse ratio to the economic value of those goods. As Professor Marshall points out in his analysis of the industrial strength of Holland[1]—" Not all of those characteristics of manufacture, to which its importance is owing, are of high quality. The substitution of repetition work in massive, standardized production, even though it be true to the thousandth part of an inch, is not an advance, from the human point of view, over skilled handicraft ; it increases man's power over matter, but it may diminish his power over himself."

If the methods of industry are to be thus subjected to a double valuation, ethical as well as economic, clearly management is called upon to readjust its viewpoint. It can no longer regard the maintenance of the present structure of industry as an end in itself. Distant ideals compel long views. In taking that long view, management may perhaps espy the time when the moulding of the spirit of the community will count as much as the production of goods.

As management, and industry generally, increase in efficiency, the expenditure of less physical effort per unit follows naturally. Management takes on more, while Labour, as such, takes on less ; more brain-work is balanced by less manual work. The necessity which compels a large proportion of the population to devote itself to unsatisfying, but often exhausting, toil will be reduced in proportion as industry becomes more efficient. The potential human effectiveness thus released may well be directed to ends which, in the eyes of an enlightened community, are higher than the material provision for its own wants under circumstances which conduce little to

[1] *Industry and Trade. Vide supra.*

the exercise of the highest human faculties.   If a community is to advance spiritually as well as materially, the subordination of its spiritual faculties to the routine toil of industrial life must progressively diminish.   However efficient, in fact, may be the material service of industry to the community, that service is not complete unless it allows the maximum opportunity to those engaged in it to develop those higher capacities which industrial life at present hardly calls into practice.   When the motive of industry is truly the service of the community, it will not only rule the methods of the industrialism we know, but will also mould the form of an industrialism of which we are yet but faintly aware.   As a community, we have come to regard the present form of industrialism as a *sine quâ non* of modern society.   At all events, we may look forward to a time when industry will be so transformed that, if mechanical and unsatisfying toil should still be necessary, the largest possible opportunity will be afforded to the worker to devote himself to other interests, in which he may use his higher faculties more profitably to the community.

These, then, are the three implications of the motive of service : firstly, that, in its present form, industry shall value its policies and methods by ethical as well as economic standards ; secondly, that industry shall aim at a structure wherein each individual gives of his best, and is called upon to express his personality, if not in the actual operation he carries out, at least in his relations with his fellow-workers and the management ; thirdly, that industry shall so conduct its business that all engaged in it have the opportunity to devote their highest faculties to what is communally the highest.

Progress towards these ideals is dependent upon the efficiency of industry.   In proportion as industry can satisfy the material needs of the community with a less degree of human effort, there will be a surplus of such effort available for higher communal purposes.   This, however, will require more highly developed management.   There is, in fact, ample scope for the exercise of higher faculties both outside and within industry. While research and invention reduce the need for human effort upon mechanical work, they continually open up paths for further research and invention. The development of industrial efficiency, in fact, makes possible the advance of society to a higher standard, where the practice of the higher faculties and virtues becomes necessary.

The amazing productivity of war-time industry is an indication of what may be accomplished in industry under the impulse of service. It has already been authoritatively estimated that the work of the world, by scientific organizing, could be performed by each worker contributing four hours of work per working day. Who knows what scientific advance may not be made which will reduce the hours of manual toil to a small percentage of the present level? Research, invention, organization, management and technical skill hold possibilities which may so radically alter the methods of industry, as to minimize to a degree we little think possible the necessity for the application of human effort in industry.

It is by no means impossible to conceive of an industrialism, infinitely more productive, operated by a tithe of the monotonous toil it demands to-day, releasing its workers for many hours of every day for interests more satisfying to their higher faculties, and only employing for whole-time work men who will be required to exercise in their work a degree of spiritual and mental ability equal to that required in any other social activity. This is the ideal which the doctrine of service unfolds. Every step which renders industry more efficient is a conscious move forward to that ideal. Every improvement in the technique of manufacture, in the organization of individual concerns, in the leadership and workmanship of labour, and in the management of all the factors of production and distribution —every such improvement may be to further, not only the good of industry, but also the good of the community.

The responsibility of management is the perfection of the machinery of production. The responsibility of the community is that, as the service which industry renders becomes increasingly efficient both materially and humanly, it shall make provision for the devotion of that energy which industry does not require, to ends which both employ the best service of the individual and subserve the highest ideals of society.

If these be the deductions to be drawn from this doctrine of service as regards the relation of management to the community, what deductions may we draw as regards the relation of management to those whom it directs ? This is, in effect, to analyse the basic principles which shall govern our labour administration.

Service to the community consists in supplying it not only with the goods it requires for material existence, but also with the citizens it requires to enable it to advance. The worker in industry, therefore, is not solely a means for the production of goods, but also an agent in social progress. His function is not only industrial, but communal. He is not only a worker, but also an individual. This is the basic principle which forms the social obligation of management—the obligation to regard the worker, not as a perquisite of industry but as an individual, loaned to industry for the betterment of the community. The tie which binds the employee to his factory is not the only one which is bound round his life. There are domestic ties, social ties, trade ties, national ties, and religious ties, over which there is no reason to suppose that the economic tie has a prior right. The economic relationship between worker and manager cannot cancel the worker's relationship elsewhere.

The task of management, therefore, is not simply the co-ordination of men and work as if the two were on the same plane. The man is infinitely more complex than his machine. Where the design of work requires technique and brains, the leadership of men calls for patience, courage, and, above all, sympathy. The human element in the factory is subject to neither calculation nor measurement. It is a whirling maelstrom of jostling colours, a jumble of perpetually changing light and shade. For one moment, as it were, management focuses the gyrating elements upon one object. To each individual it apportions a task.

This accomplished, however, the responsibility of management is not completed. Management cannot accept responsibility for the individual as worker, and deny its responsibility for him as a social unit. The two are inextricably intertwined. It is impossible to dissociate life outside from life inside the factory. The one reacts upon the other because the individual entity remains constant. Management inevitably, therefore, is loaded with responsibilities which stretch beyond the local sphere of production. The influence which management exerts upon the individual in industry cannot but react upon the same individual in his other capacities. All activity is educative. The spirit which management inspires in its workers must inevitably affect their spirit as parents, voters, and citizens.

This responsibility is the greater in that management not only directs the activities of some 34 per cent of the population, but does so, to-day, for the greater part of their waking hours.[1] No other form of social activity exercises anything approaching the same sway. The church may claim a minority of them for but a couple of hours a week ; the State may claim them for very much less. But industry claims them from morning to night, from youth to old age. Clearly, then, the production of goods is not the only service which management renders the community. It has it within its grasp to make or to

[1] Professor Bowley, in *The Division of the Product of Industry* (Clarendon Press, 1919), states that of a population in the U.K. in April, 1911, of 45,220,000, some 15,650,000 were wage-earners. This includes, of course, some proportion not employed in strictly industrial undertakings.

unmake men ; to lift them or to throw them upon the social dustheap ; to build them up or to destroy them. It may make a State great, because of its citizens ; homes happy, because of their parents ; communities highminded, because of their counsellors ; or it may crush State, home, and township under the weight of an apathetic, careless, toil-worn, degraded or selfish mentality among the mass of the people. Management requires more than production engineers and efficiency experts, more than scientists and statisticians. Its primary need is for leaders, and for the methods which conduce to the best leadership. " It takes doctors, lawyers, engineers, poets, and I don't know what to run the business nowadays, and I reckon that improvements which call for parsons will be creeping in next," observes the " Self-Made Merchant " to his son. Industry indeed calls for the service of all trades, but it demands that there shall be common to every trade the spirit which regards the work of each as a high trust confided to it by a sovereign community, and its control of the workers as a responsibility unequalled, an opportunity unrivalled, for making the work of each individual the means to a life devoted to the highest good of all.

The worker in industry is seeking a living, not for its own sake, but that it may provide for him the means to a life outside industry. Management, consequently, is not dealing simply with workers as so many " hands " but with workers as individual men—men with a multitudinous variety of interests, of an infinite complexity of temperament, endowed with widely diverse degrees of capacity in different spheres, reacting to outside influences in many varying ways, capable in the mass of wonderful feats of combined enthusiasm and dynamic action, yet individually distinguishable from the very movements of which they form a part. The concentration of such complex material upon a common task is primarily the task of that leadership which is sympathetic, yet strong ; conscious of its responsibility to the worker, yet not unconscious of the worker's obligation to it ; wholly human, yet not humanly frail ; inspired by high motives, yet not blind to everyday weaknesses ; working towards an ideal, yet profoundly aware of the gulf between the actual and that ideal. Without such leadership, management will find, as it has found, that science is of little avail, that organization may be but a hollow framework, and industry, instead of reverberating with the clangour of corporate effort, may resound with the clash of battle.

In proportion as management comes to realize the prodigious complexity of the human element it directs, it will also realize that certain principles must be admitted, certain rights and obligations recognized. The worker does not sell his social birth-right for the economic mess of pottage. Neither are his rights those of a primitive community, but rather the rights of a member of a civilized, educated, and democratic state. Both employer and worker have rights and corresponding obligations. Further, in so far as those rights are ethically dependent upon the due performance of function, the worker must share the rights and obligations of the management, if he be called upon to perform any part of the function of management, just as the manager must share the rights and obligations of the worker, if he be called upon to perform any part of the function of operation. The worker who is taken into consultation in matters of management must accept the obligation to formulate policy upon principles in harmony with the best interests of the community. The manager who assists in the processes of manufacture must likewise accept the obligation to render work of a justifiable, efficient character. In the proper performance of such obligations, the claim to corresponding rights is born, but without such performance such rights have no justification.

Every manager is required to form an opinion as to the nature of the rights which follow upon the recognition of the principle that the worker is not solely an industrial unit, but also an individual and a citizen. The recognition of such rights imposes an obligation to observe them.   In other spheres, the idiosyncrasies of the individual are tolerated.   We must remember that the worker, too, has his whims and prejudices, likes and dislikes, feelings and dreams, odd tags of sentiment, rough corners and sore spots.   Because a man is a worker in industry he is not thereby any the less a human being, shrouded in the tattered patchwork quilt with which men clothe themselves. The worker demands the courtesy and respect payable to any man who contributes his quota of service.   " In the long run," says Mr. Sidney Webb, " the British workmen of to-day will only do their best if they are not treated as slaves, not as serfs, not as horses, not even as ignorant savages, but as intelligent human beings, having equal rights to life, liberty and the pursuit of happiness, and willingly co-operating of their own accord in what they feel to be a common enterprise."[1] Nor are forms of courtesy enough.   The courtesy must be animated by a genuine sense of fellowship.   Fellowship betokens equality —an equality, not the result of the mighty condescending to tread the path of the lowly, not the outcome of the gentility of philanthropy, but the flower of a truly profound sense of common humanity, bound together in the pursuit of a common purpose.   " Justice between man and man does not imply that all men are equal," says Professor Baillie, but it certainly does imply that all men are reducible to terms of a common manhood.   Men are unequal in what they become, but are fundamentally equal in what they are.   Varying degrees of status rest upon a basic humanity, just as varying degrees of bonus rest upon a basic minimum.

The practice of the art of fellowship is the first obligation laid upon management.   Fellowship is the foundation of the life of goodwill.   It is of no avail to contend that it requires two to form a fellowship, and that the workers

[1] *The Works Manager To-day*, by Sidney Webb. (Longmans, Green, 1917.)

in industry are not prepared to join in it. Civilization has progressed, not by the leaders in any activity reducing their standard to that of the mass, but by their leavening of the mass by the force of example, often exercised with an infinitude of patience in the face of a discouraging response. The method of progress has been to build a bridge, not that the van might join the rearguard, but that the whole column might pass over under the leadership of the van. The leaders in any enterprise must themselves be the sappers who build the bridge of goodwill.

Management has, moreover, the obligation to make the most of each individual, not only that the service of industry as a whole may be of the richest, but also that the service of each individual may be developed to the highest degree. It seems incredible that the potential force inherent in the vast majority of men should, unless fortune, fate, or faculty has carved a way for them, be left unexplored and unemployed. Mute, inglorious Miltons and village Hampdens doubtless tread the floors of every factory. Yet, no thoroughbred horse heaves between the shafts of the brewer's dray. If we are to develop the best capacity in our workers and win the best results, we must at least afford them the careful study which the thoroughbred receives. The worker's employment should be such as to facilitate the best use of his individual capacity ; the character of his work should be suited to his particular temperament ; promotion should be open where ability presents itself. Where this state of things is absent, inefficiency reigns. The industrial " misfit " is but one degree better than the industrial " cast off." More pitiable than even the sensitive man exposed to rigorous toil, the dexterous man engaged upon heavy work, a rough temperament employed upon delicate tasks, a trained worker occupied on casual jobs, is the man who can find no work at all. Misemployment is, however, the precursor of unemployment, and its partner in futility.

There is an unlimited scope for psychology in industry. The pity is that every manager is not a psychologist. Its place in industry, moreover, is not as a lever of efficiency alone but also as a right of the worker. It is the due of the worker that, both psychologically and physiologically, his individual capacity should be explored and utilized to the best advantage. " Disorders on the bodily side of the organism become reflected in disorders on the mental side," writes Professor Myers.[1] Both in mind and body the entity of the individual worker demands analysis and proper usage. This is the more imperative as society becomes more complex as a result of education and democracy. " The spread of democracy brings with it, temporarily or semi-permanently, a hair-trigger organization of society, in which mental factors are capable of more immediate and powerful results than ever before."[2] As the individual becomes more complex, the necessity for an adequate study of his complexes grows more insistent. The individual worker, subjected on tne one hand to toil which his fundamental instincts, feelings and mentality reject as unsatisfying ; operating under conditions involving fatigue, hardship, strain, lack of interest, or monotony ; yet, on the other hand, outside industry, open to influences tending to develop responsibility, self-discipline, social intercourse, or moral rectitude, conscious of capacity, fired with ideals, or imbued with ambitions which industry fails to recognize or encourage—is no longer content to be merely disappointed with the order of things. Rather he may bring the whole body of society, of which he is a member, to witness that his entity demands from industry, if not the satisfaction, at any rate, the facilitation of its mental, moral, and physical aspirations. Society declares him a man, and industry must treat him as a man. It becomes more than productive policy, therefore, that

[1] " Industrial Overstrain and Unrest," by C. S. Myers, M.A., M.D., Sc.D., F.R.S., in *Lectures on Industrial Administration.* (Pitman, 1920.)

[2] Professor T. H. Pear.

he shall be provided with work suited to his capacities, that he shall work under conditions conducive to health and sound workmanship, and that his work shall affect him only for good ; it becomes a social obligation.

Democracy and education, furthermore, not only render society and the individual more complex, but also combine to create ideals. Education opens up long vistas, and democracy appears as a power whereby those vistas may be traversed. Together, they bring ideals into the life of everyday. Industry cannot deny ideals if the weight of the community supports them. " No man pretending to sanity can challenge in matters temporal and civil the ultimate authority of whatever is felt to be the general civic sense which builds up a State." [1] The ideal which the community adopts cannot be rejected by industry. If democracy is the ideal of a community, however much the control required in industry may appear to differ from the control required in the State, the obligation rests upon industry to mould its form of governance nearer to the expressed and fundamental belief of the community. " Reasoning men have protested, and justly, against that conception that what a majority in numbers, or even (what is more compelling still) a unanimity of decision in a community may order, may not only be wrong, but may be something which that community has no authority to order since, though it possesses a civil and temporal authority, it acts against that ultimate authority which is its own consciousness of right. . . . But men nowhere do or can deny that the community acting as it thinks right is ultimately sovereign ; there is no alternative to so plain a truth." [2] Industry is not external to society. The worker is justified in claiming that the principles which govern the control of himself as citizen shall also apply to the control of himself as worker. Management, therefore,

[1] *The French Revolution*, by Hilaire Belloc. (Home University Library.)
[2] *Ibid.*

is concerned in the local interpretation of communal ideals. This implies that management is required to apply only those principles and ideals which clearly march in line with accepted social standards.   Ideals are essential in the life of any progressive enterprise.   There is no greater danger to any State, or part of a State, than that it should rest contented with things as they are.   Healthy discontent is a presage of growth.   Management, therefore, must not only apply the principles and pursue the ideals which already actuate the community, but must also inspire fresh industrial ideals.   No leadership which does not continually hold aloft not only the light of an ideal but the torch whereby other ideals may be found, can expect to lead into a future of great achievement.

Ideals, moreover, are the perquisite of no one grade of society.   As education sheds light increasingly upon the path each individual treads, ideals spring into life.   Management cannot neglect those thoughts on progress which emanate from other sources, especially from the workers. The right of the educated man is to express his opinion. Industry, in face of the upward movement of the mentality of the mass, can no longer tolerate autocratic survivals from an age when autocracy in industry was perhaps justifiable.   Even if the educational standard of the people is not what it might be, management must at least prepare for changes.   We cannot wait for a highly educated democracy before installing democratic government.   We must forestall it by introducing the workers to some share in the determination of policy, and thus prepare them for a task which later they will unitedly demand.   It is not beyond the bounds of possibility to picture the commonalty of this country endowed with an education comparable to that which is at present the invaluable privilege of the favoured few who have benefited by a University training. Yet one cannot by any stretch of imagination picture the mentality, normally consequent upon such a liberal education, content to be subject to an autocracy which it has had no share in instituting. It will submit to direction only if it shares in setting up that direction and qualifying its policy. A gradual process of taking the workers into consultation, proceeding in some general ratio to their educational standard, is apparently, therefore, an obligation upon management, which it disregards at the risk of a violent rupture at a later date. What the worker claims as a right of citizenship must ultimately, after making the adaptations due to the different characters of state and industry, be translated into industry.

Two other aspects of the human side of industrial management here demand our attention ; firstly, the problem of the standard of living ; secondly, the problem, already referred to in Chapter I, of the minimum of leisure. " Increased means and increased leisure are the two civilizers of men," said Disraeli. They are closely allied, in that leisure without adequate material means whereby to use it profitably is an empty gift. Clearly, further, though both these problems are partially matters of internal administration in that both are dependent upon productivity, both are equally matters of social concern, since a low material standard affords little chance for communal progress in those forms of service which require from individuals constant thought and practical interest. The problem of the standard of living is, therefore, further considered in Chapter V under the subject of Wages. We should here, however, emphasize the concern of the community as a whole in this problem and the kindred one of hours of work.

From the social standpoint, the standard of living of the community is not a purely material standard ; rather it should be regarded as " the good life " of Greek philosophy—the combination of well-being and virtue, of excellence in living and development in character. Under modern conditions, however, a high moral and intellectual standard is largely dependent upon a certain minimum material standard. Though the two standards are in truth on wholly different planes, nevertheless a low material standard, if not actually preventive of, is certainly a deterrent to a high moral and intellectual standard. It is clear, further, that a high material standard is of little avail for those purposes for which the community requires it, unless it be accompanied by an amount of leisure adequate for the attainment of an intellectual standard suitable to the present position of civilization. The community, therefore, demands both an adequate standard of living and a margin of leisure for its members who are engaged in industry. It demands this, not as the right of the individual worker, but as a proper service which industry should render. Clearly, the extension of these benefits is dependent upon the productivity of industry. Wages, enough to provide for every worker a material standard proper to modern social conditions, can only come from industry if industry be conducted so efficiently as to be able to afford them. The standard of living is relative, therefore, not only to the social requirements, but also to industrial prosperity. The furthering of such prosperity is the business of no single partner in industry ; it can only arise as the result of united effort. The responsibility of management, however, is none the less clear because it is shared with Capital and Labour. More efficient work on the part of Labour must be balanced by more efficient management. " The call of the day is for better work, more efficient work. The call is the more persistent and clamant according to the responsibility of the worker. Efficiency in a hundred manual workers will hardly equal in result efficiency in a highly placed administrative officer. We may study the motions of a worker's hands as he operates a machine, but they are as nothing to the motions of an administrator's brain in their bearing upon output." [1]

Efficiency, moreover, has no moral justification unless

[1] " The Immediate Future of Industrial Management." Article contributed to *Business Organisation and Management*, Sept., 1920, by the present author.

the benefits accruing from it are equitably distributed. The payment of " a living wage," therefore, must remain a first charge upon industry. The offer of the coalowners in the strike of April, 1921, to make wages a first charge upon revenue, to forgo profits for a stated period, and limit profits to a percentage of wages in the future, is a striking though tardy recognition of a new conception of managerial responsibility to the community. War-time price fluctuations have obscured this responsibility. Upon such shifting foundations it has been impossible to determine what constitutes a reasonable standard. The responsibility for the payment of the highest possible wages is, however, outside the area of debate. Debate can only concern itself with the practical interpretation of that principle. In such debate, the constant pressure of the social conscience will insist that the highest possible wage is that wage which is payable as a result of the utmost application of ability, genius, science, organization, leadership, and workmanship in industry itself. So long as there is inefficiency, either in workers or managers, the community cannot be satisfied that the highest possible standard of living has been attained.

The adequate provision of leisure, however, is a necessary corollary of a high material standard, if our social development is to be intellectual as well as material. " All industrious people," says Mr. Denning, " rightly expect a good day's work to provide something more than bare necessities —some articles or services that make for the comfort, dignity, and enjoyment of life."[1] Such advantages are mainly available only as leisure is extended. The problem of the hours of work in relation to social progress has received but too little consideration; though now the general apathy is being dispelled by the miners' seven-hour day and Lord Leverhulme's six-hour day proposal.

The number of working hours is, like the standard of

[1] *Scientific Factory Management*, by A. D. Denning, M.Sc., M.A., Ph.D. (Nisbet & Co., 1919.)

living, relative to productivity. Here, the ground is shifting, for the recognition of the element of fatigue may upset many of our calculations. The Report of the Committee on the Health of Munition Workers proves clearly that long hours, accompanied by fatigue and strain, are responsible for a large degree of inefficiency. Long hours, in fact, do not necessarily mean high productivity, neither is it a certain remedy for low production to increase the hours of work. There is, indeed, ample evidence that, in certain processes, a reduction of hours, or a redistribution of hours, may not only leave the volume of production per worker unimpaired, but may even considerably augment it. It is indisputable that there are few types of work which cannot be so analysed and studied that changes lessening the incidence of fatigue upon the physique and mentality of the worker can be made without detriment to output and with advantage to the worker.[1] The progressive satisfaction of the social requirement that adequate leisure shall be assured to the workers in a measure compatible with the output necessary to meet the legitimate needs of the community, would therefore appear, at any

[1] The reader is referred to the lectures and writings of Professors C. S. Myers, B. Muscio, and T. H. Pear, also of Major Gilbreth, especially " Mind and Work " by Prof. C. S. Myers, and " Fatigue Study " by F. B. and L. M. Gilbreth. Also to the following official papers—

(a) Report of British Association Committee on the Question of Fatigue from the Economic Standpoint. Transactions of British Association, 1915.

(b) Report on The Eight-Hours Day or Forty-Eight Hours week, prepared by the Organizing Committee for the International Labour Conference, Washington, 1919.

(c) Comparison of an Eight-Hour Plant and a Ten-Hour Plant, U.S.A. Public Health Bulletin 106. Report by Josephine Goldmark, and Mary D. Hopkins, Feb., 1920.

(d) Report No. 6 of Industrial Fatigue Research Board on The Speed of Adaptation of Output to Altered Hours of Work, 1920.

(e) Report No. 1 of Industrial Fatigue Research Board on The Influence of Hours of Work and of Ventilation on Output in Tin-Plate Manufacture, 1920.

(f) Research Report No. 32 (Dec., 1920) of National Industrial Conference Board (U.S.A.) on Practical Experience with the Work Week of 48 Hours or Less.

rate, a possibility, provided management is sufficiently alive to the advantages to be derived from the psychological study of particular types of work.

There is, however, a tendency on the part of management to relegate this problem, and the consequent responsibility for its solution, to a minor position. The administrator, constantly alert and occupied in a variety of tasks demanding thought and discussion, is inclined to overlook the featureless routine, often amounting to sheer drudgery, in which the majority of workers are occupied. He is apt to regard leisure as relative to responsibility, forgetting that it must also be relative to the character of work. If the manager requires leisure because his work is mentally exhausting, the worker requires it because his work is monotonous.

Leisure, however, is not a purely internal matter of administration. It is rather that period of every man's life to which the community looks for that service which is no less essential than material service in the factory. The word " leisure " is derived from *scholê*, signifying " schooling." If leisure is truly to benefit the community, the more closely it can approximate to its original significance the more thorough the advantage to the community. The certainty that leisure will be misused, however, should form no obstacle in our efforts to ensure it. " There cannot be a great, sudden improvement in man's conditions of life ; for he forms them as much as they form him, and he himself cannot change fast ; but we must press on steadfastly towards the distant goal where the opportunities of a noble life may be accessible to all." [1] The importance of leisure is not that it can immediately conjure up a Utopia, but rather that it is the necessary provision of the means whereby the foundations of Utopia may be laid. Prolonged hours of monotonous toil militate against the beneficial use of leisure, firstly, by restricting

[1] *Industry and Trade* (Appendix P), by Professor Alfred Marshall. (Macmillan & Co., 1919.)

the facilities for that study and social intercourse which
spell development ; secondly, by rendering the worker
incapable of fully applying his faculties when work is
finished. Professor Marshall quotes Abbé, the guiding
genius of the Zeiss glass works, as follows : " The worker
suffering from the monotony of always having to work
in the same groove, whether with the hand or brain, has
his mental vision thereby dulled for anything situated
beyond his own narrow horizon, and loses the power of
utilizing at the right moment for his own particular purpose
anything lying beyond his ordinary everyday path."

Against such results of factory life, a progressive community cannot but register an emphatic protest, however
much economic conditions may be adduced in their defence.
It may at least inquire what steps management is taking
to eliminate them. " The better organization of the hours
of labour must be undertaken in order to provide the
facilities required for education and training during
adolescence. By this means only can we produce good
citizens, efficient workers, expert foremen and managers,
and provide a ladder from the Board School to a complete
and thorough education."[1]

The communal advantages to be derived from increased
leisure meet one at every turn. Not least among them must
be reckoned that mentioned by Mr. Seebohm Rowntree,
when he points out that a reduction in hours would enable
a larger proportion of the population to live in rural or
semi-rural districts as a result of longer time allowances
for travelling to and from work, thereby adding to the
freshness of the worker, increasing the virility of his family,
reducing his rent and rates, and contributing to the
solution of the problem of urban housing.[2]

Advantages to be gained, however, may appear a futile
subject for discussion in view of the urgent necessity for

[1] Lord Leverhulme in *Labour and Capital After the War*, edited
by Professor S. J. Chapman, C.B.E. (John Murray, 1918.)
[2] *The Way to Industrial Peace*, by B. Seebohm Rowntree.
(T. Fisher Unwin, 1914.)

economical and augmented production. To speak of leisure when more work and better work is an economic essential may seem idealistic. Unimagined possibilities, however, are looming on the industrial horizon as a result of the rapidly developing study of fatigue and motions, and the improved methods which these studies suggest. The output resulting from the worker's effort is not only dependent upon his exertions, but also upon other factors— light, ventilation, colour, quiet, and cleanliness—which affect his ability to put forth such exertions. Investigations are proving that the effect is not wholly determinable. " Careful observations have proved " says Professor Myers, " that the full effects of reduced hours of work may not be manifest until several months have elapsed. . . . The human organism, after becoming adapted to certain hours of work, requires time, when that adaptation is disturbed, before it can give its maximal response to improved conditions." [1]

Parenthetically, it is also important to distinguish between output per individual per hour, and total weekly output. Clearly, the output per hour, if hours are reduced, must be increased proportionately to maintain the former weekly total, and still further increased to show any cumulative benefit as a result of such reduction.

The application of psychology to industry, however, has valuable fruits in store. If it can increase the volume of output whilst reducing hours of work, it will have made as great a contribution to industrial prosperity as any single science has made since electricity became a practical proposition. The obligation of management to secure this contribution is indisputable. The community requires the services of industrial workers not only in the routine of manufacture, but in those activities which call for still higher intelligence. It can only secure such services in proportion to the capacity of industry,

[1] *Mind and Work* (Chapter II, Fatigue Study), by Professor Charles S. Myers. (University of London Press, 1920.)

firstly, to release the workers; secondly, to stimulate their self-development whilst at work.

Thus far we have dealt only with those implications of the principle that industry is primarily a form of communal service which affect the worker as an individual and a citizen. We have not considered them in relation to the specific claims which Labour puts forward for security of employment, for a share in industrial control, and for a share in the product of industry. The concern of the community in these is clearly more remote than in the subjects reviewed above. They affect rather the internal administration of industry. Yet our principle affords certain guiding directions. For instance, if a certain volume of unemployment appears to be incidental to modern industrial methods, those exposed through no fault of their own to the hardships at present associated with unemployment, cannot be left to bear a burden which is attributable to the community as a whole. If work is, indeed, service to the community, undertaken so that it may attain a fuller and richer life, the community cannot disregard the hardships which befall numbers of those who serve its higher purposes. The obligation on the citizen to render such service requires a complementary recognition of the right of the citizen to security in the performance of that service. Similarly in the control of industry and the apportionment of its product, the worker, endowed by nature with a mind and by the State with an education, is not likely to be content that his labour should be applied without his opinion being sought. " A man is not playing a man's part who is merely the tool of other men." [1] In a State where the principle of democracy has received general acceptance the industry of that State, if it recognizes its true function of service, cannot but devise a system of industrial governance in general harmony with that of the State.

Furthermore, the claim to a share in prosperity is

[1] David Stewart.

justifiable, as a direct claim, only to the extent to which the individual participates in promoting that prosperity. Profit-sharing may be desirable for the reason that it serves to remove an obstacle in the way of obtaining the full co-operation of the workers. But as a claim on the part of Labour, it can only be justified by a corresponding share in making the profits. Clearly, however, the motive of service indicates that not all surplus profits are to be divided between Capital and Labour. It is only reasonable that, beyond the point where Capital and Labour have received adequate rewards, the community as a whole should benefit from industrial prosperity. Sharing in control and sharing in profits, in fact, should march together in that both should be subject to the limitations imposed by a philosophy which regards industry, not as a social unit divorced from the life of the community, but as an integral part of that life.

Every right carries a corresponding obligation. Both Management and Labour are inclined to insist upon rights, before fulfilling the obligations which each owes to the other, and both owe to the community. Only upon a basis of good work can Labour legitimately erect an edifice of its rights. Privilege is indeed only assessable in proportion to service. If management has obligations to the workers, imposed by the community in that the workers themselves are citizens, the workers also have obligations to that same community in that they are members of it. Only as Labour renders its best service, with the control necessarily exercised by Management, may it claim privileges. At the basis of industry, whether of that part which is Management or of that part which is Labour, lie the ethical obligations incumbent upon men united in rendering a common service.

There is need to affirm the basic ethics of corporate life, so that industry as it develops may be guided by the signposts, not of selfishness, greed, and restriction of effort, whether on the part of Management or of Labour, but of service, democracy, and efficiency. Good service is only possible upon a basis of efficient co-operation. The social responsibility of management is to carve out the path of co-operation in service, so that the economic service of the community may produce not only material wealth but spiritual well-being. " While the advances made by objective science and its industrial applications are palpable and undeniable all around us, it is a matter of doubt and dispute if our social and moral advance towards happiness and virtue has been great or any," says Mark Pattison. That which has been lacking is the consciousness of a unifying motive in industry. When industry comes to be actuated in its everyday affairs by a motive which transcends self-interest, the moral progress of our community may be said to have begun. The cost of building the Kingdom of Heaven will not be found in the profit and loss accounts of industry, but in the record of every man's conscientious service.

CHAPTER IV

THE ORGANIZATION OF THE FACTORY

SUMMARY

(a) Definition of Organization ; distinction between capacity for organizing, the process of organizing, and an organization ; distinction between organizing, planning, and control.

(b) Problem of organizing grows with increasing delegation. Five fundamental ingredients of an organization : Function, Objective, Faculty, Relations, Method. Organizing is only concerned in methods of administration in so far as they affect duties.

(c) Five advantages of scientific organizing: Permanence, Concentration, Individuality, Combination, Human Standards. Test of a form of organization is its ability to provide means for best management.

(d) Form of an organization depends upon extent of delegation. Delegation involves specialization and co-ordination. Forms of organization are to be distinguished by underlying principles—the principle of Function as interpreted in the Functional form of organization ; the principle of Decentralization as interpreted in the Departmental form of organization ; the principle of Specialization as interpreted in the Staff-and-Line form of organization; the principle of Conference as interpreted in the Committee form of organization. Examples of each ; notes on the Organization Chart.

(e) Forms of organization grow ; what may be theoretically desirable may not be immediately practicable. Need for cultivation of the " organization sense." Organizing is mostly a problem of reorganization. Kindred problem of extending an organization. Power of co-ordination is the limiting factor in the growth of businesses.

(f) Consideration of the forms of organization in the light of the five advantages enumerated above.) Need for correlation of the Functional form with the Staff idea, aided by Committees. Summary of main requirements of an ideal form of organization.

ORGANIZATION has already been described in Chapter II as the process of so combining the work which individuals or groups have to perform with the faculties necessary for its execution that the duties, so formed, provide the best channels for the efficient, systematic, positive and co-ordinated application of the available effort. Mr. L. V. Estes has defined it again as " the arrangement of dependent parts or functions, so as to show their inter-relation in the structure and to provide the means whereby the efforts of a group of individuals will be directed rationally towards a common object."[1] Mr. C. E. Knoeppel has described it as

[1] Mr. L. V. Estes : an article in *Industrial Management* for April, 1919, entitled " Managing for Maximum Production."

" the proper adjustment of the relationship between human beings in an effort to accomplish certain definite ends."[1]

Five fundamental requirements emerge from these definitions—five basic ingredients of any form of organization, to be introduced into any attempt to frame such a form of organization or to reorganize any existing organization. These five requirements may be summarized as (a) work to be done, (b) an object, (c) human faculties, (d) relationships, (e) method.

The need for a clear definition of precisely what Organization is becomes the more patent the further the subject is pursued. The difficulty arises, not so much in arriving at a definition which will convey a concrete meaning, as in framing the wording of the definition in such a way as to make clear the distinction between Organization and similar or overlapping terms, such as System, Control, Plan. On this subject of Organization there is probably more confusion of thought than on any other aspect of management. Yet it is quite clear that we cannot scientifically approach our subject, unless we carry in our minds a clear-cut and definite picture of what any single term conveys. Without precise definition, any structure we may build may be wholly inaccurate, vague, or lop-sided.

Unfortunately, there is a general impression, not by any means confined to industry, that organizing is simply the application of common sense, and that common sense is a capacity which is common. There are few slights more resented than the suggestion that a person cannot organize. It is normally taken as a suggestion of a lack in everyday mental capacity. The capacity for organizing, however, is not wholly common sense any more than common sense is common. There are admirable managers with a great fund of common sense who cannot organize, and indeed cannot grasp what organizing means. On the

[1] Mr. C. E. Knoeppel : a series of articles in *Industrial Management* during 1919, entitled " Laws of Industrial Management."

other hand, there are no organizers without a full measure of common sense. Common sense is an ingredient of the organizing capacity as it is of most scientific and business qualities ; but there are other characteristics requisite in an organizer. After all, in the distinguishing of one man from another, the important items are those which transcend common sense and are not common. In industry most managers are confident that, though they may have failings, they certainly do not lie in the field of organization. Consequently industrial organization has suffered either neglect or distortion. It has either been allowed to grow wild, or has been twisted and turned to suit the particular requirements or caprices of the moment. Least of all has it been regarded as a profound scientific problem capable of analysis on a scientific plan, and of solution according to scientifically determined principles.

It would be well before going further to draw distinctions between the capacity or faculty for organizing, the process of organizing, and an organization. This may appear elementary, but much of the loose thinking on this subject may undoubtedly be attributed to the careless use of the word " organization," which is made to cover all three of the above items. How often is it said " Organization, after all, is common sense," inferring that organization is a capacity for organizing. Similarly it is said, for instance, " The organization of this concern must be a costly business," meaning that the process of organizing the concern must be expensive. Or again it is said " That is a fine organization," signifying that the form of organization as designed by the organizer, using his capacity for organizing, is fine. We have, therefore, carefully to distinguish between organization as a faculty, organization as a process, and organization as a condition of things.

It is important, further, to draw distinctions between organization in this triple sense, and other allied terms. The distinction between Organization and Management was made clear in Chapter II. There are other terms, however, with which, owing to close connection, Organization is confused as, for example, System, Control, and Planning. Organization is none of these, though intimately related to them. A system is a standard way of doing things ; it is a term applicable to any form of consistent and deliberate activity. There is a system of organizing as there is a system of control. The system of organizing, however, is distinct from the faculty for organizing, the process of organizing, or the form of organization. Control, again, is more a part of management than of organization. Organization is the framing of a fabric composed of the two elements, work and men. Control, as a part of management, uses that fabric, but does not design it. The organization may be designed to facilitate control, but does not itself exercise control. Planning, again, is not the same as organizing. Organizing provides the channels through which work is made to flow ; planning determines the volume of the work passing through those channels. It is a branch of management in that it uses the form of organization. It endeavours to put the form of organization to its maximal use, but it does not design the organization.

This definition of terms is necessary on account of both the present confusion of thought and the inherent complexity of the subject. This complexity increases with the growth of the concern. The proprietor of a small business is normally little troubled about the problem of organization. He delegates practically no authority and takes personal responsibility himself. The policy of the business is his own policy and he feels no necessity to convert others to it. Time passes, and the business grows. Authority has to be delegated ; responsibility and work have to be distributed. The proprietor finds his task is increasingly to co-ordinate and direct the activities of others. Later, he begins to realize that there is a lack of cohesion in the business, which becomes more evident as a new generation comes into the concern. Finally, he finds that the business runs largely apart from himself, that he is only required when things go wrong, and that he personally is ignorant of much that goes on and of many of those working under him. He finds wide differences in individual capacity, work unequally divided, cumbersome and overlapping methods, departmental staffs diversely occupied, responsibility in a state of confusion, and individual duties undefined. He is thus driven, if he be wise, to study the problem of organization. As he studies he finds much valuable information and theory, but also encounters a thousand conflicting elements in his own factory which render such information and theory apparently inapplicable. He is compelled minutely to investigate his own organization, and finds that though it allows management to operate it does so by slow and confused methods. He finds, in fact, that while organizations can be scientifically constructed they can also grow unscientifically. He finds that the type of management he wishes to install cannot operate through an unscientific organization.

This is the story of 90 per cent of modern businesses. The large undertakings in British industry which have built up their organizations upon a scientific plan can be counted on ten fingers. The number which to-day are endeavouring to remodel their organizations, by gradually substituting a scientific and organic structure for the haphazard growth of the last half-century, is daily increasing.

The fundamental ingredients of an industrial organization have already been briefly enumerated. These may be stated again as—

(a) FUNCTION   —or, work to be done.
(b) OBJECTIVE   —or, the ideal and object.
(c) FACULTY   —or, the human capacity in work.
(d) RELATIONS   —or, the relationships, administrative and physical, between the faculties employed.
(e) METHOD   —or, the way in which work is done.

The basic idea upon which the process of organizing

has developed has been that of function. The first essential preliminary in any organization is certain work to be performed, which is capable of being divided into related sections. This conception is by no means confined to industrial organizing. It is rapidly being accepted as the true basis for social organization, and, since the days of Plato, has been preached as the true basis for the proper organizing of the life of the individual.[1] This principle broadly lays down that for the proper execution of work involving more than one individual, the work shall be divided among the individuals according to a scientific division of the whole task, such division being made by segregating those parts of the whole which require the exercise of one faculty.

A function, however, is dependent upon an object. In order that some object shall be achieved, certain work must be done which is divisible into functions.   Clearly, the object determines what work is necessary, and which portions of that work are primary and which are subsidiary.

The discharge of functions, further, requires the exercise of human faculties, and functions are limited by the capacity of human beings, either individually or collectively, to discharge them.   Production is the sum of various functions, and to come within human compass must be divided into its constituent functions.   Scientific organizing requires, therefore, that the functions to be discharged, so that their cumulative effect may be production, must be so divided that normal human faculties can successfully discharge them.   These faculties may be exercised either by an individual such as a manager, or by a group of individuals such as a Committee of Management or Works Council.   In the process of organizing, therefore, it must be determined which functions, or parts of functions, are

[1] " We have not seen what is the underlying principle of social organization, a principle which must be distinct from the principle of community, however dependent upon it.   This principle is the principle of Function."   In *Social Theory*, by G. D. H. Cole. (Methuen, 1920.)

to be performed by individual faculties and which by group faculties.

Further, the application of certain faculties to certain functions necessarily occasions relationships. Production is achieved by the operation of many different faculties upon diverse functions. The function discharged by a factory is the sum of the functions discharged by its management and employees. To achieve this, the functions and the faculties exercised in performing those functions must be economically inter-related. The division of a task into separate parts involves intimate relationships, in terms of work, between the persons, or groups of persons, contributing their various faculties to the discharge of the various functions. No one individual performs his work wholly alone ; whatever he does is relative to what another does. An organization, therefore, is not only composed of functions and faculties, but also of the work-relationships inherent in the procedure necessary for the economical execution of work. That is, an organization is built upon the procedure by which many separate parts contribute their respective quotas to the completion of any one task.

Such relationships arise in two ways : firstly, as a result of the system by which any piece of work is to be done ; secondly, as a result of factory and office layout. In the one case, there is a relationship as a result of the costing system between the cost clerk who takes out certain figures and the manager who uses those figures. In the second case, there is a relationship as a result of the factory layout between the section which transports goods and the department which receives those goods.

The process of organizing must take account, therefore, of the layout of the factory and the procedure according to which work is passed from one individual or group to another individual or group.

These, then, in brief, are the five basic factors in organizing—function, object, faculty, relationships and method.

For clarity of thinking, moreover, it is almost as important to note those items in the factory with which the process of organizing is not concerned. The fundamental distinction here is between character and method. Organization as such has no concern with the character of the product or of the processes or of the machinery. It is only concerned with the execution of the functions whereby the product is made, the processes operate, and the machinery works. For instance, in the payment of wages, organization is concerned in the arrangement of duties between the individuals affected, so that the methods existing for the payment of wages may operate smoothly and economically. It is not concerned with the character of the payment, whether it is cash in envelopes or cheques, or with the character of the computation, whether by brain or by machine, unless different methods, involving different relationships between individuals, lead to different duties. Similarly, in the generation of power, the organization of the Power House does not take account of the character of the boilers and engines, their horse-power and capacity. It assumes those facts as fundamental, and concerns itself in the allocation of duties, so that the existing methods of operating the power plant may be properly executed. Or again, in cleaning a factory, the organization is not concerned in the nature of the cleaning apparatus. It is only affected if a change in apparatus involves a redistribution of individual duties. This applies equally to the product of the factory. The organization is not concerned in the nature of the product, except in so far as certain functions are necessary for its production.

This applies both to organization-building and to the reorganizing of an existing organization. Reorganization does not mean the alteration of everything from top to bottom. It is no business of the organizer, for instance, to consider whether the product is good, fair or bad, whether the office machinery is efficient, whether the engines are old or new, whether the workers are efficient or inefficient. Those are tasks of management. The organizer must accept these as fundamental and constant. Upon the existing product, the existing workers, the existing buildings and the existing machines he must build up his new organization. To alter these is not his concern, though he may legitimately point out any economies in organization which might accrue from alterations. On the other hand, if these should be altered, and certain changes in methods should result, then it is his business to consider what changes in duties follow upon such amended methods.

Obviously, however, not all changes in method involve changes in organization. Only those changes in method which involve changes in relationships between individuals or groups are the concern of the organizer. The fact that, by motion study, for instance, a different method of operation is discovered, by which a process can be executed more rapidly, does not affect the organization, unless thereby the duties of certain individuals are altered. From minute changes in operation, direct changes in duties will not generally result. But the effect upon the organization of several small changes in individual methods may be cumulative. Quicker motions, for instance, may lead to new processes, which, in turn, may lead to the employment of an additional foreman, or the transfer of a group of men to new work—a change which directly affects the organization. Or again, an administrative officer may keep his records in a certain way. Should he decide to keep them in another way, the organization is not affected. But should he decide that the records are to be kept by another officer, thereby affecting both his own duties and the other officer's duties, as well as the relationship between the two, obviously the organization is to that extent affected.

The process of organizing, in fact, is concerned with functions, and only with methods of operation in so far as changes in method occasion changes in duties. If it should be arranged that the dispatch of material shall be changed from one exit to another, the distribution of individual duties will probably remain the same. The character of the work will differ, in that, may be, two corridors only are traversed instead of three, but the duty of the foreman—viz., the transportation of goods—remains the same. If, however, it comes about that, in dispatching from the new exit, the issue of certain instructions is rendered unnecessary, then duties are changed and relationships are changed, so that the organization must be adjusted. Similarly, if it is found in the process of organizing, that closer relationships between individuals are possible, whereby the passing of certain orders is rendered superfluous, the organizer may legitimately suggest that such change in method is desirable, so that individual duties may be more compact. That is to say, his concern in methods is only to the extent to which methods determine individual or group functions and faculties.

It may be that this is to draw too fine a distinction between organizing and managing, but unless such a distinction is drawn the danger that organizing will be unscientific is much increased. Of course, the distinction drawn between the hypothetical organizer and manager applies, not only to such individuals, but also to one individual who may exercise two such faculties. The distinction is equally valid between the manager, in the exercise of his task of managing, and the same manager, in the exercise of his task of organizing. The same individual may practise both faculties.

An example of the prevailing laxity of thought may be taken in the false distinction which is sometimes drawn between " organization of work " and " organization of staff." The two are the same. The organizing of work can only be in terms of staff, and the organizing of staff in terms of work. The distribution of work to be done according to individual capacities is organizing just as much as the distribution of individuals according to the work to be done.   It is clear, however, that, in organizing, the work precedes the man.   The function to be performed must be decided before the faculty for performing it is brought to bear upon it.   Functions are irrespective of persons.   The grouping of related duties must be preliminary to the assignment of such duties to individuals.   However brilliant individuals may be, if they are allowed to collect around themselves duties which are not functionally related, they constitute a danger to the stability of the organization.   It is far better that an individual should school himself to fit into a form of organization, provided the organization is scientifically sound, than that he should twist the form of organization out of its scientific structure to suit his particular abilities.   Should such an individual die, or leave the business, the organization will be left distorted and stranded, by reason of the maladjustment of functions and faculties.

On the other hand, organizations grow.   No man can foresee what developments may take place in a business. Brilliant leaders may guide an ever-expanding business, until its magnitude outdistances all the dreams of its infancy.   The day, however, when this was possible, without a prepared plan of organization, is passing.   A " one-man business " requires its plan of organization, even if all the functions are performed and all the faculties provided by a single individual.   It is essential that he should distinguish, in his mind, the different functions which he performs.   Then, when delegation of functions becomes necessary, with expansion, the process can be carried out upon lines which will hold good to whatever dimensions the business may ultimately expand.   Development by the outstanding capacities of individual managers, irrespective of scientific organizing, is being superseded by development through the ability of individual managers to display their outstanding capacities through the medium of a scientific organization.   Individual brilliance is not truly effective unless it is governed by corporate requirements.

It will be legitimate at this point to ask what advantages are to be gained from an organization, scientifically built, over an organization which is the outcome of unregulated growth. Every business has its form of organization, which may be good or bad, as judged by the object it has in view. Every form of organization has also grown, and may still grow. The distinction is not, therefore, between an organization and a lack of organization, but between a scientific organization and an unscientific organization. It is suggested that the main advantages to be gained by scientific organizing may be summarized as follows—

(*a*) PERMANENCE, or the capacity of the organization to endure and develop, despite changes in personnel and methods.

(*b*) CONCENTRATION, or that ease in individual operation, that application of skill, that definition of objectives, that economy in effort, that intelligibility as regards the work of all, which springs from a proper allocation of related duties, a precise delegation of responsibility, and a concise definition of individual faculties.

(*c*) INDIVIDUALITY, or the sense of personal proprietorship of and pride in work, and the surety of responsibility, authority, scope and status.

(*d*) COMBINATION, or that close and economical working between units which results from a definition of duties and relationships.

(*e*) HUMAN STANDARDS, or the fixing of individual scope, according to the knowledge, skill, and character of normal human beings, so that not too much is required of one individual, and not too little of another.

The fundamental test of a form of organization is its ability to provide the means for the best management. Each of the above advantages is a managerial advantage. A form of organization has no advantages save those which accrue to management. Management must necessarily, to a great extent, adapt itself to channels which the form of organization provides, like wine poured into a bottle. The organization, therefore, must considerably influence the aspect which management presents to those with whom it is concerned. For instance, if there are elements in management, particularly those warm, human, undeterminable and often erratic elements, which cannot flow through the channels of the organization, those channels stand condemned—a hindrance rather than an aid to management. The advantages enumerated above, however, are clearly conducive to good management. Permanence makes possible the continuous and economical development of the best methods of management. Concentration provides the manager with every aid in the pursuit of his objective, and assures him of the place that objective holds in the aim of the whole concern. Individuality makes possible personal leadership and confidence. Combination makes possible effective corporate working. Human standards make possible a management, which, whilst efficient, is not overworked, and is so divided as to provide positions within the range of normal human capacity.

Thus far, we have surveyed the definition, scope, elements and advantages of a scientific organization. It is time to consider the forms of organization which exist or are advocated, their merits and failings, and the processes of organizing which bring them about.

The form of an organization depends upon the extent to which the basic functions of a business have been developed and distinguished by delegation. The growth of a business involves the increasing delegation of functions. The development of individual functions, again, involves the expansion of the form of organization. As the functions severally develop, the organization grows. The expansion, by delegation, of any one part means an alteration in the structure and balance of the whole.

Delegation, however, involves a dual process. It involves specialization, in that the field of each individual is carefully limited, and increasingly circumscribed. It involves, also, co-ordination, in that the various specialized groups must be welded together to achieve the common end. Specialization and co-ordination, however, are not themselves functions, but rather the paths by which functions develop. They are, therefore, inherent necessities in any form of organization, and forms of organization may be judged by the degree to which these common principles are extended in them.

Forms of organization may be distinguished by the principles underlying them. In actual practice, no single organization can be said to be founded upon one principle alone ; but for purposes of clarity, it will be advisable to consider, firstly, the forms of organization resulting from the strict application of each principle, and secondly, how these principles may be judiciously combined. The principles commonly governing forms of organization may be summarized under four heads—

(*a*) Organizing according to the principle of function, or Functional Organization.

(*b*) Organizing according to the principle of decentralization, or Departmental Organization.

(*c*) Organizing according to the principle of specialization, or Staff and Line Organization.

(*d*) Organizing according to the principle of conference, or Committee Organization.

The principle of Function may best be described in the words of Mr. L. V. Estes. " By this plan," he says, " specific functions common to all or several departments . . . are each placed in the hands of a man specifically qualified for his particular function, and instead of giving attention to all of the factors in *one* department, he gives his attention to *one* factor in all departments." [1] The functional form of organization is to be distinguished, however, from the popular *functional foremanship* of the

[1] *Vide* " Managing for Maximum Production," an article by Mr. L. V. Estes, in *Industrial Management.* April, 1919.

late Mr. F. W. Taylor. A functional organization is one which is organized, from managers to workers, according to the basic functions of production. Functional foremanship is that part of management which operates through the lower divisions of a functional organization. It is, in fact, a detailed development of a part of functional organizing. A functional organization may be described, therefore, as one where the necessary activities of production are grouped according to scientifically determined lines of demarcation, irrespective of the particular nature of the products and processes involved.

The form of organization based upon the principle of decentralization is quite the reverse of a functional organization. Whereas, under the latter the work of the factory is divided according to the various functions of production, irrespective of the various processes of manufacture, under the former the work is divided according to the various processes, irrespective of functions. One individual is responsible for everything concerning the particular processes allocated to him. He divides his department into sections. The head of each section is responsible for everything concerning his section. He again divides his section into groups, and the head of each group is responsible for everything concerning his group. This is commonly known as the Military or Departmental type of organization.

A " Staff and Line " organization differs again from these two. It is based upon a strict demarcation between thinking and doing ; between the actual execution of production, which is the " Line," and the business of analysing, testing, comparing, recording, making researches, co-ordinating information, and advising, which is the " Staff." The Staff division is, in fact, advisory and supplementary to the Line division. It involves the segregation of those activities which are not part of the routine of production, and the placing of them under officials who take no direct or executive share in that routine.

" The chief function of the Staff is to analyse and point out the road to business efficiency. The task of attaining the ideals pointed out is the function of the Line." [1]   The essential point in this principle of organizing is the non-executive and separately organized position of the Staff. In every organization there is " Staff work," but it is normally done by executive officers, either individually or in committees. These officers are also in charge of the action taken as a result of their investigations and considerations.   In the " Staff and Line " form of organization, executive work is to be performed by executive officers, staff work by Staff officers.   The principle is based upon what is held to be a profound distinction between human beings.   Some have the minds of men of action—leaders, executives.   Others have the minds of thinkers—scientists, planners, engineers.   Again, just as in the human body there are sensory and perceptive, also motor nerve centres of activity, so it is suggested that, in the organization of the factory, a similar distinction should be drawn between the planning of action and policy, with all its essential business of inquiry and analysis, and the actual direction of work.

The form of organization known as the " Committee " organization is rather a supplementary than a complete type, though procedure by committees may be introduced to such an extent as almost to constitute the governing principle of an organization.   The method pursued is to replace individuals by committees exercising similar faculties.   Committees may, therefore, be determinative, co-ordinating, or advisory, according to the individual faculties which they replace.   They may be temporary or permanent, according to the purpose which they serve. They may also be functional, inter-functional, departmental, or inter-departmental according to the form of organization of the factory.   This system has recently

[1] *Installing Efficiency Methods*, by C. E. Knoeppel. (Industrial Management Library, 1918.)

been described as " Organized Delegation "—" the distribution of authority and responsibility and interest among
as many individuals as possible."

Before proceeding to consider the practical application
of each of these principles, it will be necessary to comment
upon the charting of an organization. The normal
Organization Chart appears in the form of an inverted
genealogical tree. It is not clear, however, what precisely
such a chart represents—whether distribution of functions,
lines of authority, areas of responsibility, routine of work,
or delegation of faculties. The Organization Chart (which
is to be distinguished from a Process Chart or Routine
Chart) is composed of three basic elements—the work to
be done, the faculties requisite for doing it, and the individuals who unite work and faculties into duties. It
does not show the procedure by which duties are performed,
but rather shows for what particular duties each individual
is responsible. It is a chart of duties, not a chart of
procedure. This distinction is important since the two
are often confused. It is important also because the
Organization Chart normally requires to be supplemented
by Charts of Procedure, though the two should be kept
quite distinct. For the work of any one function, it is
necessary to have two charts—firstly, the Organization
Chart; secondly, the Chart of Procedure. The Organization
Chart should show (a) How work is divided between the
various areas of individual responsibility ; that is, the
distribution of functions. (b) How the individual faculties
are distributed between the various divisions of the work
to be done ; that is, the distribution of faculties. (c) How
authority and responsibility are delegated, since each
sub-division of functions represents a delegation of authority
and responsibility. The Chart of Procedure, on the other
hand, should show the procedure by which work is accomplished. It should show at what particular points in the
procedure individuals contribute their specific duties.
Thus, while the Organization Chart shows the relationships

between individuals as a result of delegation, the Chart of Procedure shows their relationships as a result of their participation in carrying out a function or piece of work. The Organization Chart, therefore, works, as it were, perpendicularly, and the Chart of Procedure horizontally. Though the two are mutually supplementary, it is clear that to combine them is to create confusion.

We may now review the practical application of each form of organization. Undoubtedly, a modicum of good resides in each, and it is not unlikely that the best form of organization will contain some elements of all. It is further open to doubt whether a practically ideal form of organization, applicable to any concern, can exist. Forms will vary according to the peculiarities of each business. This does not, however, discount the hypothesis that there is an ideal principle governing forms of organization, and that, in the practical interpretation of that principle, certain constant factors necessarily ensue, whatever may be the variable features in such interpretation.

For the purpose of illustration, we may assume that the business under consideration is some form of manufacturing concern, engaged in the production of a single product, such as soap, paper or biscuits, that certain raw materials go to the making of this product, and that there are five processes, which we may name, without reference to any specific industry, as sorting, boiling, mixing, drying and packing. Each process will, of course, have subsidiary processes, which in the case of sorting, we may designate as picking, listing and rolling. We thus begin with the simplest possible form of industrial enterprise, and we may observe how the different principles of organization will affect its structure.

Figure 3 represents this business organized on the Departmental Plan. Each department corresponds to one of the five processes of manufacture, with the exception of the Power House, which is necessarily common to all. Each department is responsible for the entire execution

The "Departmental" Form of Organization — (Figure 3.)

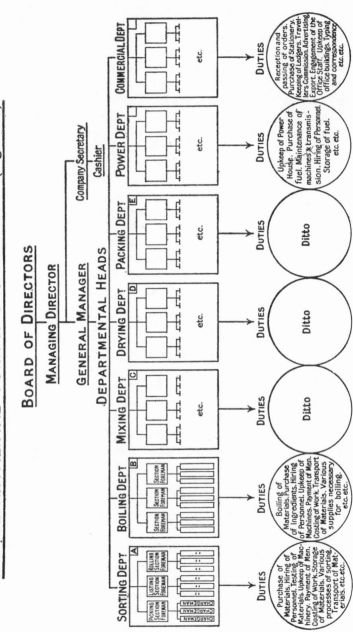

BOARD OF DIRECTORS

MANAGING DIRECTOR

GENERAL MANAGER

Company Secretary
Cashier

DEPARTMENTAL HEADS

| SORTING DEPT. A | BOILING DEPT. B | MIXING DEPT. C | DRYING DEPT. D | PACKING DEPT. E | POWER DEPT. | COMMERCIAL DEPT. |

SORTING DEPT. — PICKING SECTION FOREMAN, LISTING SECTION FOREMAN, ROLLING SECTION FOREMAN — CHARGEMAN, CHARGEMAN, CHARGEMAN — etc.

BOILING DEPT. — SECTION FOREMAN, SECTION FOREMAN, SECTION FOREMAN — etc.

MIXING DEPT. — etc.

DRYING DEPT. — etc.

PACKING DEPT. — etc.

POWER DEPT. — etc.

COMMERCIAL DEPT. — etc.

DUTIES

Sorting Dept.: Purchase of Materials. Hiring of Personnel. Testing of Materials. Upkeep of Machinery. Payment of Men. Costing of Work. Storage of Materials. Various processes of sorting. Transport of Materials. etc. etc.

Boiling Dept.: Boiling of Materials. Purchase of Ingredients. Hiring of Personnel. Upkeep of Machines. Payment of Men. Costing of Work. Transport of Materials. Various supplies necessary for boiling. etc. etc.

Mixing Dept.: Ditto

Drying Dept.: Ditto

Packing Dept.: Ditto

Power Dept.: Upkeep of Power House. Purchase of fuel. Maintenance of machines & transmission. Hiring of Personnel. Storage of fuel. etc. etc.

Commercial Dept.: Reception and passing of orders. Purchase of Stationery. Keeping of Ledgers. Travellers Commission. Advertising. Export. Engagement of the Office Staff. Upkeep of office buildings. Typing and correspondence. etc. etc.

of some particular process, not only for its technique but also its specifications and ingredients, for the purchase of the necessary materials, for the planning of the work, for the transportation of its materials, for the engagement, dismissal and payment of its workers, for the costing of its processes, and for the necessary records of output. Each department is responsible, in fact, for those seven functions of Preparation, Production and Facilitation listed in Chapter II. These functions are grouped departmentally, and are repeated in each department. Each department is a complete and self-supporting entity, irrespective of other departments. Authority is definite and absolute. The manager of the department has complete command, under the general manager, over all the factors concerned in the operation of his department. He delegates the work of the department, not by function, but by definite sections of the process of manufacture. Each section is under a foreman, who is responsible, absolutely and wholly, for the work of his section, except for those particular items which the manager does not delegate, just as the manager himself is responsible for the work of all his sections. The work being thus divided, there exists practically no inter-relationship between departments or between sections, except such co-ordination as is provided by the general manager, for departments, and the departmental manager, for sections. The faculties provided by the personnel of each department are mainly executive, with the other faculties inextricably included in the executive faculties. The main general duty of the manager is to carry out the work of his department, with what staff he requires, as seems to him best, subject to the veto of the general manager. Clerical work is done by both managers and foremen, or by staffs under these. Research, comparison and planning are done by each manager and foreman, as he considers such work is necessary. The manager is a complete master in his own house. The objective of the business is the sum of the individual objectives of the different managers, which are wholly dependent upon the general manager for any common direction to one purpose.

The same hypothetical business, organized on the " Staff and Line " plan, is shown in Fig. 4. In this case, it will be seen that the line organization—that is, the executive organization—may be either departmental or functional. The distinguishing feature of this form of organization is the organization of the staff. The staff organization may be described as a deliberate organization for thought, just as the line organization is the organization for execution. The presumption is that the executive manager, whether he be a functional superintendent as, for example, Superintendent of Equipment, or whether he be a departmental manager, as, in our example, the Manager of the Sorting Department, cannot have time or opportunity for the investigation, analysis, co-ordination of information, and constructive thinking which are necessary for progress. He, therefore, requires advice, and a staff is instituted to give that advice. In Fig. 4, the organization of the staff is shown as functional, but the principle upon which " Staff and Line " organization is based does not necessarily require that this should be so. The staff may be organized upon any plan which provides the assistance which the line may require. The essential feature of the staff organization is that it is purely consultative and advisory, and exercises no direct authority over the line. It would be a large business which could support such a staff organization as is shown in Fig. 4.[1] The staff organization is wholly supplementary in character. It is the organization of expert knowledge, for the guidance of executive officers. Clearly, its value is greater where the line organization is departmental, since the executive officers are called upon to deal with many varied subjects,

[1] The phrase " Staff Bureau " is used to emphasize the distinction between the divisions of the Staff organization and the departments of the Line organization. *Vide Factory Organization and Administration*, by Hugo Diemer. (McGraw Hill Book Co., 1914.)

THE 'STAFF-AND-LINE' FORM OF ORGANIZATION - (Figure 4.)

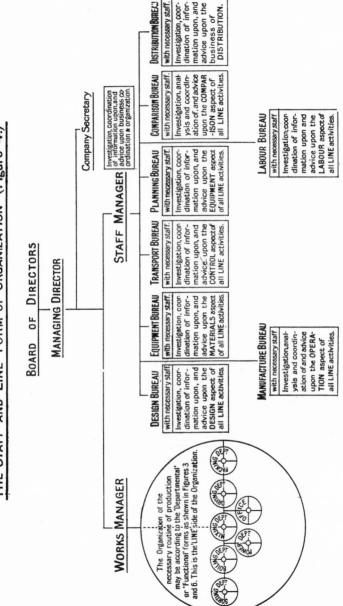

BOARD OF DIRECTORS

MANAGING DIRECTOR

WORKS MANAGER

STAFF MANAGER

Company Secretary

Investigation, coordination of information upon, and advice upon business co-ordination & organization

The Organization of the necessary routine of production may be according to the 'Departmental' or 'Functional' forms as shewn in Figures 3 and 6. This is the 'LINE' side of the Organization.

DESIGN BUREAU with necessary staff. Investigation, coordination of information upon, and advice upon the DESIGN aspect of all LINE activities.

EQUIPMENT BUREAU with necessary staff. Investigation, coordination of information upon, and advice upon the MATERIALS aspect of all LINE activities.

TRANSPORT BUREAU with necessary staff. Investigation, coordination of information upon, and advice upon the CONTROL aspect of all LINE activities.

PLANNING BUREAU with necessary staff. Investigation, coordination of information upon, and advice upon the EQUIPMENT aspect of all LINE activities.

COMPARISON BUREAU with necessary staff. Investigation, analysis and coordination of, and advice upon the COMPARISON aspect of all LINE activities.

DISTRIBUTION BUREAU with necessary staff. Investigation, coordination of information upon, and advice upon, the business of DISTRIBUTION.

MANUFACTURE BUREAU with necessary staff. Investigation, analysis and coordination of and advice upon the OPERATION aspect of all LINE activities.

LABOUR BUREAU with necessary staff. Investigation, coordination of information upon and advice upon the LABOUR aspect of all LINE activities.

SORTING DEPT BOILING DEPT MIXING DEPT DRYING DEPT PACKING DEPT POWER DEPT OFFICE than where it is functional, in which case the functional officers, concerned only in one group of activities, are presumably experts in their own line. It is not unreasonable to view this form of organization, therefore, as halfway between the full Departmental and full Functional forms of organization. It is clear, further, that the relations between the line and the staff will require careful adjustment, since, while there is room for the one to assist the other, there is also room for their respective interests to clash. The staff manager would require, therefore, a large measure of tact and understanding, while frequent conferences between staff and line are essential to this form of organization. The principle underlying it is not transgressed if the personnel of the staff are distributed among departments and work in departments. The essence of the principle is that the work of investigation, research and advice should be wholly distinguished from the routine of production, and should be under a separate control.

The so-called committee form of organization may next be considered. As already indicated, this is rather a supplementary feature of any form of organization than a separate form of itself. Present tendencies in industry, however, are inclined to render committees of such importance that, in some concerns, the actual form of the organization becomes dependent upon the place allotted to committees. The use of committees to the fullest possible extent is based on the assumption that only by extending staff responsibility to as wide an area as possible is efficient and corporate management likely to ensue. Committees, however, cannot interfere with the direct line of authority. Each departmental or functional head must still remain responsible for the work allotted to him. Some committees may be called executive, but they are so only in one sense, viz., that they are empowered to make decisions on such subjects as executive officials may wish to bring forward. Other committees may be advisory to executive officials, or co-ordinative, in that they bring officials together to ensure that each pursues, in those things which affect other spheres besides his own, a common policy. There are probably no concerns at the present time where committees are not already in existence. The Board of Directors constitutes the highest committee in any business. Below this, it is not unlikely there will be a Committee of Management, with sub-committees concerned in each branch of the business, and further committees into which representatives of the workers are introduced. It is not generally realized, however, that the introduction of a committee affects organization as much as management ; and that the institution of a permanent committee is primarily a change in organization. A liberally constituted Works Council involves not only a new method in management but also a new feature in the form of organization. The tendency to create committees, irrespective of the form of organization, may therefore be deleterious to the organization. If committees are to bring certain faculties to bear upon the work to be done, they must be as scientifically constituted as the duties of an individual. It is to be remembered, however, that committees may be much more costly than individuals who could provide the same faculties. Furthermore, being subject to scientific constitution, committees should only be located in an organization where they are scientifically necessary. The haphazard setting-up of a committee is equivalent to the haphazard appointment of a new official.

Committees can only be of four kinds ; firstly, executive, in the sense of making decisions upon matters brought before it. Such a committee can decide, but cannot act. It must appoint some officer to carry through and supervise the execution of its decision. It is only executive to the extent that it makes decisions ; their actual execution must rest with the main line of the organization. Secondly, a committee may be advisory, in that it brings together certain selected individuals to whom an official who requires special guidance in a difficult situation may refer. Thirdly, a committee may be educative in that it forms a means whereby an official may keep his staff regularly notified of events and policies, and thereby introduce them to the larger problems of management, thus forming a species of training-ground for others to succeed him. Fourthly, a committee may be co-ordinative, in that it brings together certain individuals, representing certain definite functions or parts of functions, for the purpose of ensuring that the work of each function is conducted upon lines corresponding to and harmonizing with the work of other functions.

In setting up a committee, it is essential to determine for which of these purposes it is established. If it is to be advisory, the full responsibility for the policy adopted or action taken still remaining with the administrative officer to whom the advice is given, it should not overstep the bounds of advice and arrogate to itself executive powers. This condition is necessary for the benefit of the administrative officer rather than of the committee. Every officer requires to know the area of his responsibility, and what his exact relation to any committee actually is. Committees of a purely advisory character, however, should be rare. When the duties of an individual are clearly defined, it should not be necessary for him to consult with a committee at every turn. Friendly conversation with the officials on whom he can put most reliance, when any difficulty arises, will be as effective as the statutory establishment of a committee.

Educative, executive, and co-ordinative committees have their place in an organization, however, no matter how efficient may be the management and the organization through which it works. No form of organization can be considered complete, without its sprinkling of committees. The establishment of committees should be related, however, not only to the needs of management, but also to the existing fabric of the organization. When individual duties already include the provision of means for the performance of a certain task, a committee should not be instituted to take over that task, unless the individual duties are accordingly amended.

It has already been indicated how essential committees are to a " Staff and Line " organization. They are still more so to a functional organization. Fig. 5 illustrates the application of the Committee principle to a functional organization. The location of such committees is further discussed in the consideration of the functional form of organization.[1]

In reviewing the form of organization into which our hypothetical factory would fit on the basis of the principle of function, one is treading on ground already severely trampled upon by the feet of multitudinous theorists. Fig. 6 shows the form of organization which is the outcome of this principle. The reader will, of course, realize that for so small a plant as that postulated, so heavy a burden of indirect labour would not be necessary, since certain functions would be combined. Even so, however, it would be essential to maintain the distinct entity of each function, and the primary functionalization is therefore shown in full. It will be seen that the whole business is divided according to the basic functions already suggested. The function of Manufacture is divided according to the processes necessary for the actual making of the product.[2] These processes are peculiar to any business and will differ in every concern. For example, in a plant of a wholly different type, the first department might be the Foundry, instead of, as in our example, the Sorting Department. The sub-processes might then be named the Core Room, the Foundry Floor, and the Cleaning Room. But, of whatever character the product may be, the primary

---

[1] For the Committees requisite in a " Staff and Line " organization, illustrating also the course taken by business, *vide Installing Efficiency Methods*, by C. E. Knoeppel. (Engineering Magazine Library, 1918.)

[2] The principle governing this division of the function of Manufacture is discussed in Chapter VI.

THE PRIMARY INTER-FUNCTIONAL COMMITTEES OF A FUNCTIONAL ORGANIZATION.

(Figure 5.)

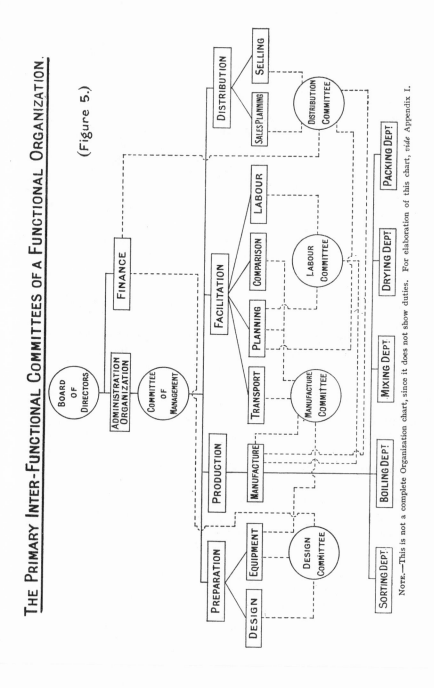

NOTE.—This is not a complete Organization chart, since it does not show duties. For elaboration of this chart, *vide* Appendix I.

The Functional Form of Organization. (Figure 6.)

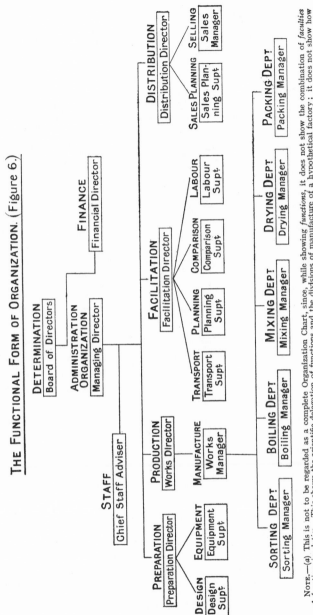

NOTE.—(a) This is not to be regarded as a complete Organization Chart, since, while showing *functions*, it does not show the combination of *faculties* and *functions* in *duties*. This shows the scientific delegation of functions and the divisions of manufacture of a hypothetical factory; it does not show how the work of each function is distributed between individual officials. *Vide* p. 140.

(b) " Staff " is included in this chart, but is not an essential part of the Functional form of organization.

functions remain constant in all concerns. The function of Manufacture, which of course forms the backbone of the organization, is then supplemented, on the one hand, by the two preparative functions of Design and Equipment, and, on the other hand, by the four facilitative functions of Transport, Planning, Comparison and Labour, each of these functions being executive in its own line. They are not to be confused with the work of the Staff in a Staff and Line organization, where the experimental and advisory work is wholly separated from executive work. A Staff organization can be added to a functional organization, if the need arises. Functional sections of a functional organization, however, are definitely executive. Each function has a functional superintendent, who is responsible for his particular function throughout all the departments of the function of Manufacture. For example, in the Sorting Department of our hypothetical factory, the storage and transport of the necessary materials will be under the Transport Superintendent; [1] the planning of the work under the Planning Superintendent; the upkeep of machinery and the supply of power under the Equipment Superintendent; the costing of processes under the Comparison Superintendent; the payment of wages under the Labour Superintendent. The head of the Manufacturing department acts as the co-ordinating agent of all functional activities affecting his department, and ensures that all co-operate to the end for which his department exists. [2]

With the corporate task thus divided into many parts, the need for committees is clearly vital. A functional organization cannot operate without committees, such committees being primarily of a co-ordinating nature. The organization being based upon a scientific distribution

[1] The title " Superintendent " is used to distinguish the head of a function from the " Manager," who is head of a department of the function of Manufacture.

[2] This relationship between functional " superintendents " and departmental " managers " is elaborated in Chapter VI.

of functions, however, it is possible to determine at any rate the essential members constituting committees, not by reason of their personalities, but rather by reason of the duties they perform. For proper co-ordination between heads of functions, as apart from co-ordination provided lower down the organization, and as apart from that co-ordination provided by a Managing Director, who will, of course, be a member of all primary committees, it is clear that, by reason of their duties alone, certain heads must collaborate with each other if one policy is to be uniformly executed. For instance, collaboration between Design, viewed as a purchasing function, and Finance is essential.[1] It may be necessary, further, to form a permanent relation between Design, Planning and Comparison, though it is more likely that the relationship here can be adequately provided by the proper routine of work, the Planning function simply indenting for quantities of materials, and the Comparison function specifying qualities. We thus obtain the necessary nucleus for a Design Committee (i.e. in a firm where Design is mainly a question of purchasing)—namely, the head of the function of Design, and the administrative head of the function of Finance, normally the Company Secretary, or a Director specially charged with the control of financial questions. Again, co-ordination between the Labour function and the Manufacture function is essential, since obviously alterations in wages or employment or welfare conditions cannot be made without affecting the Manufacture function. Co-ordination is also necessary between Labour and Planning, since the dispositions which Planning may make must materially affect the volume and distribution of Labour. The nucleus of a Labour Committee will therefore be the head of the Labour function, the head of the Planning function, and the head of the Manufacture function, who will normally

[1] Where Design is concerned in the specification of the nature of the product rather than in the purchase of raw materials, clearly, Equipment must also be co-ordinated with Design through the Design Committee.

be known as Works Manager. The same co-ordination is clearly necessary between Manufacture and Equipment, Comparison, Transport and Planning. Similarly, Distribution requires to be co-ordinated with Finance, Planning and Manufacture. We thus find four essential Committees at the top of a functional organization—the Design Committee, the Labour Committee, the Manufacture Committee, and the Distribution Committee—the main purpose of which is co-ordination between functions, the fact that the business is functionalized determining the membership of such committees. Given this original purpose of co-ordination, and this basic membership, the Committees may also be advisory or executive, as may be determined ; or other members may be added on account of special ability in committee work, apart from their strictly functional work. It is not unfair to say, therefore, that a functional organization, though based upon a wholly distinguishable principle, cannot be complete if based on that principle alone. It must also have a committee system as an inherent part of it.

Briefly, these are the forms of organization which follow from the principles stated. It cannot be too strongly emphasized, however, that the types here outlined are the logical outcomes of pure principle, which takes no account of those circumstances which surround the growth of every organization. It is just as easy to over-emphasize the logic consequent upon a principle as to over-emphasize the difficulties in the way of applying a principle. Every form of organization is a growth. Once an organization has, as it were, reached the stature of manhood, changes cannot be undertaken hastily or without profound consideration. It is better to await the right moment for a change than to impose it arbitrarily. Reorganizing requires time as well as genius. The scientific way is not always the surest way. It is often better temporarily to tolerate the unscientific than to create a ferment of human feeling. For industry is primarily human. It must not become the playground of scientist and engineer. We must often temper our zeal for what is scientifically desirable by considering whether it is immediately politic. Reorganization cannot, indeed, move more rapidly than the rate at which the individuals composing the organization can be induced to welcome it. It needs to be preluded by a long period of cultivation of what one may call the "organization sense."[1] An organization can only be the medium of good management if the latter is willing to utilize it. On the other hand, many individuals are scarcely able to distinguish the organization from the management. They lack the sense of inter-relation. Many a department persists in laboriously collecting statistics which another department already holds ; one department religiously closes its doors to the officers of another department ; the head of a department often clings tenaciously to a thousand and one miscellaneous duties, and will not admit his subordinates to a tithe of his secrets ; an old department endeavours to cling to its pristine duties although a new department has been created to take some of them over. These and similar incidents are evidence of a lack of ability to see the logical groupings into which functions fall, and the relations of one thing to another, or to grasp the significance of the phrase with which Professor Marshall prefaces his book—" The many in the one, the one in the many."[2] For such as these, the prejudice is not against this or that form of organization, but against organization in general. They can be won over only by infinite patience and the cultivation by every means of this undeveloped sense of relativity.

Though, to discover our fundamentals, we must regard the business of organizing as if in every case it were a new venture, it is apparent that the present-day problem is that

---

[1] *Cf.* " Nothing is more fundamental than what may be termed the organization point of view. The essence of this is to see things as related." E. B. Gowin, in *The Executive and His Control of Men*. (Macmillan & Co., 1915.)

[2] *Industry and Trade.*

of reorganization, which is a different thing. Organizing presumes an untilled field ; reorganizing presumes a field full of weeds and alien growths. Few firms have the opportunity of Mr. Gordon Selfridge, who planned the whole organization of his vast London store before even a door was opened to the public. Most concerns to-day are encumbered with the legacy of the Victorian era. The skill required in organization is not so much that of the draughtsman as of the fitter. It is a problem of remoulding and adapting rather than of design. While the machine runs, the cogs must be adjusted. A scientific scheme of organization, therefore, provides an ideal and a guide, but does not obviate the necessity for and the problem of evolutionary adjustment. We have to thread our way through a labyrinth of the present towards the ideal we may adopt.

No reorganization can take place without a deliberate and purposeful effort towards it, which necessarily involves as a preliminary the determination of what it is intended the organization shall become. Next comes the deliberate fostering of the organization point of view, and the interesting of every managerial officer in the larger aspects of his work.[1] Without the general feeling that reorganization is a desirable and natural process, no scheme, however scientific, can conduce to harmonious management. After such a turning-over of the ground, the next step is to bring into some intelligible shape the form of organization as it stands. A comprehensive and detailed chart of the present form of organization is wholly essential to any scheme of reorganization. One cannot reorganize a business when one does not know how it is organized now. Armed with a chart of this kind, one is then in a position to draw up another chart—an idealistic picture of how the new organization should ultimately appear. It

[1] *Cf.* an interesting article in *Factory* for January, 1920, entitled " What I Learned When Each Superintendent Inventoried His Job," by Mr. W. J. Kilpatrick, of the Burroughs Machine Co., U.S.A.

is then a problem of observing where the actual and the ideal differ, and why; of determining what alterations can immediately be made and what anomalies it would be better to delay remedying till circumstances are more propitious. This forms not only a plan for immediate action, but also a guide for the future, so that, when opportunity offers, either by the retirement of officials, changes in method, changes or extensions in plant layout, or changes in trade conditions, endeavours may be made, according to a definite scheme, to remodel the actual nearer to the form of the ideal.

Kindred to the problem of reorganization is that of extending an organization. It is often not realized, or is realized too late in the day, that every extension of an organization is a new scientific problem. New duties, committees, personnel are not to be added like fresh squares to a patchwork quilt, sewn on at any point which the whim of the moment suggests. Haphazard extensions of organization form the surest way to failure in co-ordination. Only as new branches of an organization are added in such a way as to locate them in some logical relation to the existing branches, can an organization still receive that direction from a central source which makes further extension possible. An organization requires to be built and extended to some design, so that each piece added to it does not throw the whole structure out of proportion. That is the secret of organization-building—to place every stone in some scientific relation to the other stones. Without this, there soon comes a point when further building cannot proceed, because there is no cohesion. History has no precedent for the magnitude of modern industrial undertakings. It is significant, however, that, after a certain stage, every vast enterprise finds that the problem of organization becomes the first and foremost problem of the head of the business. " There is," says Major E. D. Hine, " a distinct limitation to the size of an undertaking ; volume may be the determining condition. The operating activities of many corporations have outgrown a detailed direction from a central source."[1] This limiting factor is not the capacity of management to carry out its functions, but rather the capacity of the organization to remain co-ordinated. The only factor which can circumscribe the development of a business, apart from human failings, is the complexity of co-ordination. This stage comes earlier in a business the organization of which has been haphazardly constructed than in one where the organization has been planned, from the beginning, with a view to expansion. Expansion is a process of delegation, but every step of delegation is putting an additional strain upon co-ordination. Presuming that every delegation is the creation of a lesser sphere for the " delegatee " than for the " delegator," it is clear that a point must come where the co-ordination exercised by the head of the business will be almost nugatory in effect. Even with the most scientific form of organization, this point will come at a comparatively early stage. It is then a question not only of delegating functions and divisions of functions, but of delegating co-ordination itself. Co-ordination from the head is not the only co-ordination. There must also be co-ordination " points " throughout the organization. Co-ordination in fact becomes a function of itself, with its head as head of the entire business, and its staff located at various " concentration points " in the organization. It is suggested that such " points " are to be found at the top of each main unit of manufacturing ; that, in fact, the primary duty of the departmental manager of a manufacturing department is to co-ordinate the activities of others who contribute to the efficiency of his department, such co-ordination being functionally related to that exercised by the chief co-ordinating official, who is the head of the business. This subject is further treated of in Chapter VI.

This problem of the regulation of growth clearly affects

[1] *Modern Organization*, by C. D. Hine. (Engineering Magazine Co., 1912.)

the question of permanence, or the capacity of an organization to endure and to develop, which has been postulated as the first main advantage of scientific organizing. Permanence consists of two elements—regulated growth of co-ordination, and replacement, or the repairing of the ravages of time, fortune and death. The Departmental form of organization, by concentrating all functions under one head, may appear to offer the best chance of effective co-ordination. It must be remembered, however, that co-ordination should not be restrictive, in the sense of imposing artificial boundaries upon expansion. Its function is rather to facilitate growth, by insuring that there is room in which to grow. The effect of the Departmental form of organization is, as it were, to impose a glass-frame on sunflowers. Whilst it certainly affords effective control, it definitely prevents growth. When the manager is fully occupied, growth stops ; or, if it goes on, it continues outside the province of his control. It creeps outside the glass-frame, and is wasted. Moreover, no manager, except in the smallest conceivable department, can be expected to give full attention to every function, with the result that the functions develop unevenly ; some grow, others remain stunted. On the other hand, the danger of functional organization is that co-ordination should be lacking. Functional organization has, however, one great initial advantage—that the whole task of the business is grouped into logical sections, thus leaving the supreme executive free for the work of co-ordination alone. Functional organization recognizes co-ordination as the highest function. " Just in so far as functionalization brings the necessary and effective decentralization for action, so does functionalization of itself make essential another function. Where there are separate entities of an organization, each responsible for action and results in its own line, and all aiming at the same ultimate object, it is necessary, in order to obtain harmonious and effective ultimate action, to recognize the necessity for co-ordination, and to treat it as a distinct and basic function of the organization."[1] Functional organizing without a proper allowance for co-ordination is, indeed, infinitely perilous. It is the primary function of the chief executive, in which he may well be assisted by a co-ordination or organization expert for the sole purpose of advising him upon this subject alone.

The other element of permanence is the replacing of executive officers as they leave the business. No organization can claim the advantage of permanence which is dependent upon the ability of one man, or which places the transient advantage of allowing ability to run its own course, irrespective of the scientific grouping of work, above the permanent advantage of regulating individual effort according to a corporate plan of organization. This is a question of " understudies " or " second strings." Management cannot carry out a connected policy unless provision is made for replacement in the event of death or other circumstances. No matter what the form of organization, this necessity remains. Under the Departmental form of organization, however, it cannot be satisfactorily met. Obviously, when a manager has complete control of every factor affecting his department, and is judged only by results, he will institute methods peculiar to himself. Nor is such a manager required to any great degree to exercise the gentle art of co-operation with other officials, with the result that there is a decided tendency and, indeed, a temptation for him to retain the attributes of the autocrat. The lesson of history is that no autocracy can perpetuate itself. Autocracy bears its own coffin. Moreover, to " understudy " duties which, not being scientifically grouped, are liable to alteration at will, may be to pursue a mirage. The functional form of organization, however, maintains a standard form, which enables the " understudy " to have some definite and clear prospect.

[1] Mr. R. A. Feiss, as reported in the Taylor Society Bulletin. Vol. IV, No. 2.   April, 1919.

No matter what individuals may perish, the broad groups of work remain constant, and the "understudy" has, therefore, before him a position the requirements of which will not appreciably vary. The provision of a niche for the "understudy" in the organization is a problem for the organization-builder. "Understudying," as such, is not normally a whole-time job. It comes about, rather, by so dividing the work to be done that an official is compelled to delegate work to his immediate subordinate, who, by performing the work thus delegated, is qualifying himself for the position above him. "Understudying" is, in fact, a matter of scientific progression—a climbing from position to position, such positions being defined according to a scientific scheme of delegation.

Such a distribution of work is the basis of that further advantage of scientific organizing mentioned above; namely, Human Standards, or the grouping of work according to the normal capacity of the persons required to execute it. The tendency in many concerns is to overload the willing horse. Under the Departmental form of organization, the danger of this is clear, since each department, being a self-supporting and centrally controlled unit, divides its work according to the temperament of the manager rather than according to a scientific analysis of functions. In itself, however, functionalization, while defining the circumference of a certain group of duties, does not directly allocate duties to the individuals composing the staff of any one function. This is decided by the combination of function with faculty, as illustrated in Fig. 7. Clearly, it is not essential that every department shall have such a staff that every faculty is provided by a different person; but it is suggested that for the proper conduct of a department, the required faculties shall definitely be provided either separately or in combination. We thus obtain what Mr. Denning has described as "each person's work" and "each piece-of-work's person," which is the scientific interlocking of

"FUNCTION" AND "FACULTY" DETERMINING UNIT POSITIONS. (Figure 7.)

Faculty	PREPARATION		PRODUCTION	FACILITATION				DISTRIBUTION	
	DESIGN	EQUIPMENT	MANUFACTURE	TRANSPORT	PLANNING	COMPARISON	LABOUR	SALES PLANNING	SELLING
DETERMINATIVE									
ADMINISTRATIVE									
SUB-ADMINISTRATIVE									
EXECUTIVE	Superintendent of DESIGN								
SUB-EXECUTIVE			Sub-Manager of MANUFACTURE						
SUPERVISORY									
INVESTIGATIONAL									
COORDINATIVE									
ADVISORY							Advisory Staff Officer of LABOUR		
SPECIAL									

EXECUTIVE (bracketing DETERMINATIVE, ADMINISTRATIVE, SUB-ADMINISTRATIVE, EXECUTIVE, SUB-EXECUTIVE, SUPERVISORY)

SERVICE (bracketing INVESTIGATIONAL, COORDINATIVE, ADVISORY, SPECIAL) work-function and personnel faculty.[1] The advantage here is not alone that work is distributed according to normal human standards of capacity, but also that there is a natural and consecutive progression from one position to another, and that the work every official is engaged upon and the faculty he brings to bear upon it are defined.

The other advantages of Concentration, Individuality and Combination, described above, spring from the logical grouping of work. When both the work to be performed and the status and capacity of the person performing it are definite and standard, close and economical working is possible, since work-relationships are rendered precise and intimate. Nor does a functional organization take away personal responsibility ; it rather enhances it. When an individual is given definite and circumscribed duties, his personal sense of proprietorship is increased. It is lack of definition which blurs the outline of responsibility. This applies as much to the departmental manager or foreman—i.e. the manager of a process or department of the function of Manufacture—as to the functional super-intendent. The " Functional Foremanship " of Taylor eliminates this departmental manager, and substitutes eight functional " bosses," the " gang boss " being the executive officer in the main corresponding to the position of manager or foreman. To eliminate the manager, as understood in this country, however, is to restrict that essential function of co-ordination, already referred to, which must be discussed later.[2] The manager and foreman are essential features of British management, and it is possible to develop functionalization to a wide extent and yet retain these features.[3] Functionalization does

[1] *Scientific Factory Management*, by A. D. Denning. (Nisbet, 1919.)

[2] *Vide* Chapter VI.

[3] *Cf*. Mr. Charles Renold, of Hans Renold & Co., Ltd., speaking at Oxford, April, 1920.

" Those of us who are concerned with management know perfectly well that a good foreman is a good foreman because he is a good

not rule out, but rather increases the necessity for that leadership and co-ordination which distinguish the manager and foreman in British industry. The foreman is the imperishable legacy of our industrial history. Under the functional form of organization, as outlined here, however, his duties are somewhat changed. He is no longer the autocrat—the oracle—but rather the mouthpiece of the management as a whole.

Just as it is possible to correlate a functional form of organization with the existence of the departmental manufacturing manager, so it is possible to correlate the functional with the " Staff " idea in organizing. Both manufacturing and functional heads are executive ; there is still room for investigational and advisory work. The " Staff " idea is one of those innovations which are liable to be ruined by over-emphasis. The idea is being run to death, and is laying itself open to that most damning of all charges—the charge of creating unnecessary departments, and employing superfluous officials. The word " Staff," moreover, is being used in current theory in far too loose a sense. Strictly, it means certain officials who provide the faculties of advice and investigation. The Staff is not executive, in either production or facilitation. It is not essential that any specific individuals should compose the Staff, though in a large concern this might be necessary. In a smaller concern, several officials on the executive side might collectively provide the faculty

leader. If you replace the foreman who has complete charge of a gang of men by functional foremen, each of whom has a say over only a part of a man's work, the opportunity for personal leadership ceases to exist. . . . I have no hesitation in saying that functional foremanship is a failure. Anything which limits the scope of the foreman, or his exercise of leadership is a mistake ; and the place for functional division is in the higher ranks of management."

Cf. also Mr. A. R. Stelling, in *Taylor's Principles in Modern British Management*, in *Lectures on Industrial Administration*, edited by B. Muscio, M.A. (Pitman, 1920.)

" The devolution of the functions, of management is the keynote of the Taylor system in America, but it will not work in this country. Here again we have to deal with the psychology of the British workman. He won't stand eight bosses."

of advice for any particular function.   Or again, the faculty may be provided by the employment of an outside staff, as is a growing practice in America—" calling in the expert," as it is called.   It matters little what the form of organization for this particular purpose is, provided the faculty is in some way provided.   The " outside expert," or, as he is called, " the consulting industrial engineer " will probably not be popular in British industry.   The introduction of a stranger who even indirectly tells everyone how to do his job will never be a popular mode of increasing efficiency, even though in certain circumstances it may be recognized as necessary.   Nor would it appear that committees can wholly be relied upon adequately to provide this faculty of advice, since it involves, above all things, careful and detailed   analysis,   prolonged   study,   various   academic qualifications, and special scientific methods.

It seems, therefore, that there is a place in any industrial organization   for   definite   staff   officials—non-executive officials, whose sole business is to make investigations and recommendations.   Even under a completely functional form of organization   these   would be required, though clearly in a lesser degree, since each functional head would be an expert in his own function.   Nevertheless, each functional head would be executive, and might not therefore be able to give the time necessary for investigation.   For example, though there may be a Comparison superintendent, who is an expert in costing, it may well be necessary to supplement his work by that of a special investigator into costing methods.

This   example   of   Comparison   is   taken   because   to   a great extent this function is performing the work of what we   have   referred   to   as   the   staff.   It is the function concerned in research ; and, certainly, to the extent to which it is developed, the need for a special Staff organization is diminished.   But, there will still be room for a Staff, especially as advisory to the head of the business. As the process of transference from the Departmental to the Functional form of organization is in train, an expert staff is essential, in the sense of the " Staff and Line " organization. It may then be that, as the functional form develops, the former staff officials will themselves become functional officials. Finally, the nucleus of the former staff becomes distributed between the function of comparison and a permanent staff body, advisory to the managing director, especially upon such matters as developments in organization, new ideas in management, administrative innovations in other businesses, and the collation of information to show the corporate results of activities. This absorption of the staff in the functional organization, however, by no means eliminates the possibility which may arise for special staff work on particular subjects.   It is no reflection on the executive that this need may arise any more than it is a reflection, in certain circumstances, upon a medical practitioner to call in a specialist, or upon a builder to have recourse to a consulting engineer. Whether such circumstances are constantly arising, and thereby warrant the employment of a whole-time staff is a matter of local concern.   It is clear that, though functionalization ensures such a grouping of activities as enables the officials of the organization to concentrate upon particular lines of work, it does not guarantee that the best information, theory and advice are always available for the execution of such functions. It may, therefore, be necessary to supplement the functional organization by a staff organization, consisting of a nucleus of whole-time staff officers, supported by local investigational committees, and, if necessary, aided by outside experts.   Such an organization will certainly be necessary before functionalizat on is complete.   After that, local circumstances will decide how far a permanent organization of that kind will still be necessary.[1]

[1] *Cf.* " The New Spirit on Industry," a lecture by Sidney Webb, LL.D. at Oxford, April, 1920—

" My vision of the future of management in the years to come is an exalted one.   But this management, far from being autocratic,

To summarize, we are now in a position to enumerate the main requirements of an ideal organization. The detailed application of these requirements is for local consideration. There is no complete ideal, but the following may be regarded as necessary principles—

(*a*) The main division of the functions of the business should be based upon a scientific analysis of the work to be accomplished.

(*b*) Like functions should be grouped together and clearly defined, especially " border-line " duties.

(*c*) Positions should be determined by a proper interlocking of work and faculty, job and man.

(*d*) Co-ordination should be the sole concern of the chief executive, such co-ordination being continued lower down the organization.

(*e*) The leadership of the workers should be single, direct and intimate.

(*f*) The executive management should be supplemented, firstly, by a committee organization to provide co-ordination, facilities for advice and investigation, and the training of subordinates ; secondly, by such expert Staff organization as circumstances require.

(*g*) Positions should be determined irrespective of individuals, and so graded as to allow of a methodical progression from one to another.

(*h*) The whole form of organization should be charted, published to all concerned, and kept up to date.

will be dependent very largely on the reports of disinterested experts. Of course, there will still be emergency decisions, but management on its higher level will probably come to be more and more a competent weighing of expert evidence, involving both measurement and publicity."

Cf. also Chapters III and IV of *Factory Organization and Administration*, by Hugo Diemer (McGraw Hill, 1914), and Chapters VIII and IX of *Installing Efficiency Methods*, by C. E. Knoeppel. (The Engineering Magazine, 1918.)

APPENDIX TO CHAPTER IV

The growth of mammoth businesses has made the administration of such businesses in many respects comparable to the administration of State Departments. Moreover, the increasing regulation of industry by the State, the absorption of the State in industrial affairs, the direct control of Labour by the State, especially during the war, and the increased staffs of Government Departments have combined to approximate Civil Service conditions of administration to those we find in industry.

Two further factors of note are developing in this connection ; firstly, the growth in industrial administration of standard methods of procedure for the execution of administrative work, in many respects comparable to the routine procedure of a Government office ; secondly, the increasing publicity and consequent criticism of industrial methods—a publicity and criticism which the Civil Service has long endured, and which have profoundly influenced its methods of working. Both of these factors, as regards industry, show every sign of development. The indefinite methods of administrative working, which have long distinguished the conduct of industry from the conduct of the State, cannot longer survive in the larger industrial corporations. Standard and definite methods of carrying out the routine of administration are becoming essential in those concerns which have developed to a size where control has had to be widely delegated.

Similarly, it is impossible to be blind to the growth in recent years of publicity as regards industrial affairs—a development which cannot but influence industrial methods of management in some such way as it has for long affected the methods of Government. In the case of the latter, whilst exercising certain beneficial effects, it has also had that insidious result of perverting the sense of relative values, so that the smallest matters receive a consideration equal to the largest. The same danger confronts industrial administration. In large businesses, it is no uncommon feature to see committees and individuals devoting valuable time to the smallest and most insignificant matters. Why ?—largely because it is felt to be necessary to review every little matter with the same scrupulous care as would be given to matters of high policy, in view of the impression that might be created upon the workers in industry and the public at large. That such consideration should be given is to the good, but that it should be given irrespective of the relative value of the matters under review is an indication that the same danger confronts industrial administration, and for the same reason, as confronts the Civil Service.

This is not the place to consider in detail the organization of Government, but it will not be inappropriate to note certain tendencies and make certain comparisons, which the staffs of large businesses may do well to consider further. The comments made in the McDonnell Report, of 1914, are significant in this connection, and serve to indicate how far the war has carried industry in the direction suggested.[1] The Report advances four main reasons why the Civil Service cannot always apply so-called " business "

[1] The Report (Fourth) of the Royal Commission on the Civil Service. Part II. Cd. 7338.

methods to public administration. The first point is that public administration is not conducted for profit, and therefore commercial criteria of success cannot apply. A new motive in industry is gradually eliminating this distinction. Though industry must always be conducted for profit, there is no reason why profit should always remain the sole motive. Industry must pay its way, but so also must a Government. In any event, the utmost economy in administration is a necessity common to both. A few years have carried industry into a new atmosphere. Unlimited profits, if still taken, are beginning to be looked upon askance. Neither Press nor public are longer inclined to regard them as the only measure of successful industrial enterprise.

The second point in the Report is that departmental procedure is largely governed by Parliamentary criticism ; that, in fact, a department is constantly open to outside criticism, and must therefore carry an elaborate system of records and regulations of procedure, in its own defence and for its own justification. In industry, this same feature is developing. The greater discernment of public criticism, the easier access to the details of industrial administration, the inquisitive capacity and more intelligent and informed criticism of Labour, and, be it added, the augmented sense of public responsibility on the part of employers have tended to expose industry to the same outside criticism as the Civil Service receives from Parliament and public. The third point in the Report is that a Government has necessarily to consider its employees more than a business concern. This point was surely made before the days of welfare work, pension schemes, unemployment benefits and employment departments. Since 1914, in this direction, industry has made vast strides. The distinction drawn in the Report may still exist, but undoubtedly in a restricted and diminishing form. The fourth point is that heads of Government Departments can neither choose nor dismiss their men as freely as business managers. Again, the passage of a few years has diminished the force of this distinction. The growth of Employment Departments has brought into industry a feature not unlike the Establishment Division of a Government Department, whilst the increasing practice of establishing pension schemes has tended to modify that handling of labour to which the Report apparently refers. In general, from these points enumerated in the McDonnell Report, it is possible to observe that those differences between State and industrial administration which, in 1914, were regarded as fundamental have, in a few years, been singularly modified.

Since administrative conditions tend to approximate, therefore, in principles of organizing there must also be points of similarity. Prime among papers upon this subject is the Report of the " Machinery of Government " Committee, which sat under the chairmanship of Lord Haldane.[1] Attention may first be directed to the functions of the Cabinet, as outlined in that Report. The main functions of the Cabinet are there described as—

(a) " the final determination of policy " . . . , etc.,
(b) " the supreme control of the national executive " . . . , etc.,
(c) " the continuous co-ordination and limitation of the activities of the several Departments " . . . , etc.

[1] Cd. 9230.

—a statement which concisely summarizes the duties of that supreme industrial function referred to above as Administration, and would apply to any executive board of directors or committee of management. It will be of interest, therefore, to note the conditions laid down as desirable for the due performance of these functions. These the Report holds to be : (*a*) smallness in number, preferably ten, or, at most, twelve ; (*b*) frequent meetings ; (*c*) the supply in the most convenient form of all information and material necessary to enable it to arrive at expeditious decisions ; (*d*) personal consultation with heads of departments likely to be affected by decisions ; (*e*) systematic method of securing that decisions are effactually carried out. To these are added the desirability of a secretariat and of an organization for acquiring information and facts " preliminary to the settlement of policy and its subsequent administration." Emphasis is also laid upon the necessity that " in all departments the higher officials in charge of administration should have more time to devote " to inquiry, research and reflection before policy is defined. Each of these points has its application to the conduct and scope of the similar supreme committee—be it a board of directors or a board of management—in an industrial concern. The limitation to twelve is something more than the selection of a number ; it is a principle of basic importance. Under a functional form of organization, if each head of a function and the head of the function of Administration composed the committee, it would be a committee of ten or eleven, according to whether any special individual represented Finance or not. The need for frequent meetings, again, is equally essential in an industrial concern, mainly in order that continuous and adequate co-ordination may be secured. The third point, namely, the necessity for the convenient presentation of data, is to be linked to the fourth point— the need for consultation with the permanent heads of departments —and the further point regarding the desirability of a secretariat. Industrial committees of management are liable to waste time through ill-digested or incomplete information, and, indeed, to pass over important matters for the same reason. It is suggested that in this lies the need for the conservation of that which has been referred to as the nucleus of the Staff. The managing director requires, as chairman of such a committee, an investigational and advisory staff, which at the same time would act as the secretariat of the committee, and the head of the organization for the acquisition of information.

The last point is of special importance—" a systematic method of securing that decisions are effactually carried out." This is to draw that profound distinction between the two parts of Administration (the " determinative " element, and the " co-ordinating " element) which has already been described. A connecting link is required between the two. Many executive committees make decisions, which are imperfectly and inadequately interpreted in practice. Herein lies the vital need for an individual—normally the managing director—who co-ordinates, not primarily policies, but the administration which those policies involve. A committee may be executive in the sense that it makes decisions which are to be carried out, but cannot be executive in the sense of ensuring that in practice they are actually carried out. That is and must be the concern of one individual alone.

Beyond this consideration of the duties of the Cabinet, the Report proceeds to define the principles upon which work should be divided between departments. The tendency indicated is towards a functional form of organization. The Report observes that there are two principles only for the allocation of duties : (a) by persons or classes to be dealt with (corresponding to the " departmental " form of organization, i.e. grouping by processes) ; (b) by services to be performed (corresponding to the " functional " form of organization, i.e. grouping by functions). Under the latter, to take an instance, " a Ministry of Education would be concerned predominantly with the provision of education whenever and, by whomsoever, needed," *irrespective*, be it noted, of localities or classes of the community, just as a function of Comparison, for instance, in an industrial concern, is concerned in comparative and research work, irrespective of manufacturing groupings in departments. This principle is justified in the following terms, which read also as a justification of functional organizing in industry : " It is, moreover, only by distributing business between departments on this principle that the acquisition of knowledge and the development of specialized capacity by those engaged in the several departments can be encouraged to the full. These results are obviously most likely to be secured when the officers of a department are continuously engaged in the study of questions which all relate to a single service, and when the efforts of the department are definitely concentrated upon the development and improvement of the particular service which the department exists to supervise."

The Report concludes with a summary of recommendations, two of which appear to suggest broad principles of organizing which are true of industry as of the State. They read as follows—

" (a) Further provision is needed in the sphere of civil government for the continuous acquisition of knowledge and the prosecution of research, in order to furnish a proper basis for policy."

" (b) The distribution of business between administrative departments should be governed by the nature of the service which is assigned to each department. But close regard should be paid to the necessity for co-operation between departments in dealing with matters of common interest."

Stated in the terms used hitherto, this would appear as a recommendation for a functional form of organization, supplemented by the necessary staff organization, and welded together by the requisite co-ordinating machinery—a proposal which has already been advanced. It is, even if it is not permissible to draw comparisons, at least significant that the recommendations of such a committee upon the organization of the Government service should in broad principles coincide with pronounced tendencies towards a similar form of organization in industry. It is accordingly suggested that a study of the machinery of Government should form a part of every industrial administrator's training. The Civil Service may have many faults, but it is suggested that those faults lie rather in the traditions of the Service than in its organization. The State organization is by no means perfected, but the study to which it has been subjected and the ideas which are advanced for the direction of its development merit profound consideration from those who are concerned in similar problems in industry.[1]

---

[1] The following Reports and books are recommended for this subject—

(a) Reconstruction Pamphlets 38A, 38B, 38C—" The Business of Government."

(b) Cd. 9230.   Report of the Machinery of Government Committee under Lord Haldane.   (1918.)

(c) Report of the Joint Committee on the Organization, etc., of the Civil Service.   (1920.)

(d) Fourth Report of the Royal Commission on the Civil Service. Cd. 7338.   (1914.)

(e) *The Civil Servant and His Profession.*   (Pitman, 1920.)

CHAPTER V

SUMMARY

(a) The new spirit in industry ; danger of its becoming a catchword ; its significance to-day ; its essence of fellowship.

(b) The problem of wages ; whence increased wages can come ; profit-sharing—objections and advantages. It does not touch the wage problem. The problem of the minimum ; the necessary adjustment between economics and ethics ; relation to productivity. The minimum sets the standard for wages above minimum. Payment by results—advantages and criticism. Need for a policy as to rate-cutting. Need for wage co-ordination, and agreement as to rates.

(c) Employment work—the spirit behind it ; the engaging of personnel ; vocational diagnosis and job analysis. The maintenance of Labour ; significance of Labour Turnover ; its causes ; why Labour maintenance is worth while. The discharging of Labour ; the basis of discipline.

(d) Economic security—unemployment the converse of employment ; a problem of adjustment ; restriction of the volume ; meeting effects of inevitable unemployment ; amount payable ; place of the State.

(e) Welfare work—dependent upon a general welfare spirit ; other motives of no avail ; the field of the work, and its methods ; affects mental and moral as well as physical environment ; need for workers to co-operate in the work.

(f) Training and Education—method more important than subject ; the training of Scientific Management, value and objections ; need for true co-operation in training ; development of initiative rather than technique ; relation of management to education ; factory life forms mentality ; democracy presumes better education ; management cannot remain passive.

(g) Trade Unions—problem of their dissociation from production ; development through defence ; can constructiveness ensue ? Necessity for intimacy with unions ; possibilities of co-operation with management. Use of shop stewards.

(h) Co-operation—the basic principle of progress ; gregarious instinct of mankind ; diversity of this instinct in industry due to lack of a common motive ; management the key to co-operation in the future ; new type of manager necessary ; failure of the wage incentive ; Works Councils a beginning ; is co-operation possible ?

AN inherent danger lies in the use of " catch " words or phrases—a danger that they may either convey an inadequate significance, and occasion misunderstanding or, by excessive use, become nauseating. We have seen the term " efficiency " fall into both these dangers. It would

be a thousand pities were the phrase now being freely used—
" the new spirit in industry "—to suffer a similar fate.
For " efficiency " we may coin another less irritating term,
but for " the new spirit in industry " there cannot be any
substitute with the same significance. For the phrase is
expressive. It betokens a change, not in structure,
methods, objects, environment or conditions, but in
mentality. It stands for a new human attitude among
the various groups of beings united in an industrial undertaking. In particular, it stands for a new relationship
between management and men—a relationship determined
neither by tradition nor by economic conditions, but by
the spirit emanating from each party. It betokens,
therefore, a new attitude on the labour side of factory
management.

The problem of Labour is the " Ireland " of industry.
It is a perpetual problem, a developing problem and a
psychological problem. Like the problem of Ireland
in the political sphere, it needs not only skill, practical
statesmanship and the power of constitution-building,
but also vision and understanding. Alterations in hours
and wages, the establishment of Employment Departments,
and the encouragement of Welfare activities may too often
resemble many of the overtures which have been made
to Ireland. They may lack the spontaneity of a spirit
informing them with honesty. The need is not primarily
for schemes and departments, but for sympathy and insight.
We often fail to realize that our present factory system
is the mushroom-growth of a century, and that to attempt
to stabilize conditions in the midst of growth is to emulate
Canute. Industry is evolving ; we cannot foretell to
what it may attain. But we may be sure, to adapt a
phrase, that " evolution was not aiming at *the present
stage of Industrialism* when it set out on its long journey
from the flaming mist of the nebula." [1] The present in

---

[1] *Vide : The Mirrors of Downing Street.* By " A Gentleman
with a Duster." (Mills and Boon Ltd., 1920.)

no sphere of human activity can ever be the permanent. The present is rather the stepping-stone to the future ; it is the playing-field rather than the goal. A new spirit means a reinvigoration of the sense that further steps must be taken. It indicates not only a refreshed vision, but also a different line of approach to the problems of to-day. It does not involve a vivid portrayal of an industrial Utopia, any more than the Christian spirit involves a panoramic view of the Kingdom of Heaven. It gives a broad principle for everyday conduct, a general attitude to daily routine.

The essence of the new spirit, as opposed to the old spirit of the " iron hand," is fellowship. The old spirit said, in the words of one of the characters of Mr. Galsworthy's play " There is only one way of treating men—with the iron hand. This half-and-half business, the half-and-half manners of this generation, has brought all this upon us. Sentiment and softness, and what this young man would call his social policy. You can't eat your cake and have it ! This middle-class sentiment, or socialism, or whatever it may be, is rotten. Masters are masters, men are men ! " [1] The new spirit turns away from the old ; it does not attempt to regard the present as the goal of progress. Seeing that progress is the outcome of the development of human attributes, it puts humanity before wealth. It erects neither the present nor any future condition of things as an ideal, but rather argues that, if the future is to be an improvement on the present, the way to it is the highway of conciliation, fellowship and mutual understanding. The finger-post of progress points to the path of co-operation.

Labour management brings us to the cross-roads. It compels us to decide which road we shall follow. If we go on, we follow a road of infinite difficulty but also of infinite hope. A new spirit in our management will not immediately remove difficulties, but maybe it will ultimately solve them.

[1] *Strife*. By John Galsworthy.

In this chapter we shall consider the operation of this spirit in the main fields of Labour management—Wages, Employment and Welfare.   One cannot condense a volume into a chapter, but one may perhaps state problems and suggest paths for management to follow.

WAGES

The problem of wages is the determination of that part of the proceeds of industry which is payable to Labour. This inevitably involves the determination of that other part which shall be paid to Capital in the form of interest. But, unfortunately, the task before us is not in what proportions to divide a given cake, but how to divide a cake the size of which is not given.   Wages and profits are, as it were, the sides of a triangle, with a fixed apex, the base of which is production.   If the base is short, the sides are contracted.   If the base is long, the sides are extended.   Wages, as also profits, are conditioned by production.   Even " the minimum wage " must be based on an assumed minimum of productivity.

Whence, then, can increased wages come ?—for that is the crux of the problem.   Increased wages may come from one or all of the following sources : (a) Reduced profits, (b) increased selling price, (c) reduced cost of raw materials, (d) increased efficiency and harder work.   Each of these is strictly limited, save the last.   The rate of profit is limited by the necessity of attracting capital.   An increase in selling price is limited by the public demand, and in any event cannot, speaking generally, increase real wages The decrease in the cost of raw materials is limited by scarcity, transport costs, and the costs of cultivation or extraction.   But the efficiency of industry is limited only by the unknown boundaries of human genius and toil. It is, therefore, mainly to this source that we must look for the means whereby the remuneration of those engaged in industry can be augmented.

The main problem, however, leads to secondary problems : Firstly, the determination of the minimum upon which higher wages shall be based ; secondly, the determination of the relative wages to be paid to different grades and classes of workers ; thirdly, the determination of the machinery by which wages shall be fixed. The whole problem may, therefore, be stated under four main headings : (a) The distribution of proceeds between Capital and Labour, (b) the minimum wage, (c) the distribution of wages between grades of Labour, (d) the machinery of wage settlements.

To deal with the first of these problems, there has, within recent years, been a recrudescence of enthusiasm for schemes of profit-sharing and co-partnership.[1] In the first ten months of 1919, twenty-nine new schemes were put into operation, and, at the end of that year, 164 firms, covering about 243,000 workers, were using some profit-sharing or co-partnership scheme. These schemes, however, do not touch the basic problem of wages. They presume a " standard " remuneration for both Capital and Labour—for the former, the minimum of profit necessary for its attraction and for the continuance of the business ; for the latter, the current wages for the types of labour employed. The schemes deal with that debatable volume of proceeds which is still surplus after Capital and Labour have been paid respectively on the lines indicated above. The actual fixing of wages, therefore, remains governed by the old idea of a " contract " between two bargaining parties. On the other hand, in so far as profit-sharing attempts to formulate an acceptable balance between standard wages and standard profits, and endeavours to distribute the surplus upon an agreed

---

[1] *Vide : Co-partnership and Profit-Sharing*, by Aneurin Williams (Home University Library), for a general review of the subject. Also " Report on Profit-Sharing and Co-Partnership in the United Kingdom," 1920, published by the Ministry of Labour. Also *Sharing Profits With Employees*, by James A. Bowie, M.A. (Pitman, 1922.)

principle, it goes some way to limit bargaining to a restricted area. Profit-sharing, however, does not obviate the necessity for fixing wages according to the powers of the two parties. It is, therefore, supplementary, but not an alternative, to bargaining. Neither can profit-sharing be regarded as any very considerable stimulus to increased productivity. The payment bears no direct relationship, as does payment by results, to the effort expended. It is, further, difficult to calculate and is paid some long time after the effort. It is not, therefore, an immediate and vivid incentive. The value of any scheme is more likely to reside in the concession to the claims of justice which it represents than in the immediate results of the payment. Such psychological value may, however, be of greater importance than the more questionable economic value. If profit-sharing can materially contribute to the development of a sense of justice in industry, its value may be immeasurable.

Yet we cannot overlook the fact that the general attitude of organized Labour to profit-sharing is, though different in various localities, for the most part hostile. The dangers to Trade Unionism are obvious, since there might easily be an attempt through profit-sharing to weaken the solidarity of Labour, by attaching the profit-sharing employees to their own firm rather than to their organized fellow workers. There is the further danger that profits might be manipulated, by the setting aside of reserves, etc., so that the portion accruing to Labour would be insignificant. Again, as Mr. W. L. Hichens points out, " there would be glaring inequalities, amounting to injustice, as between one firm and another." There is, again, the very real danger that profit-sharing, by a union of Capital and Labour through their respective organizations, might be made a weapon against the community. The degree to which industries are united amongst themselves, in Employers' Federations and Workers' Unions, makes it possible that, by both parties compounding upon a scheme of sharing profits, the community might be mulcted and have no means of redress.

Labour, in fact, would rather receive direct wages in some proportion to work performed than agree to wages on a standard basis and a hypothetical bonus out of profits, over the assessment of which it has no control. [1]

There remains, however, a further alternative. Industry is not only a business conducted by Capital, Management, and Labour for their own benefit. All three are contributing service to their common master, the community. It is not unreasonable to suggest, therefore, that in the distribution of profits the community has a claim for a share. Profit-sharing, in fact, may not only be between employer and employee, but also between these and the community—the community benefiting after the industrial partners have received both their standard remuneration and a bonus for service, such benefit being proportionate to the volume of profit.

At the same time, any profit-sharing scheme must be based upon a sound foundation of wages. It represents not a substitute for but an addition to wages, and cannot act as a palliative of low wages. The wage problem, therefore, still remains, i.e. the problem of wages apart from any addendum to them which may accrue as a result of a redistribution of profits. The wage question is, in the first instance, a question of the minimum. It is important to bear in mind that the case for a minimum wage is, though based upon an assumption of productivity, not relative to it. The primary case for a minimum wage is that it is the right of every citizen of a civilized community to be assured the means to a reasonable scale of living according to the general standard of the community. No progressive community can hold that its industrialism is contributing to the full that service it owes, if a proportion of those engaged in industry are condemned to so low a

[1] *Vide: The Works Manager To-day*, by Sidney Webb, page 83. (Longmans, Green & Co., 1917.)

material standard of living that their efficiency as social units is negligible. Taking a community as a whole, apart from exceptional individual cases, a low material standard involves a low intellectual and moral standard. If the latter standard is to be raised, the former must also be raised. While the material welfare of some social groups may thrive upon the low remuneration of unskilled labour, the general intellectual and spiritual life of the community cannot but suffer. In other words, before an adequate material standard of living can help a community to achieve an ethical standard proportionate to its stage of development, that material standard must, to some extent, be a common standard, a standard which cements and does not disintegrate society. Prosperity is to be measured by degrees of capacity and character rather than by degrees of luxury. True national prosperity means not sporadic luxury, but general development in capacity and character, and thus involves a juster balancing of material well-being, so that equal opportunity in the exercise of the higher human faculties may be afforded to all. The case for the minimum wage is, therefore, primarily ethical. That it must also be economic is obvious. But to deny it because, in an economic sense, it is not immediately possible, is to avoid the primary assumption that, economically possible or not, it is ethically right. If we are to progress, it will not be by subordinating the ethical to the economic, but rather by adjusting the economic to serve the higher ends of the ethical.

Clearly, advance must be governed by the extent to which we can make that adjustment. It is not possible, nor would it be immediately politic, to raise the material standard of the workers by sudden leaps and bounds. The process must necessarily be slow. Under present circumstances, therefore, how may we determine what that minimum shall be ? Mr. B. S. Rowntree has defined it as a wage " which would enable men of ordinary ability to marry, live in a decent house, and bring up a family of normal size—which I here assume to be a family with three dependent children—in a state of physical efficiency, while allowing a reasonable margin for contingencies and recreation."[1]   This he estimated to be, for a man 35s. 3d. per week, for a woman 20s. per week, with prices at the level of 1914. This means a wage of 70s. 1d. and 39s. 1d. per week for men and women respectively at the level of prices ruling in December, 1921. The criticism that it is unfair to take as a basis a man with a wife and three simultaneously dependent children (Professor Bowley states that only 18·7 per cent of male workers over 20 years of age are in such circumstances) does not invalidate the main contention that such a wage has not been even approximately possible in any single industry as a whole. Yet it is a wage of barely tolerable subsistence. [2]

The view that the payment of a minimum wage is communal and not wholly economic, in basic theory, is supported in the " Maintenance of Children Bill, 1919 " of New South Wales, which provides that the basic minimum wage for male workers is to be a living wage for man and wife, determined annually according to the cost of living, plus an allowance per child, *payable to mothers*, from a central " Children's Fund," maintained by the contributions of employers, according to the cost of keeping a child and the estimated number of children born to industrial workers. The payment direct to mothers strikes the keynote of the minimum wage theory. The employer, as a mere economic entity, is solely concerned in obtaining an immediate supply of adequately efficient labour. Even

---

[1] *The Human Needs of Labour.* By B. Seebohm Rowntree. (T. Nelson & Sons, 1918.)

[2] Mr. Rowntree allows only 5s. per week at 1914 prices for " personal sundries," 2s. to 2s. 6d. of which he estimates to be expended on Health Insurance, Trade Union subscriptions, additional subscriptions to sick clubs, etc. This leaves only 3s. a week for " newspapers, incidental travelling, recreation, occasional presents to the children, beer and tobacco, subscriptions to church or chapel, burial and sick clubs for wife and children, and the multitude of small sundries, such as stamps, writing materials, hair-cutting, drugs, etc."

if he knows that the efficiency of his workers must progressively deteriorate while he pays a wage insufficient to meet their legitimate requirements, it does not concern him, since if the workers deteriorate beyond a certain point, he can dismiss them. His own interest, as a cog in an economic machine, is simply to pay a wage in return for the productivity of the earner. That the wage paid may be inadequate to maintain a tolerable standard of living, though the first concern of the community, clearly is not, and cannot be, anything but a secondary consideration to the employer. The inherent problem of the minimum wage is, therefore, to determine the extent to which the community is entitled to impose its own general and ultimate interest upon the immediate interest of the employer. No community, however, can make demands which cause its industry to be conducted upon an uneconomic basis. The problem accordingly follows as to how far the productivity of industry can be increased, so as to enable the employer, without economic risk, to offer the worker at least such a wage as the interest of the community requires.

Though wages cannot be divorced from productivity, productivity may be made subservient to wages. Wages are not charity ; they are a payment for services rendered, normally measured in terms of product or result. Hence, increased productivity is hardly to be expected unless some proportionate increase in wages or benefits accompanies it. Increased production is not to be sought for its own sake, but for the sake of those benefits which accrue from it. A wage, moreover, is not only a payment for, but also an incentive to, effort. For labour, like any material commodity, may be purchased cheaply, but the quality may be in inverse ratio to the price. Low-paid labour may indeed prove more expensive than highly paid labour, if the former should prove incapable of so increasing its productivity as to earn a higher minimum. It is, in fact, better to pay a worker five units of wage for five units of work than three units of wage for three units of work. Efficiency is always cheapest in the long run, and the revelations of medicine and psychology have gone far to prove that the incidence of a low wage is amongst the prime reasons of poor productivity.

It is also to be borne in mind that a minimum wage tends to a more equal distribution of purchasing power throughout a community, which, in turn, opens a wider and more stable market for home products. Greater diffusion of wealth means a more general advance in the standard of living, and consequently creates a wider demand for those commodities and services which a higher standard involves. A minimum wage, in fact, may result in an increased trade.

Apart from economic considerations, however, if industry is to be conducted primarily for service, the impulse to increase productivity and thus augment earnings, must come from a conviction that the payment of wages is not to be based upon the least that can be disbursed under pressure but rather upon the most that the industry can afford. The limit to wages should not be the obstinacy or incapacity of the employer, but the solvency of industry. An industry which, through obstinacy, or through ineffective management, will not pay the wage of which, when operating at its highest efficiency, it is capable, is denying its responsibility to the community. But the motive of service requires from the workers, no less than the employer, a high standard of efficiency. Given able management, it is within the workers' own hands to increase their earnings. Clearly, therefore, a high minimum wage involves the elimination of ineffective workers. It is socially more desirable that an industry should be operated by the most efficient workers, adequately remunerated according· to the communal standard of living, whilst ineffective workers are treated as a separate problem, than that an industry should be carried on, as it were, by a chain of links of unequal capacity, the minimum wage being based upon the strength of the weakest. It is better that industry should be efficient and able to pay an adequate wage and provide reasonable conditions, than that it should carry on its wage-bill the burden of inefficiency. This applies to management and labour alike. Efficient management can influence production far more than efficient labour. The productivity of the worker is dependent not alone upon his personal effort, but also upon the use to which management puts his effort. Wages may often be low by reason of inefficiency over which the worker has no control. A minimum wage compatible with modern requirements, therefore, is conditional upon not only operative effort and skill, but also managerial efficiency and enlightenment.

Management and workers together, then, are set the task of so conducting industry that the minimum requisite for a tolerable standard of living becomes economically possible. We have to solve our economic problem on lines which promote an ethical end. We may, therefore, expect the extension of the compulsory minimum wage, fixed by statutory bodies, representative of industry and the community together—such wages being based rather upon the estimated capacity than the present practice of the industry. It then remains for the partners in industry to unite in the effort to transform that estimated capacity into actual volume.

Clearly, moreover, a minimum wage forms the basis for wages above the minimum. According to the level of the jumping-off ground will be the height to which it is possible to jump. Minimum wages are naturally based upon a principle wholly different from that determining wages paid for responsibility, effort, hardship and skill, above the minimum. The one principle is to be regarded as a protection against conditions conducive to both industrial and commercial inefficiency ; the other determines the reward for services above the basic productivity of the low-grade worker. Wages above minimum, other than extra wages paid for responsibility, hardship or skill, can be determined only according to output.   This distinguishes such wages from minimum wages which, whilst necessarily presuming a certain given output, are not fundamentally relative to it.   The most obvious form of such payment is the straight piece-rate.   Theoretically, no more equitable basis of payment exists.   There is a mistaken notion that Labour objects to piece-work as such.   This is by no means true.   Labour resists, rather, the concomitant conditions of piece-work, in that it clings to the " lump of Labour " fallacy, and fears the risk of rates being cut.   Such fears are by no means groundless, and more than mere promises of good faith on the part of management are necessary before they can be removed.   But an assurance of constant employment, or adequate maintenance in unemployment, and a standard piece-work list would remove many Labour objections.   Modern management, moreover, views rate-cutting with far more distaste than its forbears.   The risks inherent in rate-setting based upon experience or unscientific computations have become so formidable that a thorough analysis of the job is becoming the normal mode of such assessment.   Accuracy can only be obtained by analysis of each process, its division into its component elements, the determination of the time taken over each element, and the time to be taken over all the elements in combination, and the fixing of the allowance to be made for necessary rest intervals.   Scientific rate-setting is an essential condition, not only of maximum productivity but also of wage justice.

This is the more so when the setting of rates is based upon calculations of time irrespective of volume, as in the case of the Premium Bonus system.   Briefly, this system means that a scientifically determined *time* for a process or piece of work is arrived at, which forms the basis for the rate.   If the process is accomplished in a less time than that determined, the worker receives a bonus in proportion to the time saved.   The time saved is not paid for *pro rata*, but in some proportion, according to the agreed method of computation, such as the Halsey or Rowan methods. This amount paid to the worker, over and above day-rate, varies from 25 per cent to 33⅓ per cent of the *pro rata* payment for the time saved. Such a system may also, of course, be applied on a collective basis, the premium, in terms of hours saved, being shared amongst a group of contributory workers, according to the time worked by each.

Carried a degree further, it is possible to base the payment by this method not only upon the execution of the job under the standard time allowance, but also upon its execution according to certain scheduled instructions for the most efficient way of performing it. Payment is made, therefore, for adherence to instructions as well as for time saved. Of this character is the Gilbreth " Three Rate " system, which assesses the wage upon a triple basis: (*a*) The basic day rate, (*b*) the efficiency rate for adherence to instructions, irrespective of time saved or increased output, (*c*) the bonus rate when the work is done both according to instructions and within the standard time.

Payment by results, in fact, may take multitudinous forms, which it is impossible to describe here.[1] Management, however, apart from the particular form which it chooses to adopt under particular circumstances, must determine its general attitude to such payment. Such payment has indeed a dual aspect : Firstly, as payment for material results ; secondly, as payment for human effort.

[1] *Vide : A Rational Wage System : Some notes on the method of paying a worker a reward for efficiency in addition to wages.* By Henry Atkinson. (G. Bell & Co., 1917.)

Also *Work, Wages and Profits.* By H. L. Gantt. (Engineering Magazine Co., New York, 1916.)

Also *Adjustment of Wages to Efficiency.* (American Economic Association Economic Studies, Vol. I.) (The Macmillan Co., New York, 1896.)

Also *Incentives to Efficiency under Scientific Management.* By Henry Atkinson. (Industrial Reconstruction Council, 1919.)

Also *The Wages of Labour.* By William Graham. (Cassell & Co., Ltd., 1921.)

Also *The Premium System of Paying Wages.* (Office of *The Engineer*, 1917.)

To judge only by results is to miscalculate the dependency of such results upon the effort. The two aspects are interdependent. Payment by results may in practice achieve little, if the form of payment does not stimulate and encourage the necessary effort. To concentrate wholly upon the results accruing from any particular system is to neglect the very important factor of justice. Injustice in wage questions is, irrespective of systems, forcibly and directly repressive of energy, productivity, and effort, and breeds all the germs which destroy co-operation. Wage efficiency means, therefore, not only that rates shall be fixed scientifically, so as to ensure a full return in productivity, but also that they shall be fixed according to the most equitable standard and in the fullest co-operation with the workers themselves. It is only when rates are equitable and agreed that they stand a chance of being productive. The need of the employer for output must be balanced by the need of the employee for justice. The combination of a scientific assessment of output with equitable rates constitutes wage efficiency.

From the point of view of the management, the measure of the value of wages is output. Wages, of themselves, are meaningless except as representative of a certain volume of output and as expressed in terms of the cost of production. Increased wages and decreased costs, in fact, are not only not incompatible, but are rather indicative of the highest wage efficiency. This end, however, is only to be attained by a more economical use of effort. Monetary incentives may not evoke that effort unless they are founded upon a sound basis of justice. Wage justice requires two vital things : Firstly, a policy with regard to rate-cutting ; secondly, wage co-ordination. As regards the first, clearly more scientific rate-setting in the first instance would obviate the need for subsequent alterations. On the other hand, if it should become necessary to cut a rate, it should only be altered by agreement between the management and all the workers affected—that is, not only the workers operating under the particular rate, but also other workers operating under other rates, to whose earnings the earnings of the workers under the rate in question are disproportionate. That, indeed, is the only substantial reason for rate-cutting—the disproportion between the earnings of those working under the rate in question and those working under other rates. Rates cannot be cut on grounds of high labour costs, for, if high earnings are accompanied by high output, the labour cost per unit remains constant. But if high earnings rise to an extent where they are wholly out of proportion to the earnings of workers on other rates, then the whole wage situation is rendered topsyturvy. The sound policy would appear, therefore, to set rates in the first instance with the greatest analytical care, or, in co-operation with the workers concerned, to set an experimental rate for a given period, with the option of revision at the end of the period, and only to revise rates in agreement with the representatives of the workers in the factory, or, if the rates cover an industry, of the workers in the industry.

As regards wage co-ordination—the second element in wage justice—it is to be remembered that justice is largely a matter of efficient organizing and straightforward methods. The problem is that of balancing the earnings of those working on different processes, involving various degrees of skill and various amounts of output. The larger the business and the greater the variety of processes and rates, the more complex becomes the problem. A factory is a unity, however manifold its parts. Injustice cannot be hidden or suppressed ; it spreads and infects the whole. Widely diverse earnings on different processes, requiring comparable skill and effort, occasion bitterness and resentment. Such conditions cannot be remedied departmentally. A central authority is necessary to ensure justice in payment between all grades and sections of workers. The centralized co-ordination of wages is essential in any large business.

In the settlement of both day and piece rates, moreover, agreement between management and workers is also necessary. This involves the present system of bargaining. Under a system of scientific rate-setting, bargaining as to the character of any process is reduced to a minimum. But there is still the field for bargaining as to the price per piece or per day. When bargaining is between the representatives of thousands of organized workers on the one hand, and of groups of employers on the other, the method is not only beset with difficulties but also bristles with dangers. The place of the community in wage settlements has not yet been developed to the degree which our philosophy indicates as possible. If we assume the right of the community, exercising its powers over one of its communal services, to restrict the profits accruing to Capital, we must further assume its right to insist that Labour shall not appropriate a wage disproportionate to the earnings of the business or industry. In no province of human activity is the right of any section recognized to be the final judge in its own cause. All industry is one body. The settlement of what wealth an individual business shall take to itself and divide between its constituent parts is not a matter for itself alone to decide. An agreement between Labour and Capital in any one industry might ruin the community. It is not inconceivable, for instance, to imagine such a body as the Building Trades " Parliament " compounding upon wages and profits which would form a menace to the general public.

It is, indeed, largely because Labour and Capital are in opposition that the legitimate function of the community in the settlement of wages has never been emphasized. When a fair settlement can be arrived at by means of bargaining, the need for the explicit agreement of the community to it does not arise. Only when the bargainers cannot agree, or agree upon an unfair bargain, comes the summons to the State, as representative of the community.

As an instance of this, we have seen the State called in to compose the differences of miners and mine-owners. The principle of State intervention is widely deprecated. If, however, we recognize that the State is representative of the ultimate sovereignty of the community, which it is the purpose of industry to serve, it seems both logical and right that it should wield the final power in the settlement of the division of the proceeds of industry.

Employment

If the first main task of the labour side of management is the proper execution of a wage policy, its second task is that of applying and maintaining an efficient labour force. Broadly, it may be said that employment work is concerned in the movement of personnel—the engaging, transferring and discharge of the workers—as distinct from welfare work, which is concerned rather in the conditions surrounding the same personnel at work. The work of the two, however, must necessarily overlap—not only because their respective duties are intimately connected, but also because the spirit of both branches must be the same. While both are exercising functions of management, and thereby form necessary parts of the factory organization, both stand for that spirit in industry which places the man before the machine. For employment work is essentially the application of a spirit, as well as a necessary piece of managerial organization. Too often an Employment Department is set up like a new piece of plant, and expected to operate with the precision of a machine. As such, it achieves little, for it crystallizes no human spirit. The primary requisite in an Employment Department is that it shall stand for all that is human in a factory, linked closely to welfare work, and constantly bringing before the management as a whole the human effects of its policy. It cannot, indeed, relieve management of its conscience, but rather represents one active function of that conscience which, watching over the life of the factory, slumbers not, nor sleeps.

Employment work places the human capital of our factories before the material capital. It informs the business of production with a human spirit. It cannot, at the outset, be too strongly insisted that all the methods and machinery of employment work will achieve nothing in the direction of humanizing industry unless the work is imbued with the spirit which aims at making industry a great concerted human effort, in which the primary agents are men and women, in which the binding forces are co-operation and justice, and the motive is the better service of mankind.

There is little need to emphasize the necessity for employment work to be organized as a distinct department. The engaging of personnel alone is a highly specialized function. It cannot be regarded as incidental to supervision. The discharge of personnel, again, if we are to regard the worker as something more than a cog in the machine, cannot in justice be left wholly to the will of individual foremen. The movement of personnel within the factory, again, requires a central organization to effect the necessary transfers between departments.

So many firms, both here and in America, have instituted Employment Departments that we may presume this form of organization as established. The first problem of the employment manager, then, is the engaging of the personnel of the factory. In this, he owes a duty both to the firm and to the prospective employee. He will set a high standard, only selecting those applicants whose character and ability approximate to that standard. He will study the labour conditions of the locality, keeping in touch with employment agencies in the district. To the applicant he will display the courtesy and directness due to a man who may be about to throw his life into the work of the factory. He will select men for work most suited to their capacities. He will receive them in an atmosphere of welcome, and, should he engage them, he will ensure that they are set to work with a suitable introduction to work-mates and foremen, and a proper explanation of their work and their place in the whole. He will insist upon a medical examination to ensure that the present employees are exposed to no risk. He will endeavour to imbue the new worker with a high conception of his duties, with an interest in his work, and with something of the spirit of the factory. In his selection, he will be guided by the results of such psychological tests as are suitable for the work upon which the new employee will be engaged.

The engagement of personnel is indeed a combination of spirit and science. The instinctive discernment of the naturally able employment manager requires to be supplemented by scientific psychological tests. Such psychological analysis works in two complementary ways: firstly, by analysing types of work and determining the predominant characteristics requisite for the work; secondly, by analysing the qualities of the applicant by tests directed to that end, with a view to determining how far he possesses the qualities necessary for the efficient execution of the work. The gradual collection of data ultimately results in standard tests being formulated for specific jobs. [1]

The consequences, deleterious to the interests of both employers and workers, of putting square pegs into round holes have never been fully realized. An ill-fitting screw receives the immediate attention of the mechanic, but an ill-placed man is left to work his own way. We trust too much to the adaptability of men. Men are not adaptable

---

[1] *Vide : Lectures on Industrial Psychology.* By B. Muscio, M.A. (Routledge, 1920.)

Also *Vocational Psychology.* By H. L. Hollingsworth. (D. Appleton & Co., 1919.)

Also *Psychology and Industrial Efficiency.* By Hugo Munsterburg. (Constable, 1913.)

Also *Mind and Work.* By C. S. Myers, M.A., M.D. (University of London Press, 1920.) Etc., etc.

as regards their fundamental characteristics. A clumsy man can never become dexterous. An intelligent man will never be content with unintelligent work. Even if men were adaptable, we should still have the waste due to the rubbing off of fine corners and the discontent arising from an unsuitable application of effort. We see this wastage in terms of poor workmanship, lack of zeal, high labour turnover statistics, and absence of co-operative vigour. But we often overlook it. " We can see our forests vanishing, our water powers going to waste, our soil being carried by floods into the sea, and the end of our coal and iron is in sight. . . . We can see and feel the waste of material things. Awkward, inefficient or ill-directed movements of men, however, leave nothing visible or tangible behind them." [1] This waste of human potentiality will continue until we can bring a more scientific method to bear upon the selection of our workers. The time cannot be far distant when a psychologist will be a regular member of every management, and the chief assistant of the employment manager.

Following the task of engaging employees is that of maintaining the labour force. Clearly, success in selection will reduce the volume of work under this head. Even so, however, there will always be a constant leakage of employees out of the factory. The measure of this leakage is the " labour turnover " figure—a figure corresponding to the death-rate of a community, the index of factory human conditions. Labour turnover is normally stated in the form of a percentage, and may be defined as the ratio of the total number of terminations of employment, for whatever reasons, in a given period, to the average number of employees on the payroll for the same period. [2] A high

[1] *Principles of Scientific Management.* By F. W. Taylor. (Harper Bros., 1914.)
[2] *Cf.* (a) *A Statistical Study of Labour Turnover,* 1921. Published by the Industrial Fatigue Research Board. (No. 13.)
(b) *Annals of American Academy of Political and Social Science,* May, 1917. Vol. LXXI. (No. 160.) *Stabilising Industrial Employment.* Etc., etc.

turnover represents not only a financial loss to the employer, by reason of the time wasted on engaging and training, but also a feature of industrialism which is obviously undesirable for social reasons. Permanence of employment for efficient workers should be the objective of all employment work. A high turnover figure calls for immediate investigation. Why has such a large proportion of our workers left within, say, the last year ? How many have left for reasons which the management might combat—dissatisfaction, shortage of work, end of temporary employment, etc. ? How many have left for reasons which a more judicious selection of workers might have prevented—inefficiency at work, bad timekeeping, drunkenness, etc. ? How many have left because of unsatisfactory conditions of work—domineering foremen, bad ventilation, etc. ? How many have left to go to other firms where conditions are better ? How many have left for social reasons which industry might help to remedy —lack of housing, difficulties in transportation to work, or poor home conditions ? From which departments have most gone ? At what period of the year was the incidence of terminations greatest ? What service had those who left ? Why have so many left with less than six months' service ? Is poor management, lack of prospects, poor selection, bad conditions, unsympathetic foremanship, or unhealthy home environment the main reason ? What is the age of those leaving ? Why are so many under twenty ?

Postulating these queries, the employment manager will seek to answer them, and remedy what requires alteration. He will endeavour so to regulate wages as to afford an adequate and fair reward for services rendered. He will do his utmost to ensure that work is so arranged that employment can be maintained, as far as possible, at a steady level. He will try to keep in touch with the home difficulties and conditions of employees. He will inspire the welfare workers to provide the best possible conditions of work and the most refreshing recreative facilities. He will initiate schemes to remove the fear of old age, sudden death, involuntary unemployment and chronic illness. He will do his utmost from the first day of employment to imbue every employee with the spirit of goodwill, enthusiasm, loyalty and justice. He will promote physical efficiency in every direction. He will keep an open door for every employee with a complaint, a trouble, or an idea. He will induce departments to make openings for likely men, and endeavour to bar the path to " blind-alley " occupations. He will constantly present the human viewpoint in all questions of debatable policy. He will inspire heads of departments to give full weight to human considerations. He will assist welfare work in its business of decorating and brightening workrooms, reducing noise and other disturbing factors, ensuring ample fresh air and sunlight, providing comfortable seats, lavatories, and washing facilities, arranging rest periods, encouraging friendly relations among workers themselves and between foremen and workers, and in what is perhaps the greatest task of welfare—the stimulation of interest in work. He will promote recreational facilities, and institute clubs, educational classes, canteens, competitions, sports and entertainments.

The maintenance of the labour force at the highest point of efficiency is, indeed, a supremely human undertaking. Is this employment work worth while ? one may ask. Judged by results, its cost is indeed small. For the results are great if contentment, goodwill, and wholehearted effort amongst the workers can be counted great. Moreover, it has now taken on the garb of necessity. The considerate treatment of the human agent in industry is no longer optional. The scientific mastery of the methods of production cannot compensate for the loss resulting from a disregard of the human element. Moreover, society is beginning to demand a relationship between employer and worker widely different from that of war. It is beginning to recognize as the true leaders of industry only those whose service, on the actual field of operations, has promoted industrial peace and progress. In its assessment of merit, the more enlightened part of the community is looking for a truer balance between leadership and material results ; it is concerning itself in the factory spirit as well as the business profits, the service to the higher needs of the community as well as the service to its material needs.

The final aspect of employment work is the control of the discharge of personnel. Circumstances of trade, of seasonal fluctuations, or of misconduct on the part of the employee contribute to the ebb and flow of personnel which to some extent is inevitable. Discharges, however, are not lightly to be effected. Every discharge is a social responsibility—a responsibility not only as regards the factory as a whole, but as regards the individual discharged. Of this responsibility an employer cannot divest himself ; it is inherent in leadership of every kind. Justice in this respect is essential ; there can be no healthy factory life where any other principle rules. In the determination of the laws arising from this principle and in the settlement of particular cases coming under such laws, the workers themselves may take a share. In social life, the individual is governed by laws of his own making and tried by juries of his peers. There is no reason why a similar course should not be followed in industry. Where circumstances demand discharges, however, over which neither management nor workers can exercise control as, for example, in circumstances of trade depression, reductions of staff must be effected on the basis of efficiency. The most inefficient worker must go first, except where inefficiency is attributable to age. When, however, degrees of efficiency are equal, other considerations may have play— single men before married men, the man with no family or dependents before the man with a family, the man with short service before the man with long and honourable service, the man with no domestic troubles before the man who is overburdened with them. In all cases, the co-operation of the representatives of the workers themselves will ensure equity. As for discharges for purely personal reasons such as those connected with discipline, the employee may legitimately claim that his case shall be considered by his fellow workers as well as by his management. Management will lose nothing, but will rather be reinforced by the support given to its actions by the public opinion of the factory.

In general, employment work affords the machinery, on the one hand, for the maximal use of the capacities of every worker; on the other hand, for the creation of a factory spirit of high endeavour based upon justice. It animates the activities of the factory with a pulsating sense of humanity. It makes production human, the worker a man. It promotes efficiency, not for efficiency's sake alone, but for that ultimate good which efficiency subserves.

SECURITY

The problems of unemployment and under-employment are the same problems which we faced before the war. No doubt, exceptional circumstances have rendered them abnormally acute, but their essential nature has not altered. Unemployment, indeed, has always been a feature of the factory system.

It is customary to regard unemployment as if it were detachable from other features of industrial life. · In truth, it is but the reverse of the picture of employment. Work and lack of work are two sides of the same coin. Whatever may be our philosophy of the one will apply equally to the other. If we regard work as a fortuitious occurrence in the economic life of the worker, equally shall we regard lack of work as a mischance associated with the present circumstances of production. On the other hand, if we regard work as the duty which every citizen owes to the community, we shall regard involuntary lack of work as a matter of immediate concern to the community. If the community requires work of its citizens, it must ensure that work is available, and if for the moment it cannot provide them with work, it must maintain them till it can.

Under any philosophy, it is impossible to imagine that the volume of work to be done is so limited as not to provide employment for all. The time when it will not be possible to employ usefully the whole of our labouring population, as Sir William Beveridge says, " has not come ; it is not within sight ; it can barely be imagined." Wealth is produced by the three factors of land, labour, and capital. It is an egregious misconception to imagine that there is too much labour, when one even casually considers the vast reserves of land and capital which exist, though clearly, the volume of labour applied in any one field will not always need to be constant.

The problem of unemployment, then, is one of adjust-ment—of so organizing industry that, as far as possible, labour is made available and is economically employed wherever required, and that, where periods of unemploy-ment are inevitable, its menace disappears. It is not possible wholly to eradicate unemployment. The adjust-ments necessary to provide every worker at all times with tasks of economic value are beyond the bounds of achieve-ment. Moreover, if every worker were fully employed, obviously any business requiring extra workers could not obtain them, except by paying an exceptionally high wage or offering other abnormal inducements—a policy which, if generally pursued, would dislocate the whole labour market. What is possible, however, is, firstly, to set about the reduction of the incidence of unemployment by a better adjustment between the contributions made by land, capital and labour in the process of producing wealth ; secondly, frankly to recognize that it may be necessary at times that a man shall not work at his accus-tomed task, and to make provision for such a contingency. These, therefore, constitute the two problems which must be solved if the present volume of periodical unemployment and the hardships incidental to it are to become things of the past.

It is no longer practical politics to maintain that the solution of these problems does not lie within the province of management, and that it has no concern in the fact that its employees are subject to discharge at a day's or week's notice. To do so is both bad policy for the business and a shirking of social responsibility. " Ca canny " is the reply of the workers to managerial indifference. The physical, mental and moral effects of unemployment, moreover, under prevalent conditions are such, if the period of unemployment be even a little protracted, as to render the workers unfit for work should they again be required. Unemployment, especially amongst young workers, leads to an inevitable deterioration of physique and character.

Management must, therefore, both from the point of view of efficient production and also from that of communal responsibility, apply itself to the reduction of unemployment. For instance, work may be re-arranged so that there is a more even flow throughout the year ; or again, the possibilities of " short-time " working may be explored. Apart from these palliative measures, every step forward on the road of efficiency implies ultimately an extension of employment. While costs are high, demand is restricted. Increased production without reduced costs will not solve the problem ; it may even accentuate it. A necessary preliminary is a reduction in costs. Just as economical production offers the most hopeful way to higher wages, so also it affords a way to more general and steady employment.

A certain volume of unemployment, however, cannot be avoided. If industry is to be efficient, it cannot afford to employ either those workers whose capacity falls below the normal or those efficient workers whose services are not immediately required. These two quite distinct reasons for unemployment imply two different problems. The problem of the inefficient worker is one which industry by itself cannot be expected to solve. It is by no means wholly an industrial problem. When workers become inefficient because of their industrial service, as in the case of accidents, old age after long service, or bad health due to working conditions, clearly industry must accept responsibility. But when inefficiency is attributable to causes outside the direct sphere of industrial influence, industry can only accept that share of responsibility which it is called upon to take as a part of a complex community. This is a problem for the community as a whole to solve.

For that margin of unemployment, however, without which industry cannot progress, it is clear that industry must accept, if not all, at any rate the major responsibility. If industry requires a constant labour market as a necessary part of its organization, it must maintain that market.

Maintenance of efficient workers during involuntary unemployment is mainly an industrial function. Whether this maintenance is the business of the employer or of the employee, or of both in conjunction, however, raises fresh problems. It seems obvious that, so long as the workers have no responsibility for the conduct of a business, they cannot be called upon to take part in shouldering any burdens thrown upon the business through circumstances outside their sphere. If this be accepted, the burden becomes one for the employer to bear. This again, however, does not represent the whole truth, for if industry is conducted for the service of the community, some responsibility must rest with the community. When a business, therefore, achieves the standard of efficiency required of it by the community, it is legitimate that the employer should receive from the community such assistance as his service merits. It is suggested, in fact, that the basis upon which the community shall share in the maintenance of the workers during unemployment is the efficiency of the industry concerned. This again requires qualification, since it is clear that in certain industries, apart altogether from efficiency, the volume of unemployment must be larger than in others. Seasonal trades, for instance, are likely to have a larger burden than trades in which work is constant. It would appear reasonable, therefore, that the contribution of the community should be based, firstly, upon the general volume of unemployment ; secondly, upon the variations between industries, and that the contribution of the employer should be based upon the incidence of unemployment in his particular industry, minus (or plus) that amount which distinguishes the volume in his own industry from that in other industries. As regards the amount payable to the individual worker during unemployment—that is, the worker of average efficiency during involuntary unemployment—it is clear that the amount must be such as to maintain a man in good health, whilst affording no encouragement for him to malinger. In practice, it is suggested that the amount will vary according to his family; a single man, for instance, receiving half his normal earnings, and a married man an additional 10 per cent on behalf of his wife, and 5 per cent for each dependent child, up to a maximum figure of 75 per cent of normal earnings. [1]

WELFARE WORK

What is true of employment work is true also of welfare work—the spirit of the work cannot be functionalized or departmentalized, since both are actuated by a common motive—the humanization of industry ; both are inspired

[1] For general authorities on unemployment, *vide*—

(*a*) *Unemployment.* By Sir W. H. Beveridge. (Longmans, Green & Co., 1919.)

(*b*) *Unemployment.* By A. C. Pigou. (Home University Library.)

(*c*) *The Unemployed : A National Question.* By Percy Alden. (1905.)

(*d*) *Unemployment : A Social Study.* By B. S. Rowntree and B. Lasker. (Macmillan, 1911.)

(*e*) Draft Convention concerning Unemployment by the General Conference of the International Labour Organization of the League of Nations. (1920.)

(*f*) *Unemployment and Industrial Maintenance.* By G. D. H. Cole. (1921.)

by a common belief—that the man is greater than the machine ; both are suffused with a common spirit—the spirit of concord and fellowship. Welfare does not attempt to monopolize or to be the only exponent of that motive, that belief, or that spirit. Indeed, unless the spirit is shared by the management as a whole, no amount of welfare work can make factory life in essentials any more human, more corporate, or more brotherly. The spirit of welfare, like that of employment work, cannot be concentrated in a Welfare Department. If welfare work is to succeed, the welfare spirit must prevail throughout the factory. In externals, progress may be made without such a general dispersion of the spirit, but it alone makes progress possible in the fundamental relationships of factory life. The first condition of successful welfare work is a universal welfare spirit—the spirit which regards factory life as a cross-section, as it were, of all the individual lives composing the human element in the factory.

The concentration of welfare " work " is a matter purely of organization. In the small factory, the manager himself may do his own welfare work. Just as management has, of necessity, to be divided into several functions, which, in turn, must again be divided, so that function of management which we have termed Labour must take over from the general body of management certain specific duties such as employment work and welfare work. But the motive and spirit of the work cannot be thus segregated. It is only in proportion to the diffusion of the spirit that the functionalization of the work can succeed. The spirit must precede the work. Welfare work will not engender a spirit unless the spirit has first engendered welfare work. It is no reply to the query " What are your relations with your workers ? " to answer " We have a welfare section which looks after all that."

Without that strong human spirit of co-operation behind it, welfare work may still appeal to certain employers : firstly, because it pays ; and secondly, because it is good advertising. Such appeals, however, are opposed to the spirit of true welfare work. It may be said to pay, but the basic motive of honesty is not a nice balancing of " pros " and " cons." It may be said to be good advertising, just as *The Pilgrim's Progress* may be said to have " boomed " the name of John Bunyan ; but John Bunyan's motive was not to make his name a household word for all time. Such indirect consequences are to be most definitely distinguished from the motives of welfare work. If they become motives, the work must suffer, just as industry as a whole, actuated by motives which are rather advantages accruing from the carrying on of industry, is to-day suffering from dislocation and internal strife. Welfare work will pay, just as fighting for the right paid in the war. But we did not fight for the right because it paid, nor should we adopt welfare work because such a procedure finds a satisfactory reflection in the ledgers. Without a motive which is disinterested welfare work is a fraud. Neither the world nor that part of the world we call industry will be rendered one whit the better by appraising in terms of cash what is intrinsically a human ideal, or by setting out to make financial profits from an outlay of human spirit.

Welfare work has been defined by Miss Proud in the following terms : " Welfare work consists of voluntary efforts on the part of employers to improve, within the existing industrial system, the conditions of employment in their own factories." [1] This is a definition of welfare work, not of the spirit actuating it. If the workers in industry have a right, as individuals, to conditions of work which are physically healthy, mentally stimulating, and morally sustaining, the counterpart of this right, within the existing industrial system, is a duty laid upon the employer and his management. Welfare work undertaken in response to this call partakes of neither the materialism

[1] *Welfare Work.* By E. M. Proud, B.A. (G. Bell & Sons, 1916.)

of profit-making nor the condescension of pseudo-philan-
thropy. " Most employers keep philanthropy and business
in different compartments of their mind," says Professor
Marshall. The need of this new industrial age is that
employers should cease to regard philanthropy as a moral
luxury, and find in it a practical obligation. Not in
industry alone, but in our whole social life, we are too apt
to commend ourselves for acts of so-called philanthropy,
when, in fact, we have but done our plain duty.

It is imperative that management, as a professional
body, should thoroughly grasp the inwardness of welfare
work. It is too often regarded as the whim of an influential
and large-hearted director, or the palliative introduced by
a Labour-harassed Board. It is but too rarely regarded as
an integral part of the science of management. It is no
novelty born of war-time conditions. The novelty is in
its organization as a separate part of management, but its
existence is as old as organized industry itself. Welfare
work, when the master worked in the shop alongside his
men, was a matter of daily intimacy. As the factory
system developed, the master became increasingly separated
from his workers, until a generation came into the mill
to whom the employer was but a name. There was nothing
personal in the relationships of the various grades contributing to the common work of the factory. The weekly
pay-packet came to take the place of the daily familiar
greeting. The inadequacy of this substitute to create the
same corporate spirit as existed in the early days soon
became not only apparent, but a danger to our industrial
stability. Industry became racked with a strife born of
misunderstanding, nurtured in ignorance, and matured
in suspicion. It has thus become necessary that an
absorbing and convincing new impetus should sweep the
whole field clear of conflict. That impetus is coming
from a new motive in industry. That motive places human
relations before all else, and requires that the work of
welfare shall be so organized as to rank as at least equal

to other parts of any industrial organization.   The factory
manager is not absolved from the responsibility of super-
vising the well-being of his employees by the appointment
of a welfare worker, any more than he is absolved from the
responsibility of keeping his manufacturing costs low by
the appointment of a cost-accountant.   Welfare and
Costing are essential parts of one homogeneous factory
policy.   They are not divorced from such factory policy
by the mere necessity of delegation.

Welfare is essentially a corporate enterprise.   Though
the responsibility for it must rest with the management,
it is that part of management in which the workers are
immediately concerned, and in which their claim for
control may first find practical application.   The volume
of output, the cost and the quality are matters which only
indirectly affect them, but the conditions of work are
their hourly concern.   They form their lives ;   they are
the tissue of every day.   Welfare work, therefore, cannot
succeed except by co-operation.   It cannot be conveyed
into a factory like a load of steel.   Men can only be made
healthy in mind and body when there is a will to be healthy.
The workers must be convinced before the conviction of
the management can succeed.   They will never be convinced by being informed that welfare work pays.   They
will never be convinced by an employer who ascribes to
himself a large-hearted generosity.   To seek to establish
welfare without co-operation is to follow a path which
will soon be strewn with the debris of schemes that have
failed.   The stimulus of welfare must be corporate, springing from a common conviction that factory life must be
conducted upon a plane fitted for men to whom life may
afford prospects nobler than the satisfaction of material
needs.

Clearly, welfare concerns the workers in their mental
and moral as well as physical aspects.   It is too often
regarded as dealing simply with the last—the provision of
good lighting and ventilation, of canteens and rest-rooms,

the decoration of workrooms and the provision of medical treatment. It is very much more. It deals with fatigue of mind as well as of body, with monotony of work, and the nervous effects of working conditions. It is concerned with the atmosphere, the " tone " of the workrooms. It combats sullenness and strife as it combats monotony and disease. It aims at good fellowship as well as good health, justice as well as cleanliness, interest as well as efficiency, comradeship as well as comfort, high character as well as high spirits.

In the pursuit of these aims, clearly the life of the worker outside the factory must be reckoned with as well as his life inside it. Here the need for a strong factory impulse is essential. The more the workers can organize their own welfare, especially out of factory hours, the keener will be their interest. Management runs the factory, not the whole life of the workers. But it should so run the factory that the time out of it is spent profitably. Then factory clubs, social and athletic, will be spontaneous growths. Welfare work will foster the factory spirit, and the factory spirit may be left to raise the factory football team. Inside the factory, welfare is a function of management, but here also the workers themselves should be left, as far as possible, to direct the work. They will soon learn to conduct their own canteen, to determine the decoration of their workrooms, to recommend devices for their own safety, and to inaugurate and direct their own societies and educational facilities. The welfare worker will be wise to regard himself as a factory Town Clerk—an executive officer, acting for the factory community, giving advice where required, pointing out new lines where the old seem exhausted, encouraging the disheartened, but leaving the direction to those for whom the work is done. The days are past when the workers could be regarded as the willing beneficiaries of a benevolent employer. They are independent and ready to shoulder responsibilities. They require their experts, as management requires its cost-accountants and chemists, and the London County Council requires its architect and engineer. They require their welfare worker qualified and trained in the work. Management and workers together should appoint him and direct his work. Without such co-operation, welfare work will fail, because management itself as a body has failed to establish a bond of fellow feeling. When management learns the golden lessons of co-operation, it will find in every field, and especially in welfare, a new welcome easing its path. When it puts off its divinity and humbles itself to the level of the worker, it will find that it is working on a plane infinitely higher than the pedestal upon which it took its stand in the past. The welfare spirit will permeate all the conditions of factory life—wages, hours, health, self-development, foremanship, and environment—with a new significance. Flourishing in an atmosphere of co-operation, it will render welfare, not simply a new duty added, but a new way of regarding all that goes to make up the life of the factory, the healing of an old sore, and the opening of a new vista.

TRAINING AND EDUCATION

It will obviate any confusion if it is made clear that, in this present discussion, the term " Training " denotes that technical training by which a worker is rendered more efficient at his work, and the term " Education " denotes that more general, humanistic education by which an individual attempts to satisfy his thirst for knowledge, to equip himself for his responsibilities as a citizen, and to find opportunities for self-expression. (*Vide* Report of Adult Education Committee.) The distinction thus drawn between vocational and non-vocational education is to some extent false, since the test of any education is not the subject taught so much as the method of teaching. It is as possible to train the intelligence and the character in the teaching of shorthand, housewifery or farming as in the teaching of the classics or orthodox science. The

modern presentation of what is known as " Scientific
Management " has, however, emphasized the distinction
between humanistic education and technical training, by
its insistence that there is no operation in industry which
does not require teaching, and no work which can properly
be called " unskilled."

" Scientific Management," according to its original
exponent, Mr. F. W. Taylor, involves the addition of four
new duties to the task of management : (1) The development of a science for each element of a man's work ; (2)
the scientific selection and training of men ; (3) co-operation
with the men to ensure the adoption of the scientific
methods ; (4) an almost equal division of work and responsibility between workers and management. The training
of the worker is the most outstanding contribution of
" Scientific Management " to modern industrial problems.
It forms, indeed, the principal basis of its methods. Time
and motion studies, the standardization of the job, the
making and issue of the Instruction Card, the definition
of the Task, and the theory of the " Task and Bonus "
system of remuneration are, one and all, based on the
assumption that the worker can be and will be trained to
do the job in the prescribed manner and the scheduled
time. Without training, the whole fabric of " Scientific
Management " is impossible. Mr. McKillop, indeed,
summarizes the whole general principle of " Scientific
Management " as " the process of transference of skill from
the management to the worker." [1]

The management, by time study and research, determines the best method of doing the job ; it standardizes
the method, and issues an Instruction Card, stating in
the minutest detail exactly how the job is to be done, and
what time is allotted for the performance of each of its
constituent parts. Upon this basis, taking either efficiency
in operating or time in operating, it fixes its Premium
Bonus system of payment. It is not to be anticipated,

[1] *Efficiency Methods.* By M. McKillop. (Routledge, 1917.)

obviously, that the performance of the job in the prescribed manner and time will come naturally to every worker. The management, therefore, arranges for " functional foremen," of whom a proportion (four, on the Taylor system) are in the shops. These four are teachers rather than foremen in the old sense. The " inspector " teaches the quality of the work ; the " speed boss " teaches the quickest method of working ; the " repair boss " teaches the proper care of the machines, and the " gang boss " teaches the correct tools to use, the correct sequence of jobs, the correct materials, etc. " Scientific Management," in fact, institutes its own scheme of training, its own teachers, and its own standard tasks.

In so far as " Scientific Management " has emphasized the need for the training of the workers for every industrial occupation to be more scientific than at present, it has performed a valuable service. Too long have we been content merely to allot a task to the worker and let him choose his own methods ; to make him the arbiter as to ways of operation, be they as old as Adam and as slow as the tortoise. Management has offered no help. Greater output has been obtained by greater persuasion, not by greater assistance. Management has expected the worker to " pick up " his technique, if it ever realized that there was a technique, as best he could, and if he failed to attain a given standard of output, he was flung back on the labour market to continue the process of " picking up " elsewhere.

The folly of this " hit and miss " system " Scientific Management " has ably demonstrated. The system which it would substitute, however, may be open to generalized criticism. It would be the merest beating of the air, in any way to belittle the valuable researches of Major F. M. Gilbreth and others, which have already revolutionized the outlook of many progressive managements. In so far as such researches aim at the elimination of unnecessary effort, no word can be said which is not wholly laudatory. It is, however, not a little dangerous to draw conclusions too speedily from work which is experimental in character. Because a way of performing an operation is discovered which will, if adopted, produce treble the previous output, there is no valid reason for supposing either that the average worker will adopt it, even under the highest monetary incentive, or that the methods of setting and performing the task are universally or socially desirable. There are indeed grave psychological objections to the suggestion that there is " one best way " of doing a job. It is not inconceivable, and is indeed probable, that most tasks may be performed with equal efficiency in different ways by different persons. The Instruction Card may assist one worker and hamper another. Methods, again, are learnt in different ways by different people. Granted, for the moment, that there is a " standard best," one worker may be able to apply the Instruction Card procedure by memorizing it, another may be psychologically incapable of learning in that way, his whole manual work being guided by the rhythm of movement, known as " the muscular sense." It is not unlikely that the different methods of assimilating training may result in different methods of operation.

The training essential to the methods of orthodox " Scientific Management " may be considered, however, from a wider point of view. " Co-operation with the workers to ensure the use of scientific methods " is hardly likely to succeed, when management sets the pace and the workers do the running. As Mr. Lee says: " I do not see how anyone short of being an archangel could bear the official title ' Speed Boss ' and carry with him those who are to be speeded up."[1] Co-operation can only come about by a sharing of responsibility. The workers need not only to know how the schedule is arrived at, but also to share in formulating it. The training must be in operative methods determined upon by mutual agreement after combined research. Without such co-operation, the whole success of the policy is jeopardized.

[1] *Management.* By John Lee, M.A., M.Com.Sc. (Pitman, 1921.

Training which is directed to enforcing standard methods purely by an incentive of monetary reward is the antithesis of co-operation. To neglect this fact is to forget our motive in the whole conduct of industry. Output may be desirable, but only if the methods of production are desirable. Is greater output to be achieved by a training, wholly enforced from above, in which the worker is permitted no critical or creative interest—a narrow, dogmatic training in one particular set of motions and operations—a training undertaken with the object of achieving a rigid standardization ?

If factory life is to engender communal intelligence, if industry is to enrich the community, not only by the products it makes, but by the mentalities and characters it forms, such training is clearly neither stimulating nor humanizing. Mr. Hoxie must have had this in mind when he wrote : " We do not wish the training of the worker to be centred in the hands and under the control solely of the employer. It seems that what we really need, as a supplement to scientific management—so that we may avail ourselves of its beneficial possibilities and eliminate or minimize its possible evil effects—is an adequate system of industrial education socially launched and socially controlled—an integral part of our public school system." This is a picture of a universal apprenticeship system, communally controlled. Its lesson, however, is that an enforced training, even if it should succeed in its object of increasing output, may yet be socially undesirable. Thus, whilst " Scientific Management " has contributed greatly to our realization of the emphatic need for more detailed training in industry—teaching us much as to the position of management in regard to the work of every individual, the need for definition, the value of job analysis and craft skill, the relation of applied psychology to industrial operations, and the distinction between both teaching and control, and teaching and skill—yet it has perhaps underestimated the co-operation essential to such training.

Training is pre-eminently necessary, but it must be conducted with the co-operation of the workers, and aim,
not only at increasing their output, but also at widening
their intelligence, stimulating their interest and developing
their personality. Standardization, secured only through
the incentive of gain, may involve not only the physical
subordination of the individual to methods not of his own
making, but also the hardening of his mentality into a
mould which he himself has not fashioned.

This leads one to query the concern of management in
the humanistic education of the workers—that education
which broadens the mind and fits a man to fulfil his duty
in a progressive community. To debate the value of such
education is unnecessary, but it may not be clear how far
it is the function of industry to provide it. The position
of industry should be rather to facilitate than to undertake education. Education is not alone a question of
books, but also of environment and influences. " Education
is the act of drawing out of a man all that is best and most
useful to him, so that it may be employed to the advantage
of the community, and of himself as a member of it." [1]
Clearly, conditions of work which are physically deadening,
mentally degrading, or morally perverting are detrimental
to education in this sense. The factory is, indeed, a school,
as all experience is a school, and can, therefore, aid in the
education of the workers. By inspiring interest, by sharing
responsibility, by setting an example of high endeavour, by
arousing enthusiasm, by giving work a thrill of social
significance, by following high principles, by preferring
co-operation to autocracy, management can make of
industry a school which there is no educational body
but may emulate, whilst paving the way for that more
directly educational work which is performed outside the
factory.

From such education, industry has everything to gain.
Education, indeed, is part of the great movement for the

[1] Rt. Hon. H. A. L. Fisher.

exploration of human economy. " Modern industry," said a speaker at a Pottery Conference, " cannot be carried on without better education, both of masters and men." The cause of most of our industrial difficulties is " mutual ignorance and misunderstanding, far more than deliberate choice of wrong," said Dr. A. L. Smith recently. " It is in darkness or half-lights that collisions occur," he added. Modern movements in industry—the growing necessity of co-operation, the entry of the workers into certain branches of control, the increase of leisure, the rise in wages, the sharing of profits—presume a proportionate advance in education. Democracy, whether in State or industry, without education is a bomb in the hands of a child. All our great industrial problems depend for their solution upon the degree of enlightenment and matured judgment of the main parties concerned. The solution of any one of these problems, as we daily observe, is not to be found in any simple scheme or self-evident panacea. It will only be hammered out on the anvil of co-operation by the blows, intelligently placed, of skilled workmen. The way to the industrial Utopia is the path of knowledge. Faith will help ; toil will help—but without knowledge, faith may be misplaced and toil unavailing. " It is not the lack of goodwill that is to be feared. But goodwill without mental effort, without intelligent prevision, is worse than ineffectual ; it is a moral opiate." It is only the open mind which can pick out the path to the city of Truth.

In education, therefore, both for its own purposes and for those major purposes which it serves, management cannot remain passive. Too long has industry traded upon a false division, a hypothetical gulf between itself and communal life. There is no such gulf. We cannot demand education for the people and deny education to the workers, for the twain are one. Management cannot disclaim social leadership as if it were in a different field from factory leadership. If education is requisite for our social progress, management, in its own sphere of influence, must give it and, outside that sphere, must facilitate it. The Act of 1918 will make a call upon the patience, ingenuity and sympathy of management, but unless those qualities are forthcoming, management itself must stand condemned. Through the life of the factory, management can take its share. It can develop initiative and interest ; it can remove monotony by liberalized vocational training and the cultivation of shop interests ; it can stimulate individuality by sympathetic foremanship ; it can expand individual adaptability by providing the means for each worker to share in many activities ; it can develop the sense of responsibility by enlightening the workers on such daily facts as output, costs, and general trade and factory developments ; it can fashion character by straightforward treatment and fine example ; it can stimulate enthusiasm by the facilitation of promotion and the proper reward of merit ; it can encourage responsibility by handing over to the workers the control of welfare work. These are essentially educational lines of progress. As such education proceeds, true co-operation becomes increasingly possible.

In the past, education has mainly sprung from two motives—religious and civic. It is for industry to realize that its own motive should be, in essence, civic or communal, and that the enlightenment and development of those who work within its sphere is as great a form of service as the delivery of those goods of which the community stands in need. This development of the workers it should be the duty of management to further : Firstly, by adopting a liberalized form of vocational training, so that both interest in the job and the wider interests of the worker are stimulated ; secondly, by providing those conditions of work which are of themselves broadening and conducive to self-development.

TRADE UNIONS

The day is long past when Trade Unionism could be either neglected or idly condemned. It is a force in industry which the philosophy of the industrial future cannot afford to minimize. Preluded by a history of staunch perseverance and idealistic courage, progressing with the strength of an inspiring past and a great present organization, it stands out to-day in the Labour world as the greatest power for good or for evil, the one prodigious leviathan of a turgid sea. It has accomplished more than any other factor in bettering the lot of the workers of this country. No other body in our domestic history has achieved the same pitch of success in the development of the spirit of sacrifice in association.

It is a matter for serious reflection, therefore, and, to the body of management in industry, a matter of urgent concern, that a corporate entity, developing from such a past, moving forward with such strength, and representing to so high a degree the spirituality of fellowship, should be found divorced from the interests which the daily business of its members, as workers, should normally engender. The basic problem of Trade Unionism does not lie in its strength, its motives, or its aims, but in the fundamental fact of its divorce from factory life. Why is it that the worker is led not only to place the interests of his union before those of his factory, but even to regard the two as almost necessarily antagonistic ? Why is it that his innate desire for association should find expression in a form of association only indirectly concerned with the interests of his daily work ? Why is his " group-mindedness " something apart from the " group " which forms the major portion of his life ? That is the problem which management must face. It finds Labour expressing a basic human instinct in a way which passes over the most obvious mode of its expression. The management of any factory cannot hope to succeed unless it can determine upon a constructive policy with regard to the solution of this problem—the problem of enlisting that instinct in a new corporate body in which the life of the factory and the life of the Trade Union have equal play. Too often the union is regarded as an inevitable evil. Such an attitude serves only to perpetuate and accentuate an intolerable state of affairs. In no other field of management is one of the prime factors in the situation disregarded in this way.

There are several elements in the Trade Union movement which the management of any factory must bear in mind in determining its policy towards the particular unions of which the workers with whom it is concerned are members. Firstly, it is to be remembered that the strength of the unions has developed in the course of a long campaign of defence. Their aims have been negative throughout—opposition, redress, and mitigation. Their share in the business of industry has been to right wrongs, not to establish, create or develop an order of things. They have had no opportunity, indeed ; their constructive work has been the elaboration of a vast machine outside production. One cannot attribute this solely to Trade Union policy ; the policy was largely dictated by circumstances. There is no logical reason why the association of workers should not have been founded upon a basis of industrial constructiveness, an " association of producers " like those of the Christian Socialist period. It was the fact that the natural impulse of the workers towards combination met with immediate opposition that turned the Trade Union movement away from industry into the fields of criticism and self-defence. There is no logical basis for assuming that a Trade Union, properly regarded by management and properly led by its executive, should not find a *raison d'être* for its association in the common interests of the industry of which its members form a part, as well as in the common interests of the class of workers for which the union caters. It is inconceivable that Trade Unionism should continue indefinitely to be merely an outside, disturbing force, venting its criticism and delivering its attacks upon industry. Negative forces in life tend either to become absorbed in the positives to which they form negatives, or to perish.

Trade Unionism and Management alike must recognize that constructiveness is the seed of progress, that the joining toge†her of the workers in unions cannot persist indefinitely unless their association leads to something concrete and established, some progressive activity which will benefit not only Labour, but industry and the community as a whole. This will not be accomplished by any external attitude of criticism, attack, or interference. It will come rather by a united effort from within industry, by co-operation and unity of purpose.

Secondly, management should realize that the gulf of status between itself and the Trade Union is being rapidly filled in. The more management approximates to a profession, the more does it necessarily share the interests of Trade Unionism. The Trade Union leaders are, to an increasing degree, facing salaried officials like themselves across the tables where disputes are discussed. They are not grappling at the throats of the capitalists ; they are face to face with other employees like themselves. Neither are the Trade Union executives the untrained men of forty years ago. Trade Unionism has enlisted its brain-workers, its own " management "—often men of the highest ability and erudition in their subject. This modern development, indeed, means that the conflict takes the form of a controversy between two sets of professional men, both engaged on the selfsame task of labour admin- istration. The situation is new, but its novelty suggests hope. Here are individuals in each locality or in each industry, often of comparable ability, to a considerable extent engaged upon similar work, and making their living on similar lines, yet persistently in opposition. Is it not possible to catch a glimpse of a new order of things where Trade Unionism shall become a partner with management in the administration of the factory and of the industry ?

Thirdly, it is to be remembered that Trade Unionism represents not only specific grievances and disputes, but a deep-set, almost inarticulate, consciousness among the workers as a mass that the dictates of a purged social morality would bring to them a higher standard of material living, and a more equal opportunity for that " good life " of which every community dreams, and towards which every community strives. There is indeed a moral impetus behind it, a force set upon the righting of wrongs which are primarily social, and only industrial in so far as the whole society is based upon its industrialism. It has an inchoate mission of reconstruction. True, its leaders have formulated programmes, but the reconstructive spirit of the whole movement roves fancy free, climbing and stumbling towards an order of things of which it can form but the vaguest conception.

The settlement of wage-rates, of working hours, of individual grievances, is the immediate, daily business of the unions, and probably absorbs the conscious interests of nine-tenths of their membership. But management would commit an egregious blunder were it to imagine that, if these things were divinely settled for ever, the associations of the workers would crumble into nothingness. Such a beatific intervention would only serve to open the way for that wider, more nebulous, but more impelling motive of association, which operates when men unite together to think out, work out, and achieve their material redemption, not for its own sake, but rather for the sake of some higher ideal which dawns upon their spiritual vision.

Without some comprehension of these predominating features of Trade Unionism, the picture is one of unrelieved gloom. Yet to comprehend them involves closing one's eyes to a hundred facts and tendencies where union action has belied them. The only alternative to a prolongation of the present division of what should be a common enterprise is the linking of Trade Union leadership with the profession of management, and the welding of the aims of both into a common ideal. It was management in the past which excluded the legitimate associations of the workers from any constructive interest in their own industries. It rests with management accordingly to lead the organized workers back to a participation in the furtherance of their own industries. There is no advance to be made by each charging the other to repent ; there can be no progress along the lines of protracted strife. Industry needs not a mere pact of conciliation, but the peace of co-operation. Such co-operation is to be gained by a re-direction of " associativeness," and it will ill befit management to be the laggard in its achievement.

This analysis of fundamentals may well indicate the progressive steps to be taken. These steps may briefly be stated as, firstly, the full recognition of the union— a recognition not only of its right to represent the workers, but also of its ability to assist in practical management, and to contribute its quota to the formation of policy ; and secondly, the willing and honest effort to appreciate the union attitude and to cultivate an intimacy with its aims and methods. This leads to understanding rather than condemnation, to co-operation rather than opposition. Management, doubtless, will be called upon to overlook many grounds for bitterness—petty leadership, inter-union jealousy, false economics, paltry advantage-taking. The objective, however, is great, if the way be stony. That objective is the unifying of interests. Unity, however, springs from intimacy. A joint council in London does little to unify interests in the factories of the country. We need intimacy in the factory—not only the intimacy of a works council, but the real intimacy of management, with union leaders on the one hand and rank and file workers on the other. This may begin by recognizing in each section of the factory some union representative with whom the management can co-operate, and who at all times may be regarded as the legitimate mouthpiece of the workers in that section, and the normal person with whom to discuss problems which may arise. Clearly, no progress is possible if such a representative is left to initiate all the business between the management and himself. He should be kept in touch with managerial policy, be consulted on problematic points, and be intimate with departmental statistics. The way of co-operation is to lay the cards on the table.

The problem of management is to link that spirit of association, which the unions embody, to the factory. Those qualities of group consciousness, loyalty and interest which are now largely the monopoly of the unions, industry as a whole needs for itself. We must aim at forging some strong link between the interests of the workers as members of unions and their interests as members of individual factories.[1] Such a coupling together as is here suggested is not beyond the dreams of to-day, and may yet be reckoned among the achievements of to-morrow. It is a problem, not of machinery, but of spirit ; a problem, not of coercion, but of leadership ; a problem, not of destruction, but of the welding of two into a unity.

Co-operation

" Without the sense of solidarity, of community, of fellowship, the fortunes of man in this world would be low and brute-like," said a Scotch philosopher. This sense of community is a primary human instinct. Man, in all history, has never been a solitary animal. From the earliest times he has lived and had his being in a community, subjecting himself to the requirements of that community, both consciously, in the exercise of his daily business, and unconsciously, in the acceptance of the limitations imposed upon his habits, beliefs and routine. The community of

[1] *Cf.* Report of the Royal Commission on Trades Unions, 1868, half a century ago, " The habitual code of sentiment which prevailed between employers and workmen in the times when the former were regarded by law and usage as the governing class is now greatly relaxed and cannot be revived. A substitute has now to be found for it, arising from the feelings of equity and enlightened self-interest and mutual forbearance which should exist between contracting parties who can but promote their several chances of advantage by aiding and accommodating each other."

family and of locality is followed by a community of profession, of religion, of sport, or of politics. In each activity of his mind, he tends to gravitate towards and unite with those whose interests and ideas coincide with his own. He will belong, at one and the same time, to a local borough, a religious denomination, a sporting or social club, a trade union or employers' federation, a scientific society, and a political party. Almost every action he takes is in collaboration with or in support of some body of individuals, united with him in a bond of fellow feeling. He does not act alone ; his every action is at once pigeon-holed into a scheme of things, and he thereafter bears the title of the particular pigeon-hole— a Socialist, a Church of England man, a Conservative, or a Trade Unionist.

In industry, the instinct of association has been diversified. The instinct has not operated vertically by industries or by factories, but horizontally by trades—as it were, by cross-sectional groupings. Employers are linked together in associations. Managers and technical staff are linked together in scientific and professional institutions. Workers are united in unions. But the grouping of representatives of each of these within a single factory constitutes no solidarity or community of interests. The interests of the economic classes override the interests of the economic units.

Why ? It is not so in other spheres. A church is not divided because it has grades of ministry. A locality is not liable to violent disruption because it has classes of voters. Yet a factory is often a body in internal dissension. Each grade of worker has interests which he places before those of his factory. That which is present in other human associations, a predominant and generally accepted motive, is lacking in factory life. Other social associations are governed by strong motives—religious, philanthropic, or civic. Industry lacks a sufficiently compelling motive to give rise to free association. It represents a higgledy-piggledy conglomeration of motives—from one standpoint it is regarded as a project to be exploited ; from another, as a mere source of income ; from another, as a field for professional practice. There is no corporate spirit, no community of ideals, no brotherhood of endeavour, no " team-work."

Without some general motive, the appeal for co-operation in industry is a voice in the wilderness. The motive for co-operation must be accepted before co-operation can become effective. A society cannot be formed without an object to which all the members can subscribe. The present motives in industry are not adequate. Instead of affording a basis for co-operation they instigate divisions. The motive of the employer has been profits ; the motive of the worker has been wages and security. Neither motive as such can contribute to the creation of the factory commonwealth. Alternate periods of high wages and unemployment can never give rise to anything but the consciousness of class. It is only because both motives have been tempered by certain human feelings that industry has found any binding power at all within itself. Distrust is rampant. No settlement between employers and workers is based wholly upon the honour of the two parties ; for every provision of an agreement there must be safeguards. The need for such safeguards arises from distrust which, in turn, arises from the absence of any unifying object or common incentive.

Industry, above all, requires a motive which will weld its component parts into one commonwealth. The need for a high objective, an incentive to work, based neither on privilege nor on custom, neither on fortune nor on status, is pre-eminent among the requirements of industry. It must be stronger than the motive of self-interest, though embracing it ; it must be of general application, omitting neither director nor worker. Is it impossible to picture it ? —a motive comparable to that which wafted the sails of

the *Mayflower* from Leyden ; comparable to that which
added pillar to pillar, buttress to buttress, stone to stone
of our great cathedrals ; comparable to that which, by
the passing of innumerable feet, made a way to the shrine
of Canterbury, and a path across the desert to the Holy
City of Mecca ?   The motives of the past, which have
impelled mankind to the achievement of men's noblest
endeavours, have been motives of love, of devotion, of
ideals.   The impulse of a great ideal has ever excelled the
motive of self-interest.   Industry to-day yearns for the
thrill, the unifying impulse of an ideal, which shall lead
all its workers of every class to cast aside their fishing-nets
of mercenary gain, to leave the Galilee of self-interest, and
to set out upon the stony pathway after a common ideal.
This is the inwardness of co-operation.   In war we have
seen it ; is it incapable of resurrection in peace ?   It was
not discipline alone, nor profit, nor glory, nor self-seeking,
nor thoughtlessness which filled the transports crossing
the Channel.   There was more ; there was the love—
inarticulate, nervously suppressed, laughingly denied—
of England, of justice, of what is straight and honourable
in life.   Precious in war, that motive is priceless in peace.

Were industry the mere battleground of two antagonists,
such a dream might seem hopeless of realization.   We are
witnessing, however, the gradual stabilization of a new
entity in industry—management.   Is it not possible that
this new entity may breathe into industry the thrill of a
new ideal ?   The spirit in which management—the new
management of a new age—sets about its task is our one
great hope.   If management can stand for the high motive
of service to the general commonalty of the world, the
whole spirit of industry may yet be changed.   The attitude
of management, as it develops into a professional body
with its own standards and methods, is the key to the
future.

If management is to stand for this new motive, the
manager of the future must be of a new fibre.   Technique,

disciplinary power, accuracy and reliability in work will no longer be his primary qualifications. The first requisite must be the gregarious instinct, the instinct for co-operating with other men, attracting them to him, welding them together. He must be less of a technician and more of a " captain " ; less of a " boss " and more of a leader. Being loyal-hearted he will inspire loyalty. Being intimate with his men he will gain friendship. By appreciating subordinates he will enlist their support. Being a captain he will form a team. He cannot be passive ; there is no half-way between hostility and co-operation. He cannot hide what he is. The factory is a compact corporate consciousness, which resents deception or concealed motives. Indeed, the more scientific the factory organization, the greater is the opportunity for management to spread its example and disseminate its spirit, and the greater, too, the opportunity for the workers to detect dishonest motives and paltry ideals.

A new motive on the part of management, however, will not of itself transform industry. There are roots of the past which must be eradicated, growths springing from distrust which must be removed. Prime among these is the conception that co-operation can be secured on the basis of wages, which may or may not be forthcoming. Co-operation cannot, under any conceivable circumstances, be secured whilst unemployment remains a constant menace. You may force men to work hard by the threat of discharge, but in a time of booming trade you will be stranded, and you will never find your factory working like a football team. The incentive of high wages, as is only to be antici- pated in an age not yet wholly free from the materialistic self-seeking of the preceding era, has been incredibly over-rated, especially in America. Wonder is often expressed that Labour should resist piece-work, or that many piece-work schemes should end, by the strategy of the workers, in a " dead level of mediocrity." The wonder is that we should be so short-sighted. When men see no moral reason why they should work harder, no harder work will be done whatever the wage incentive. To keep his fellows in employment, the worker forgoes the extra wage he might earn by extra effort. His economics and reasoning may be wholly astray, but his spirit is right. What would not many an employer give to find the same spirit of solidarity, of community and of fellowship applied to the factory ? This spirit, however, will not come through higher wages. The incentive they offer diminishes as the wage rises. Were it not that education is continually opening up a wider horizon, the incentive of wages would already be within a measurable distance of extinction.

The wage incentive, in fact, whilst it remains the primary bond holding the component parts of industry together, may actually retard the progress of co-operation. The " wage nexus " must be relegated to a secondary position, and other bonds must be forged. Were all wage settlements made upon a national basis, under the direct supervision of the State, the " wage nexus," as between the individual employer and his workers, would become a matter no longer solely of factory life, but of the life of the community as a whole. The forging of the other links whereby industry is to be bound together would then be the task of management—for co-operation will come not by management sharing in the work, but rather by the workers sharing in the management. Only in sharing it will Labour find its opportunity to forget the dissensions of the past and to mould the factory consciousness into a living, corporate spirit of brotherhood. Works Councils are a beginning ; many firms have extended considerable legislative, executive and judicial powers to them. [1] Unfortunately, in many instances, these have been introduced before the more fundamental preliminaries are in train—the change in the status and the motive of the management, the removal of economic insecurity, and the

[1] *Cf. The Human Factor in Business.* By B. S. Rowntree. (Longmans, Green & Co., 1921.)

relegation of wage settlements to an external body. They mark a beginning, however ; there is little hesitation on the part of the workers to support them. Not the least among their advantages has been the bringing into prominence of certain workers gifted with critical or administrative qualifications.

Whether the form of the works councils as determined under the Whitley scheme is the best is debatable, but the principle upon which they are founded is sound. The time has come when the workers must be given a greater incentive to exercise their gregarious instincts inside the factory, must be allowed some control over their own economic lives, must be united with management by bonds other than that of wages. As their share in management extends, it is for those who offered it to inspire them with their own high motives. If the management of to-day can hold aloft the torch of service to the general community to illumine the highway of progress, the management of to-morrow—a management which will be the corporate expression of a spirit of co-operation to a common end—will find all industry following the light, pressing forward in fellowship, united in a common endeavour, which makes each man's toil his contribution of effort to the good of all.

CHAPTER VI

SUMMARY

(a) Necessity for a greater volume of more economical and better quality production ; volume without quality is not the best service. Production is composed of human and material agencies ; need for more efficient use of the impersonal factors in production.

(b) Need for scientific attitude to manufacturing problems ; contribution of Scientific Management in this respect ; place of industrial Research, in the function of Comparison ; Pure Research and Applied Research ; relation of Research and Costing ; relation of Research to the manufacturing management, place of Research in the factory.

(c) The nature of Costing ; lack of attention to the subject ; reasons why Costing is now imperative ; characteristics of a costing system ; the elements of cost ; the problem of indirect cost. Costing conduces to Standardization. Definition of a standard ; application to material, process and equipment ; the universal applicability of standardization ; results in economy ; the basis of scientific control.

(d) Need for scientific planning to relieve foremen and managers ; the duties of a manager ; the analytical aspect of planning ; analysis of products and processes ; analysis of constants and variables ; scope of planning ; planning necessary by reason of inter-relation of departments ; co-ordination other than by committees ; written instructions for management and operatives ; use of time-study in management ; the battle against waste waged by science.

(e) Distinction between manufacturing and other functions ; the disintegration of manufacturing ; the higher control of industrial concerns ; need for a single head ; duties of such a head ; duties of the manager under a functional organization ; functions are supplementary to manufacturing ; co-ordination of functions by the manufacturing manager ; examples of its operation ; his second duty of leadership ; his third duty of knowing the facts ; the personality of the manager.

THE time for discussing the necessity for increased production per unit of labour is now past. Labour requires guarantees and safeguards, but, in general, accepts the economic truth. Post-war conditions, both at home and abroad, have removed any doubt that, given those safeguards, increased production is not only desirable, but an imperative necessity. As the war recedes into

199

the past, however, has come the vivid realization that increased production is of no avail without an increased capacity for consumption. The production of goods which cannot be consumed is the direct road to stagnation. We need, therefore, increased production at prices which will bring the goods produced within the reach of the ordinary consumer. Increased production must be accompanied by economies in production, so that the costs of manufacture may be sufficiently low to allow of prices being reduced to a level at which increased consumption becomes possible. The potential demand is almost unlimited—for houses, clothes, food, and all the necessaries of a higher standard of living. Our problem, therefore, is to transform the potential into an effective demand by greater efficiency in production and distribution. Production, moreover, must not only be greater and cheaper, it must also be better. Quality is as essential as quantity. Indeed, the one without the other cannot be said to constitute that maximum service to the community, as consumers, which is the function of industry. Mere volume of material goods is not enough. The last century has witnessed a tremendous increase in sheer output, but the progress of the well-being of the community, measured by standards other than material, has been little or none. Greater material resources may be used with equal facility for greater good or for greater ill. But if those material goods are of a finer quality, a higher degree of skill is required in the producer and more discrimination on the part of the consumer. More art in industrial products means more spirituality in the maker and the purchaser. More scientific research into the quality of goods means higher intelligence applied in the production and the purchasing of those goods. Only if the production is of things worth producing can a factory claim to be rendering its fullest service.

Both quantitative and qualitative production, however, depend upon the combination of two agencies—the human agency and the material agency, or, as Mr. A. R. Stelling has called them, the Personal Factor and the Impersonal Factor. Increased and more economical production may come by more efficient use of effort, through either or both agencies. Increased production from the human agency alone, however, without any corresponding increase from the mechanical factor, implies a greater demand upon the individual, either by greater exertion of hand and brain, or by a re-arrangement of his physical methods of operation. In popularizing the " Gate to More " idea, we have been too apt to consider that the latch will only be lifted by greater physical effort, that the personal factor was the only factor which counted in productive energy. We must revise our views to include the potentiality of the Impersonal Factor. The more humane our administration of industry, the less physical demand should we make upon the individual, and the greater demand upon the machine. Labour is justified in claiming that the impersonal side of industry—the machinery, the buildings, the methods of transport, routing, planning, buying, dispatching, inspecting, manufacturing—should be of the most efficient character before a demand is made upon it for increased effort. Industrial efficiency may be improved, to an extent of which we cannot foresee the end, by the more efficient utilization of the impersonal means of production.

The business of the present chapter is, therefore, to review this impersonal side of industry, its equipment and administration—those factors in production in which the human energy of the workers is not directly concerned.

Mr. F. W. Taylor and his fellow exponents of " Scientific Management " have rendered a great service to the cause of industrial progress by their emphasis upon the necessity for the scientific treatment of manufacturing problems. Modern economic conditions have raised the labour cost of our products to a point where it is essential that all possible economies in manufacture should be effected.

The lesson of Scientific Management is that our attitude should be one of inquiry. We must be more sceptical of our methods of manufacturing. We need a more analytical outlook. Self-satisfaction in the face of modern economic conditions is sheer lunacy. Pride in achievements must be superseded by research into possibilities. We want a scientific attitude—the attitude which approaches every problem from a standpoint of detailed inquiry, divides the problem into its constituent parts, disentangles every maze, advances only where proof is absolute, builds upon assured foundations. Progress does not come in the mist of half-knowledge, but rather in the hard-won illumination of truth. Hitherto, we have traded on the chance which turned out well, the circumstances which happened to be favourable, the habit handed down from the past. But times have changed ; the methods of chance, circumstances, and custom, which were inadequate even before the war, are now in many instances prepostei ously unfitted for modern conditions. It is true that Scientific Management has perhaps erred too much on the side of recrimination. It has ridiculed, stormed at, trounced, and condemned the " hit and miss," " rule of thumb " methods of pre-war industry, as if the past had nothing to bequeath to the future. The scientist may, indeed, begin his inquiries *de novo*, but industry cannot begin again *de novo*. Scientific Management, after all, can only hope, by research and re-construction, to adjust the details of a form of industry which is the outcome of years of development. It can help to mould the growth of the future, but it would be un-scientific indeed if it cast aside the whole heritage of industrial knowledge because it found parts of that know-ledge were opinion or prejudice and not fact. Scientific Management may revolutionize industrial methods, but it can only do so on the basis of the past and by the continual adjustment of the present.

Its great and essential principle, however,—the principle of research—is unassailable. Improvements in machinery and operative and administrative methods cannot be attained except by deliberate research. Improvements in the past have largely been obtained by the sheer pressure of circumstances or by the haphazard discoveries of those engaged on the work. The demands made upon industry to-day, coupled with its growing complexity, make a more exacting call upon research, so that it becomes necessary for it to be regarded as a special branch of production whose scope is limited to no particular workroom or department. Scientific method is not restricted to particular subjects ; it is universally applicable. Industry is innately conservative. When a manager wishes, as he puts it, " to get at the facts " or insists on " knowing where he stands," he takes out costs. Costing is the only scientific treatment of facts generally accepted in industry. Every manager lives in the hope of showing a profit. His inquiries into industrial processes are therefore in terms of cash. He measures in costs only ; his research is as to the probability of profit. Costing is, however, only one branch of research. Modern costing developments show clearly that costing is increasingly concerning itself with matters far remote from accountancy. It brings to notice factors which scientific inquiry, apart from a cash measure, could more easily have revealed. It will reveal " waste time " on machines, high costs in trucking, bad leakages in power distribution, which machine research, traffic research and power research would have shown in a more direct way. The valuable results obtained from efficient costing are indicative of the need, not for more elaborate costing, but for the elimination of the waste of effort so revealed by the application of scientific method to all branches of manufacturing, so that costing may become more a measure of financial success than an index-finger of material or human waste. Conditions in manufacturing are not to be stated only in pounds, shillings, and pence. Truth is presentable in a garb other than a cloak of gold and silver. The instinct to *know* is sound ; but to know only the cost is to be acquainted with but half the house of knowledge. Every day there are decisions to be taken ; only a proportion of them, and these often inadequately, can be stated in terms of cost ; other factors remain a matter of guess-work and speculation. It is a roundabout way of finding out the inefficiency of a machine to calculate its operating costs ; mechanical research and measurement would reveal the facts immediately.

This is simply to say that the first step in the better utilization of the material factors in production is the development of that function of Comparison, outlined in Chapter III. This is the function, primarily, of Research, of Standards, and of Measurement. The research ends in the establishment of a " standard " (a standard method, a standard mixture, a standard quality, etc.) ; practice is compared with the " standard " by a process of measurement. It is indeed significant that this function, which we postulate as the first necessary step in increasing the efficiency of industry, has been that most neglected in the past.

Research is of two types : firstly, that which is known as Pure Research ; secondly, that which is known as Industrial or Applied Research. For the purposes of this chapter, we must eliminate that side of research which concerns the human element—the research into the efficiency of human effort as regards motions, strain, rhythm, and into the mental, physical and moral equipment of the workers ; into the reasons of Labour Turnover, its volume and incidence ; into the factors which underlie the relations of Labour and Management, the powers which sway the " group-mind " of the workers, and the influences within and without the factory which mould their mentality. " The other more usual requirements of a research organization " says Mr. A. P. M. Fleming,[1] " are those relating to the development of new tools, processes, and methods ; the elimination of difficulties arising from time to time in

[1] " Industrial Research." By A. P. M. Fleming, O.B.E., M.Sc., M.I.E.E., in *Lectures on Industrial Administration*. (Pitman.)

manufacturing operations ; the data required for new designs ; the establishment of means of recovery of by-products, the utilization of waste, and similar economic considerations. Further, a continuous check is necessary on the quality of raw material supplied, and the establishment of standards of quality which will enable purchases to be made, as far as possible, in the open market."

The development of this impersonal research is not solely dependent upon the application of the scientific method to particular problems. The process begins in pure research—research instituted for its own sake without any specific application of the knowledge gained. The industrial research worker applies pure science to the particular objects of the factory processes ; the manufacturer ultimately puts the knowledge gained into practice. There is a tendency to overlook the place of pure research. It should never be forgotten that, without pure research, applied research is operating with an insufficiency of data. Normally, pure research will be carried on by the Universities and by the Research Associations set up for particular industries, under the Department of Scientific and Industrial Research, but it is important that there should be the closest co-operation between such bodies and the research workers in factories or groups of factories.

It is essential, further, that the management as a body should appreciate the services which the research workers may render. The self-sufficiency of the old departmental manager dies hard. Nothing which he himself does not control, is of much use to him. He is apt to resent even well-intentioned intrusion. It is this attitude which is the bugbear of functionalization. The manager is too inclined to regard research as an infringement of his legitimate province, a reflection on his capacity. This attitude must go. It arises from a misunderstanding of both his own duties and those of the research workers. Co-operation between one function and another is of the essence of a functional organization. Research exists to help, not to criticize. The manager and foreman must learn to appreciate its help—to view its inquiries and recommendations as the equivalent of costing in terms of mechanical, chemical, and electrical science. After all, a machine may pay yet be inefficient. It is a question of viewing one's work as capable of measurement in the terms of the science underlying the work. Mechanical work can be measured in mechanical terms ; electrical work in electrical terms. Costing is financial measurement for financial purposes. The problem is to inculcate the desire, the feeling for the necessity of accurate and detailed knowledge of every activity of the factory. It is the cultivation of the scientific attitude, the reliance upon facts alone, accurately presented, scrupulously tested, correctly applied.

There is room in every factory for a properly organized research unit, charged with the investigation of processes, materials, labour and layout, with the object of improving the quality of the product, of reducing the costs of manufacture, of standardizing the methods of manufacture, and of facilitating the workings of the various functions of management. Like all functional activities, such local research work is to be regarded as supplementary to the management of the manufacturing department, the investigations resulting in certain recommendations to the management. It is for the management to realize that it has neither the time, opportunity, nor qualifications to conduct such detailed research, and that, therefore, the work of such a research unit, subject to the approval of the management, can cover ground and suggest improvements which could not otherwise be attained. It is equally for the research unit to realize that the final responsibility for the activities of any manufacturing department rests with the management of that department, and that, therefore, it must not only work in the closest co-operation with that management, but also must accept the right of the latter to criticize and even veto its recommendations.

Clearly, in research work of this kind the costing of

processes is only equal to other forms of measurement. The engineer, the chemist, and the time-study man will use their own forms of measurement to guarantee efficiency. Costing is to be distinguished from these. It is rather a secondary measurement after the direct measurement in other units has been made. Costing, however, has not been unduly emphasized in modern theory and practice. The fault lies, rather, in that other statistical and comparative methods have been underrated. Costing is not primarily a measure of general efficiency, except financial efficiency, which is the capacity to show profit. Costing will show that a certain process, unit, or department costs so much, and that, at that cost, it is profitable or unprofitable. This, of course, is vital—for industry under any imaginable system must pay its way. On the other hand, costing, though it may not be a measure of efficiency, is undoubtedly a guide to it. It is a first step towards the securing of better results. It indicates where waste may lie, and points the way for research. It may be said, therefore, to have a double purpose—the indication of a reasonable selling price, including profit (eliminating the other factors in selling price, e.g. competition, mutual agreement, etc.), and the revelation of where the more obvious wastes in production processes actually lie.

The serious lack of attention to costing in this country is now happily passing. The Report of the Committee appointed by the Board of Trade in 1918, to inquire into the position and prospects of the Engineering trades, reads as follows—[1]

" Of course, all efficient firms in this country have proper systems of costing. We think, however, that the essential value of a careful system of costing to ensure the maximum economy has not yet received from many houses the attention it demands. Certain large works are known to have no system of costing at all. Other large

[1] Report of the Departmental Committee on the Engineering Trades, 1918. Cd. 9073. (H.M. Stationery Office.)

works are known to have a system of costing based upon conventional rates of wages current in those works some years before. It may be assumed that most small works have only a costing system more or less reduced to a rule of thumb. Whilst we are inclined to think that the very elaborate costing systems in the United States tend to be reduced to the fanciful, we are quite convinced that a proper system of costing introduced throughout the works of this country would inevitably lead to the furnishing of valuable information to the heads of the firm, and to the stoppage of waste before it had had time to establish itself as a fixture. We are not believers in an elaborate system of costing for small firms. We are satisfied that it is possible to introduce a satisfactory system at very reasonable cost in all firms having an even moderate turnover."

Since the above was written the situation has changed for the better. The statement of Mr. Whiteford [1] appended below, after the passage of two years, requires some little qualification. The economic situation has definitely changed. In 1919, progress appeared to lie in increased production at any cost. It is now clear that progress lies in cheaper production, and that a low manufacturing cost is as important as a high production volume. It has become necessary to investigate waste, further, in view of the new moral impulse in industry. Labour is rightly demanding that waste due to inefficient manufacturing methods shall be eliminated before wages are reduced. Costing, as indicative of such waste, has therefore assumed a fresh tactical position in the conduct of industry. The point made by Mr. H. A. Evans [2] is also of the greatest importance—

[1] *Factory Management Wastes.* By J. F. Whiteford. (Nisbet & Co., 1919.)
" It is estimated that not more than 5 per cent of the manufacturers in the United Kingdom know the actual costs of the various products of their factories. It is further estimated that not more than 1 per cent know their costs within sufficient time for the information to be of real benefit."
[2] *Cost-keeping and Scientific Management.* By Holden A. Evans. (McGraw Hill Book Co., 1911.)

that lack of knowledge of costs is a disturbing factor in trade. " The competition which is most feared by a well-conducted establishment," he writes, " is that of the establishment which does not know its costs. It is often the case that a well-conducted, efficient establishment, which has figured on a moderate profit is underbid by a less efficient establishment, and the work taken at a price below actual cost. It is no satisfaction to the efficient establishment to know that the successful bidder will soon go into bankruptcy, for there will be someone else in the field with as little knowledge of real costs. These conditions demoralize business, and they will continue until actual costs are known. This situation explains what otherwise might be considered remarkable variations in bids submitted for the same work by a number of establishments located in the same vicinity and working under approximately the same conditions. It is not unusual to see such bids vary from 50 per cent to 100 per cent."

These factors, taken together, have raised the business of cost-finding to a position of primary importance in productive control. The elaboration of a costing system becomes, therefore, essential. There is no universally applicable system. The system depends upon the nature of the work and the manufacturing methods of the business. It is obviously necessary to know what exactly is to be costed, and precisely what information with regard to such items is required. For the detection of waste it is clearly useless to know only the cost of the completed product. The management needs to know how that cost has been built up, and what sections of the process of manufacturing have contributed most to the final figures. The system must therefore view as separate units for costing the largest possible subdivision of processes that can be distinguished the one from the other. The system, further, must cover all expenditures, and must allow of their correct allocation. For this, there is no theory ; there is room only for practical common sense. The elaboration of theoretical costing has been apt to lead students to believe that the whole system can be put into operation anywhere without consideration of local facts. Costing is eminently pliable. It can be distorted to any purpose. The only possible means of guidance, when a problem presents itself, is to ask " What would ordinary practical sense dictate ? " For instance, in the allocation of those expenses known as " Indirect," " Expense Burden," or " Overhead," all kinds of theoretical methods have been promulgated. The most common, and the most misleading, is to add a percentage for each item of indirect costs to the job being costed. Clearly, in some cases the percentage will be too high, in other cases too low as compared with the actual facts. Common sense would say : "Allocate to each job, process, or article being costed an amount proportionate to the benefit derived from or the services rendered by the items of indirect cost." Or again, in some systems, interest on capital is held to be an item of indirect cost to be allocated to each item costed. But obviously, if we are endeavouring to define the cost of each article being manufactured, the interest paid on capital is outside our scope. Certainly it will be included in the determination of selling price, but cannot enter into productive costs, since interest on capital is an allocation of profits after they have been made, and not a charge on the processes of production whereby those profits are made.

Costs are composed of three elements—Direct Labour, Material, and Indirect Charges. The direct labour cost is the time spent on the job. The material cost is the original invoice price plus the expenses incurred up to the point where costing begins. Indirect charges consist of all those costs of running the factory, which are not directly attributable to any single job. For the costing of direct labour, some clear, accurate and simple system of registering time is essential. If this item is inaccurately recorded, the whole system may be invalidated, since several items of indirect cost are necessarily allocated according to such time records. Material cost depends upon an efficient store-keeping system, and an accurate system of registering the allocation of material to jobs. Indirect cost is a question of scientific analysis, and for the rest, common sense. Some items can be allocated scientifically ; for example, rent charges can be based upon an accurate survey of the factory premises ; power can be allocated, with something approaching accuracy, by use of a machine power consumption device (though, of course, the cost of generating the power cannot be included on this basis). Other items as, for instance, depreciation of plant, etc., selling expenses, and rates must depend upon a common-sense distribution in some proportion to benefits derived. The cost incurred through depreciation, for instance, can only be determined by estimating the useful life of the building or machine, and its " scrap " value, if any, at the end of the period, and spreading the difference over the intervening period of life.

The problem of indirect cost is certainly complex. There is a mistaken impression that a high indirect cost in relation to total cost is suicidal. The impression can only arise from ignorance of what goes to make up indirect costs, or from an antiquated notion of shop methods. It is not generally realized that much labour cost, and a smaller proportion of material cost are included in " over-head," since they cannot be allocated to any one specific job. There is no fixable ratio between overhead and prime costs. There is no reason why the overhead should not equal the prime cost, if thereby greater efficiency is attained. Drastic reduction of overhead expenses may lead to poor supervision, worn machines, inadequate lighting, etc. Equally, not allowing overhead expenses to swell legitimately may throttle expansion. An improved system of planning, involving extra clerical work to the relief of individual workers, may well be an extension of overhead charges which the resulting efficiency will fully cover. " The overhead charges are in no sense a measure of the efficiency of a plant ; the measure of efficiency is total cost, and not a part of total cost." [1]

Accurate, detailed, and immediate cost-finding has its re-action on factory methods. In so far as it points the way to the elimination of waste, it conduces to standardization of product, of machinery, of productive methods, and of means of production. Standardization is the result of the search for the one best way, stimulated and measured by costs and other forms of statistical measurement. Costing and research together, in fact, give birth to standardization. Standardization is the determination of the best material, the best equipment, the best process discoverable at any given time—until a better be found. It is not rigid, but is the confirmation of each step of progress. If management, in Taylor's definition, be " the art of knowing exactly what is to be done," how much simplified is the task if a large proportion of it is reduced to a standard practice ! How much simplified is production if both the character of the product and the processes of manufacture are standardized, so that every suggested improvement can be accurately weighed against the standard.

The definition of a standard by Mr. Morris L. Cooke conveys the best idea of the principle underlying standardization. [2] " A standard under modern scientific management," he says, " is simply a carefully-thought-out method of performing a function, or carefully drawn specifications covering an implement or some article of stores or of product. . . . The idea of perfection is not involved in standardization. . . . There is absolutely nothing in standardization to preclude innovation. . . . Safeguards are erected to protect standards from change for the sake of change. . . . A proposed change in a standard must be scrutinized prior to its adoption. . . . Standardization

[1] *Cost-keeping and Scientific Management.* By H. A. Evans. (McGraw Hill Book Co., 1911.)
[2] *Academic and Industrial Efficiency.* Bulletin V of the Carnegie Foundation for the Advancement of Learning.

practised in this way is a constant invitation to experimentation and improvement."

We have yet to realize how important a place in industrial development the principle of standardization is destined to fill. Harrington Emerson[1] has shown that efficiency is based upon twelve principles, of which three are concerned with standardization—standard conditions, standard operations, and written standard-practice instructions. If one quarter of efficiency is based upon standardization we have a long road to travel to it, for standardization is a thing to which our national temperament is singularly antipathetic. We all like our own way of doing things, and this is normally not the best way. We have to learn to do things in the best known way, to rely upon research in which we ourselves may not have shared, to accept what is most efficient in preference to what best pleases us or falls in with our habits.

Standardization in industry, apart from the standard product, applies principally to material, equipment, and methods, both mechanical and human, and culminates in the standard task with its written standard-practice instructions. British industry will find this last hard to assimilate, nor is it likely that it will be assimilated, unless those called upon to perform the standard task are allowed some voice in the determination of what that task shall be. This, however, does not negative the immediate desirability of applying the principle. It concerns only the method of arriving at the " standard." A standard is the outcome, first, of analysis, then of synthesis. The expert, set upon the standardization of some process, will first analyse the process into its component parts ; he will then subdivide each part into its elementary constituent parts. He will examine each part and devise the most effective way of operating it. He will then begin to rebuild, adding part to part, adjusting where necessary to fit the parts together,

[1] *Twelve Principles of Efficiency.* By Harrington Emerson. (Engineering Magazine Co., 1917.)

till he has fashioned the process into a synthetic whole. Similarly, he will analyse the material to be used in the production of any article, and the tools, machines, and speeds employed in the process. Finally, he will record what he has found to be the best way of performing the process, the best materials and equipment to use, taking into account the variables of working conditions, of varying outputs, and of the human agent. Adherence to these written instructions then becomes the duty of the management and workers.

We are normally apt to discuss standardization as if it were an item of purely local interest, of this or that process. A new vista is opened up, however, by the Annual Reports of the United States Bureau of Standards, especially when one reads, as Mr. A. D. Denning [1] quotes, " the self-imposed definition of its functions—

" The development, construction, custody and maintenance of Reference and Working Standards, and their inter-comparison, improvement, and application in science, engineering, industry and commerce."

" After all," says Mr. Denning, " why should not each industry have its own Standards Association like the engineers, and from time to time issue approved definitions and specifications ? " Every day those of us who have the opportunity to study the science of industrial management are faced with difficulties due to unstandardized conditions. We require standard names of things and people in industry ; we require standard methods of administration, to avoid wasteful covering of ground and to facilitate the direction of the administrative machine ; we require standard ways of performing operations, for an industry, for a factory, or for a department ; we require standard forms of measurement, standard specifications of quality, standard procedures, standard parts of machines, standard relations between departments, standard symbols

[1] *Scientific Factory Management.* By A. D. Denning. (Nisbet, 1919.)

of location, and a thousand and one standards for both large and small phases of industry.

Above all, standardization results directly in economy, since the use of predetermined standards renders possible a scientific assessment of efficiency. The value of costs and other statistical methods is small, unless those costs or figures can be compared to some definable standard. It is the bugbear of every high administrative officer that the figures presented to him as the means whereby he may check efficiency are uninformative, since they are comparable with nothing reliable. He may compare them with similar figures of a year previous, but there is nothing to show him that the figures of a year ago were any more indicative of efficiency than those of the present. He needs a " standard "—something concrete, concise and definite, scientifically compiled, exact and accurate. Only so can he draw reliable conclusions and trace inefficiency to its hiding-place.

Standardization, moreover, is the basis of scientific control. "The less the variety in equipment," writes Mr. F. A. Parkhurst,[1] " the better the control and the greater the efficiency." Upon standards alone may the whole task of planning the work of the factory, and combining materials and men in the performance of the common task in the most economical fashion, be built up with some prospect of success.

Efficient planning of work depends upon analysis of the work, and the standardization which such analysis renders possible. Before control of what is to be done, how it is to be done, and when it is to be done can be established, there must exist some comprehensive knowledge of the detailed features of the task. The more constant those features are, that is the more they can be standardized, the simpler is the work of control. This fact increases in importance in proportion to the complexity of

[1] *Applied Methods of Scientific Management.* By Frederic A. Parkhurst. (Chapman & Hall, 1912.)

the task.   One often hears the comment that planning is impossible owing to the complexity of the business, and the number of variables in the local processes of production. That is all the more reason for instituting scientific planning. Planning exists at present in some form in every factory. The progress of work through any factory is not purely a matter of chance.   There is always thought behind it— but it is often unscientific, unco-ordinated thought ; and, often, thought by the wrong persons.

Indeed, one of the main reasons why scientific planning or production control is so pressing a problem in every factory is because it is so often an extra burden upon administrative officers whose proper main business is not planning.   The making of all the arrangements for work is, in practice, more often than not the duty of the manager or foreman.   The manager is told to produce goods ; he is told the approximate volume that is expected from his department ; he is informed of the special varieties of goods which the sales manager can most effectively put on the market.   After that, he is left to work out the detail and do his best.   It is of no concern whether the production of the particular plant is for stock or for delivery ; whether the articles are food, machinery, or pins.   The fact remains that the task of delivering the goods to the shipping department on a scheduled day, or of maintaining the stock in the storerooms at a certain level, is left to the manager of the producing department. It is further to be noted that a single product, be it a product which is the assembly of many parts into one unit, or be it a product which is the outcome of many processes on one or more component materials, is normally the result of the work of several departments, each of which, we may imagine, endeavours to plan its work in the most effective way for its own purposes.

We may observe, therefore, the double drawback of localized planning in the normal productive business. Firstly, the manager or foreman does his own planning, and, secondly, he plans largely irrespective of the plans of other managers or foremen who play an equally vital part in making the ultimate product. Thus, on the one hand, we often have ineffective management, since the manager or foreman is occupied on work which takes him away from the constant supervision of his department, or sacrifices the work of planning to the requirements of shop supervision ; on the other hand, however effective local departmental planning may be, it does not allow of comprehensive control from the reception of the order to its completion. The sum of several good departmental planning arrangements may not be at all good planning as a whole.

Some higher administrative officers in industrial concerns are still inclined to be deaf to the eternal cry of scientific reformers that the departmental manager has too much to do. They see him working the same hours as themselves, and rather doubt in their hearts whether he actually has enough to do. We need to be quite clear as to what the duties of a manager should actually be under a functional organization. His primary duties may be stated briefly as follows—

(a) Co-ordination of functional activities in so far as they affect his department.

(b) Responsibility for producing the planned output with the maximum of efficiency.

(c) Responsibility for the effective workmanship and team spirit of his workers.

(d) Responsibility for the quality of the product.

Beyond that, all the administrative work incidental to the work of the department should be of an auxiliary functional character. If the manager can effectually carry out the above duties, the task of planning his work may well be left to others, except in so far as it is his business to co-ordinate planning with other functional activities in the department.

The main reason for planning is, however, neither the overloading of the departmental manager nor the lack of co-ordinated planning as between departments, but the necessity for the scientific treatment of control.   Planning is the business of ensuring systematic, complete and detailed control of production.   This necessitates the division of planning into three parts : Firstly, the accumulation of data to show how the work of the factory is carried out ; secondly, the elaboration of a plan to cover the whole process from the reception of the works order to the delivery to the stockroom or shipping department ; thirdly, the establishment of the administrative machinery necessary to notify the planning department of the adherence to or divergence from the plan.   These three stages in planning may be described as the analysis of productive methods, the creation of the plan, and the checking of its operation.

The analytical aspect of planning may engage our attention first—both because it is an essential preliminary to drawing up any schedule of operations, and because it is the aspect which normally receives least care.   As Mr. A. H. Church[1] points out, " co-ordination of work in shops should be based not on what should happen but on what does happen.   The latter is the only safe guide to determine what should happen next."   Much factory planning (and here it would be well to make it clear that by " planning " is meant the business of directing and controlling the processes of production to a given end) is based on the assumed means, in place of the actual means to that end.   Every industrial administrator has had experience of instructions from either a planning department, or some individual charged with making the necessary arrangements for the progress of work, which are based on inaccurate or inadequate data.   This arises from either inadequacy of analysis or inelasticity in planning.   The former is by far the more frequent reason.   Instructions are issued without sufficient

[1] *The Science and Practice of Management.*   By A. H. Church. (Engineering Magazine Co., 1914.)

knowledge and investigation of what is involved. We need something in industry comparable to the signalling system of a railway—some system which directs and controls according to a predetermined schedule, based upon an analysis of the traffic volume, and which is capable of dealing with an extra volume of traffic in exceptional circumstances. The basis of any effective control is reliable data.

Analysis for planning purposes may be divided into two parts : Firstly, analysis of what is to be made—the quality and quantity ; secondly, analysis of how it is to be made—the machinery, the processes, the time taken. All such information will, of course, be supplied by the Comparison function. This may again be divided on a different basis into (a) analysis of those elements in the processes and products which are standard, and can be reduced to routine ; (b) analysis of those elements which are indeterminable and subject to particular circumstances that may arise. Analysis is a process of subdivision. The whole business of production is reduced to a series of distinguishable units ; each is dissected and studied, firstly as a self-contained unit, secondly, in relation to neighbouring units. With adequate records of each unit—the detail of the process, the possibilities of its capacity, the time taken —an effective plan may be built up, culminating in a definite working schedule for each unit.

Upon such a basis of adequate analysis, planning may begin. The analysis will have revealed how much of the manufacture can be rendered automatic, and how much must remain undeterminable and liable to alteration according to the character of the works order. The first step is to determine the best procedure and routes for the production of the required commodities, whether those commodities be for a definite purchaser's order, involving the determination of a delivery day, or for stock. Next comes the necessity for ensuring that the scheduled means of manufacture—material, labour, and appliances—are provided and obtainable.   Following this comes the control of material, so that each item in the assembling of the product, or each successive process in its treatment, is brought into play at such a juncture as leaves no room for delay or opportunity for congestion.   Meanwhile, a record of work waiting to be begun should be kept, so that the time for beginning each job can be determined and a date for delivery promised.   Finally, each order is completed, if the schedule has been correctly drawn up and faithfully carried out, on the date for which the product was promised.

The basis for drawing up a plan of manufacture, therefore, is the time taken at each successive stage.   In carrying out the plan, according to schedule, the main factor is location. Production is, indeed, a process of movement, punctuated by the necessary halts to enable operations to be carried out.   Planning, therefore, may be described as the control of operation traffic, in such a way as to ensure (1) that there is no block in the progress through any one unit being overloaded ; (2) that the movement from unit to unit is the shortest and most economical ; (3) that every order is passed to the shops, and every fresh component ingredient brought into the processes to fit in with the points of progress reached by materials already in circulation ; (4) that orders are forwarded to the shops in sufficient time to allow of their completion by the scheduled date ; and (5) that in the event of breakdowns the traffic is diverted in the best available way.

Obviously, therefore, scientific planning of work requires not only a complete and accurate schedule of processes, but also immediate records of the positions which all orders, or their component parts, have reached.   Progress from unit to unit must be controlled by the planning function, so that the routing of material and the inception of fresh orders may be based upon an immediate knowledge of the facts in the shops.

The idea of scientific planning of work has received

tremendous impetus from the study of " Scientific Manage-ment," as advocated by the late Mr. F. W. Taylor.   British manufacturers will, however, be well advised to formulate their own schemes

Taylor himself, in fact, always emphasized that any particular factory must devise its own system.   His own expedient of eight " functional foremen " operating as the executives of the planning system is clearly quite contrary to the psychology of British industry.   The British worker likes one " boss " ;   the multiplication of " bosses " he regards, with some justification, as a " pillar to post " business.

Scientific planning, however, is best left alone unless it is to be comprehensive.   The " Progress Departments" which some concerns have instituted, set out with admirable intentions but inadequate knowledge.   The scientifically determined schedule of operations, which is planning, cannot be replaced by a " chasing " system based on no scientific data, and relying upon the capacity of its agents to browbeat the foremen and extract from them illusory promises.   Only planning which is scientific, reliable, and all-embracing, is of real value.   It is better to trust to the ability of the foremen themselves, than to harass them with instructions from insufficiently informed officials of a department which is out of touch with the facts.

Our problem is, therefore, to bring the scientific planning and control of work into an economical relationship with the essential conception of departmental responsibility and authority.   It is the problem that arises in all functional organizing—the determination of the relations between the function and the operative department.   It arises particularly in planning, however, since this has been the traditional duty of the foreman from time immemorial. He is often prepared to hand over the purchasing of his materials, the installation and maintenance of his equipment, the costing of his processes, the timekeeping, hiring and discharge of his labour, and the merchanting of his products to central functional departments. But the determination of how the work of his department shall be done is a matter which he reserves to himself ; without it, he feels that the last shred of his authority has vanished.

This is the crux of the problem of functionalization. The growth of any industry has been largely the result of the work of managers and foremen. Their ability has founded a tradition which innovators disregard at their peril. The foremen, by sheer worth, have established themselves as the central points of factory administration, and it is, therefore, useless to change the methods without first converting them to the proposed changes. Every innovation must accordingly be preluded by the persuasion of the foremen that it is necessary. The foreman has been accustomed in the past to " a free hand." Loyalty has been his outstanding characteristic—always provided that he was left free to discharge his responsibility in his own way.

Modern methods of production have broken down the barriers between departments of the same plant, and the foreman is no longer a departmental autocrat. The planning of work, however, has in most plants remained in his hands, though it has changed its features. Production has been infinitely subdivided, and the processes by which the final product is completed are normally split up over a number of departments. Foremen have accordingly been compelled to keep in touch with the work of other departments in order that the work of their own departments may fit in with the whole scheme. In other words, co-ordination of manufacture has become necessary. The foreman has recognized that his own work is not independent, but is largely governed by the work of other departments. This holds good, no matter what the products of the business may be. In order, therefore, to provide this manufacturing co-ordination, foremen are compelled to meet frequently, to set up committees and conferences, and to establish some machinery for notifying each other of how work is progressing or what changes are being made.

Such methods are clearly wasteful. It is not the job of the foreman to be continually in consultation away from his own department ; neither is it his job to be studying the progress of work in other sections of the factory. This is all the more true when it comes to be realized that a large part of such work can be eliminated by a central control, which can reduce such matters to something approximating to routine. There is a healthy and inevitable demand in industry for co-ordination. We need to remember, however, that co-ordination can be obtained in more than one way. To co-ordinate does not necessarily mean that a committee must be established. Co-ordination by committees is only necessary where the subjects to be co-ordinated are constantly variable, and discussion is essential. Where those subjects can be rendered wholly or in a large measure standard, co-ordination is better obtained by establishing machinery whereby it may be rendered almost automatic. For the purpose of determining policy, co-ordination by committee is probably necessary. In executing that policy, co-ordination by the establishment of the necessary machinery is more normally effective. For instance, in determining whether a new product shall be put on the market, co-ordination by discussion between the sales, manufacturing and planning departments, is clearly necessary. But, in the business of making that new product, co-ordination between the manufacturing departments concerned in the various processes can best be obtained by one central authority issuing the necessary directions and exercising the necessary control. Indeed, it is not wide of the mark to say that the present tendency in industry to multiply committees and conferences is, in some large degree, due to the lack of proper executive machinery.

If, however, it is agreed that the central planning of work is necessary, it is still a matter for debate how far such a central authority may interfere with departmental arrangements. It is possible to admit that a central authority shall make the arrangements for the passage of work from department to department, and determine what part of the whole each department shall perform, but still to deny that such an authority shall have power to determine how each department shall perform its allotted task. This, however, is to deprive the central authority of any power to make accurate delivery dates. It cannot be expected to state when an order shall be completed, when it has no say in the methods adopted in departments for dealing with that order. It is like throwing a bottle into the sea and attempting to estimate when it will float to the shore. Planning, in fact, cannot be effective unless the same system of planning applies throughout the whole route. This still leaves to a department, however, the responsibility for carrying out its internal planning according to the central system. The real division, therefore, between the planning function and the manufacturing department is that the former determines the methods of planning and the data upon which plans are to be made, but the latter, through its local planning section, is responsible for its own internal planning according to such methods and data.

" Where then does a foreman come in ? " one may be inclined to ask. As Mr. Stelling puts it, " What are his duties under this devolution of functions ? Does he not become a mere policeman, an automaton governed by an impersonal planning department ? "[1] If so, then clearly planning of this character may be regarded as generally unsuited to British factory conditions. Were planning the primary function performed by a foreman, this would be true ; but in so far as it is at present one of his many functions, it is not true, since, where many functions operate side by side for the achievement of a common purpose, there will always arise the necessity for

[1] " Output Planning as a Function of Management "—a series of articles in *Engineering and Industrial Management*. By A. R. Stelling. (January, 1920.)

co-ordination between them. This is the duty of the departmental foreman. He is responsible for the effective combination of functions within his province in carrying out the plan of production. In a large plant, planning will normally be organized in the form of a central planning office, with subsidiary offices in each manufacturing department. The personnel of such departmental offices will be under the department for discipline and the execution of planning work, but under the central planning office as regards their methods of work. Any difference between the planning office and the department will naturally come to the appropriate co-ordinating committee for settlement.

Planning, it must be remembered, as a function, is the assistant of the manufacturing department, but its services are such that they cannot be efficiently executed unless directed from a central source. It follows, therefore, that local alterations cannot be effected without the sanction of that central authority, though both the central office and the department will be subject to the control of the managing director or such committees as may be appointed to provide co-ordination between the two. In this way, it is suggested, functional activities may be logically carried out, whilst at the same time the foreman loses none of his authority.

Whatever may be the practical difficulties in carrying out a scientific scheme of arranging for the progress of work, however, planning, as an attempt to deal with a problem which grows more pressing as industry becomes more complex, emphasizes that feature of management which is so conspicuously lacking to-day. What management is most in need of, for the execution of its impersonal duties, is method. There is plenty of enthusiasm and initiative in post-war industrial administration, but there exists a serious lack of a sense of proportion in the executive side of management. The three basic principles of impersonal management may be described as Analysis,

Experiment, and Measurement. These three in combination give rise to a working method. There is no qualification in the manager of the future more clearly requisite than a methodical mind. Our manufacturing holds too many elements which are the result of guess-work, and too few which are the result of an established scientific and impregnable method of working. If management is indeed a science, it must accept scientific ways and means of working. It must adopt definite methods to achieve definite ends. Just as there are formulae for chemistry, so must there be formulae for management. " The chemist mixes a definite quantity of this and a definite amount of that, and he has what he knew would be the result of the combination of the elements," says Mr. C. E. Knoeppel. " The manufacturer mixes tons of this, feet of that, so many machines, some money, men, and knows absolutely nothing about the real outcome as regards cost and efficiency until the product is completed."[1] This is a revelation not only of lack of accurate and immediate knowledge, but also of lack of that type of mentality which can map out a course for its activities and proceed methodically to follow that course.

Method is normally condemned as " red tape "—a condemnation considered as a complete and final disposal of the subject. The use of graphic control methods, planning boards, forms for this and that, " move slips," " written instructions," records and diagrams is held by the average manufacturer to be the acme of " officialism," and wholly inconsistent with the necessary elasticity of a business concern. Yet modern industry can no longer be conducted in the slip-shod manner of a decade ago. We have grown too fast, the facts to be known are too manifold and complex for reliance any longer to be wholly placed upon individual memory, initiative and adaptability. A methodical way of doing things, based upon an analysis of

[1] *Installing Efficiency Methods.* By C. E. Knoeppel. (Engineering Magazine Co., 1918.)

and a proper allowance for variable factors, does not crush
initiative, but rather relieves executive officers, so that
they may the better develop that essential quality. There
undoubtedly exist minds which inevitably revolt against
the conduct of the business of management by the soulless
methods of a machine. Such minds have their place in
industry, but that place is not in control of the combination of multitudinous factors contributing to a common
product. It is the difference between the inventor and
the engineer, the minister of the Crown and the permanent
head of a department, the architect and the builder. The
one originates the idea, the other sets all the contributory
factors in motion to achieve it.

Written instructions form an essential part of planning.
Of course, their value may be over-stressed by enthusiasts.
But the main fact remains that unless individuals or groups
of individuals performing the same work are perfectly
clear as to the details of their duties, there is bound to be
confusion, overlapping, or omission, and scientific planning
thereby becomes impossible. " Scientific Management "
has emphasized the need for " written instructions " for
operatives, but what is of greater importance is the need
for " written instructions " for executive officers. In many
establishments, high officials only know their duties in a
general way. They do not know with any exactitude the
detailed methods by which their work is to be executed.
This is equally true of foremen and clerks. There is no
attempt to define that procedure which is the combination
of defined individual duties. There is a wholesale lack
of definition ; the administrative picture is a blur, not a
design.

The same holds good of the work of the operative, but
the effect is less disastrous. Lack of definition in the duties
of administrative officials is calculated to occasion greater
inefficiency than a similar lack in the duties of the workers.
In many processes, however, particularly in engineering
and allied shops, the technique of the operative may have

a profound effect upon the quality and volume of the product. Where this is so, there is every reason for reducing the methods of operation to a written series of instructions. This, then, becomes an essential basis of planning, for if the various sections of the factory are to work upon the right material at the right time, it is necessary to know the right way in which that work should be done, and the time which such methods should take. This can only be achieved by an analytical study both of machines and of men. This aspect of " Scientific Management " has been thrust to the fore in such a way that the application of such study is resented by the workers, and regarded with a wholesome suspicion by employers generally. There is a prejudice in British industry against any attempt to make factory life and methods of work mechanical. Nothing could be more disconcerting to the average man than the sensation of being watched by a time-study man, stop-watch in hand, as if he were a fly-wheel or a steam-hammer. Irritation would be certain to ensure when, later, an " instruction card " was issued to the man, telling him how his work should be done and the time allowance, to a fraction of a minute, for each element of it.

It is this psychological effect of time-study which makes it the subject to be treated with the greatest care of all in any application of scientific management. It is useless to employ it unless the co-operation of the workers is first secured. It is also of little use unless the management is efficient. Time-study, like research in other directions, is not an end in itself, but a means to an end. That end is the smooth and efficient working of the factory, as directed by the management. It is clearly useless to time-study an operation, when the routing of material is so faulty that the material necessary for the operation is sometimes not ready for the operative's use. It is equally useless if the work of the operative is not planned out beforehand, or if he is an unsuitable operative for that type of work. The economical working of any operation may, indeed, be wholly negatived by managerial inefficiency. Time-study is, therefore, to be regarded as a means not only to operative efficiency, but also, and this is of even greater importance, to managerial efficiency.

The outcome of time-study is a " standard task " or " schedule time." This means that the work of the operative is performed as economically as possible. But it also permits management to put its house in order— a matter of far greater importance. The " standard task," firstly, enables wage-rates to be fixed upon a scientific basis, thus obviating the need for rate-cutting ; secondly, it enables planning to be conducted according to accurate and reliable data ; thirdly, it enables costing to develop its value by permitting that necessary comparison, for which costing exists, between actual costs and the costs of the standard task ; fourthly, it enables the engagement of personnel to be made on the basis of an accurate knowledge of the jobs for which such personnel is being engaged : fifthly, it enables an organization to be built up, founded upon a detailed analysis of the work involved in every operation. It is in these directions, even more than in the direction of operative training and efficiency, that the true value of time-study lies.

This consideration will ensure that time-study is not pressed to extremes where it ceases to pay for itself. In the glow of scientific inquiry, the temptation is to pursue such study beyond the point where it is economically valuable. Unless, however, the processes of a factory are highly complex, constantly repeated, or performed by a large number of persons, it is probable that nothing beyond the more simple features of motion and time-study will be of real productive value. Clearly, where work is of a " labouring " type, non-repetitive and simple, good foremanship and a sound system of time-recording will provide the same efficiency as time-study, with its resultant " standard tasks," and " instruction cards."

Time-study, however, is to be sharply differentiated from machine-study. Machine time-study—or mechanical research—lies in a different field. The two cannot properly be united. The study of the human factor in production calls for wholly different methods from those requisite for the study of machines and materials, though research as a whole is not complete without the study of all these three factors. The essential ingredient of time-study is the co-operation of the worker himself. It is a problem of humanics, as machines form a problem of mechanics. Just as machine research calls for an engineer, and material research for a chemist or metallurgist, so human research calls for a psychologist. It is not, of course, necessary that every time-study should be made by a trained psychologist, but it is necessary that the time-study men should be trained psychologically and be under the direction of a trained psychologist. The work, of course, would require to be correlated intimately with research in other directions, but the qualities and the methods necessary are so distinct from those required in other research that they cannot legitimately be grouped together. The organizing of research, speaking generally, therefore, is not the organizing of specific individuals under the function of Comparison, but rather the organizing of certain activities by individuals belonging to various functions. Research is the grouping of the engineer, the chemist or the metallurgist, and the psychologist, drawn from their different functions, to concentrate upon their respective branches of investigation—the whole being co-ordinated by a research supervisor, who alone is the distinct member of the Comparison function. It is also to be borne in mind that all such research work must be conducted with the co-operation of the management of the department in which this research is taking place.

The relation of time-study to vocational selection makes this form of organization doubly imperative. Though the " standard task " is of primary value to planning, costing, wage-setting and organization, it is most intimately connected with the selection of employees. Clearly, whoever has analysed and determined the human characteristics—the motions, the fatigue, and the time—of a job is most capable of selecting the type of individual best fitted for the execution of the job. Again, it is not practicable to distinguish motion- and fatigue-study from time-study. Inherent in motion-study is the timing of the job. Motion-study is not a mechanical process; it requires even more than common sense. It calls for the capacity for winning and interesting the worker; it calls for the qualities of sympathy, humour, and understanding; it calls for a knowledge of muscular and mental reactions. It is, in fact, the task of men trained by and working under a psychologist. In determining the motions, the element of time is as important as the element of fatigue. Time-study cannot, therefore, be divorced from motion-study—both call for psychological capacities. Both, also, contribute the data for the selection of employees. Psychological analysis of the job and psychological analysis of the worker for the job are interlocked so that they cannot be divided. The fact that the results of such analysis are utilized for other purposes, and that the work must be conducted in close conjunction with other aspects of research does not invalidate the contention that time-study and vocational selection must be grouped together, under a psychologist, as a part of the function of Labour. Without the human point of view constantly guiding and informing the work of time-study, it cannot achieve the ends for which it set out.

Research, Planning, Costing and Time-study are four of the agents in the battle against factory waste. This waste is fourfold—waste in personnel; waste in operative methods; waste in machinery, materials and layout; waste in management. Waste, we are coming to realize, must be combated with the weapons of science. Science is organized knowledge, and in attacking inefficiency we cannot know too much of the facts. In management, waste can be eliminated only by a more detailed analysis of each aspect of management and a more methodical control, based upon reliable data. Waste in personnel must be combated by those methods of employment work and welfare, already outlined, applied with a knowledge born both of psychology and of experience. Waste in operative methods can be arrested by the psychological study of the worker at his task, his conditions of work, his movements and habits in working, and the incidence of fatigue, together with an investigation as to where machines can replace handwork, and the time-study of both mechanical and hand operations. Waste in machinery, materials and layout must be overcome by accurate measurements of volume, speeds and time, and by the making of such adjustments as the data thus furnished will suggest.

The warfare against waste is a guerilla form of fighting. It should go on continuously, ever inspired by a profound conviction that waste exists and that the actual efficiency falls far short of the best possible. To maintain this attitude we need not only a specific part of the organization devoted to research, but also a common, corporate eagerness to probe to the bottom of things, to know and measure the facts. In addition, we need the constructive capacity to build up on these facts a productive system which shall aim at attaining the most efficient use of every human and material factor in production, so that our products shall be of the best possible character, manufactured in the best possible way. Progress towards this ideal can only come by successive steps of consolidation, research, and construction. No step forward is possible unless the present foothold has been established. Standardization is the necessary preliminary to progress. Haphazard so-called improvements are as likely to occasion chaos as progress. The standardizing of what is best up to the present is essential to subsequent alterations of such standards. This applies both to the technique of management and to the technique of operation.   It is often assumed that if Standard Practice Instructions are determined upon for the proper working of the process of manufacture, the methods of management can be left to function as before.   It is just as necessary, however, for management to have its standards.

It is as important that the procedure for the control of a shop should be " standard " as that the actual processes in the shop should be " standard."   This is, indeed, the foundation of scientific management as distinct from scientific operating.   It is towards this object that the development of a " science of management " is striving.   Indeed, if the battle against waste is to succeed, management must not only devise means whereby the efficiency of workers and machines is brought to the highest pitch, but must also ensure that its own managerial methods are at a similar point of efficiency.   The main lesson of research and of every endeavour—by costing, by planning, by recording, by measuring, and by time-study—to determine the efficient working of a department or of a factory, is that the greatest economy is not to be obtained by rendering the individual worker more efficient, but rather by increasing the efficiency of the personnel by whom, and the methods by which, the work of the operatives is guided, controlled, and arranged.   Efficiency in industry is overwhelmingly a matter of efficiency in management.   When management can be said to be 100 per cent efficient, it will be found that the workers have achieved approximately the same efficiency.

It is clearly impossible here to discuss the detailed methods of each function of management.   An attempt has been made broadly to indicate the scope of the more recently developed activities such as research, costing, and planning, and the standardization which is an essential ingredient of these three.   We must now turn to consider the relationships between functions, which constitute the main problem consequent upon a functional division of the duties of management, and which, for the proper working of a functional organization, must be defined.

The form of organization which has been sketched thus far comprises three main divisions : Firstly, the higher control, consisting of the managing director, the works manager, and other similarly placed officers ; secondly, the functional divisions of the factory such as planning, comparison, and selling, with their functional heads and staff ; thirdly, the manufacturing division, with its direct hierarchy of manager, sub-manager, foremen, charge-hands, and operatives.

Manufacturing itself can hardly be regarded as a function comparable with other functions. It is not so much a function as a basis ; not so much one of the several branches of the tree as its trunk.   From it the functions branch off, drawing their life from it, and serving it.   Each function is subordinate to the main business of manufacturing ; indeed, the development of each function has been, in a sense, a disintegration of manufacturing to the advantage of both.   Time was, in most factories which have grown out of small beginnings, when manufacturing included practically all the functions.   It costed its own work, directed its own operations, investigated its own methods, engaged its own labour, paid its own wages, sold its own products.   Gradually, all these functions developed and became separate entities like the diverse branches of a tree, distinct both from the main trunk and the other branches.   This came about, firstly, because the work of each function became so large that it could no longer remain an integral part of manufacturing ; secondly, because the work of manufacturing became so complex that it not only could no longer cover those functions which could be clearly distinguished from it, but also had itself to be subdivided.   It was no longer the simple business of one shop or department, but a multitudinous number of processes often highly technical, and in many cases producing a vast variety of products.

Manufacturing became, therefore, subdivided into departments in accordance with the variety of its products, the variety of parts of a single product, or the processes in manufacturing, such divisions being normally based upon the simplest treatment of the greatest complications. For example, in a plant manufacturing many similar products by complex processes, there would be division by processes ; in a plant manufacturing one product of many parts, division by parts ; and in a plant manufacturing a wide variety of separate products, division by products.

We have, therefore, in the modern industrial concern these three factors developed to a high degree—the higher control, with an intricate machinery for collecting data, consulting with officials, and issuing instructions ; the functional administration, in separate bodies, engaged upon distinct yet inter-related lines of work ; and the manufacturing management, divided, by either product or process, into several groups, each with its own staff and operatives, premises and machinery.

In taking a bird's eye view of the business of production, it will be seen that, though a consideration of each function is of importance, the first problem for thought is the constitution and inter-relations of these three main divisions of administration—the higher control, the auxiliary functions, and the manufacturing.

It has not, perhaps, been fully realized how the higher control of a business is affected by the process of functionalization. This subject has already been discussed in Chapter IV, when it was pointed out that co-ordination in functional organizing is essential to effective administration. We have here to consider, however, how best that co-ordination can be effected to cope with the growing specialization of the factory activities, and what steps are necessary to ensure that such co-ordination is effective in promoting efficient management.

At the head of the administration of every business it is essential that there should be some centralizing agency.

Such an agency cannot consist of a committee; it must be a single individual. If the directors of a business are executive heads, it must be a Chairman of Directors. If the directors are non-executive, it must be a Managing Director. The futility of a committee requires no demonstration. Clearly, if the heads of functions collectively constituted the actual summit of the business, the functional divisions of the works would end at the top, each in mid air, like the strands of a rope. Those strands must be brought together by some individual charged with the co-ordination of all functions and the direction of the organization to some single objective. Certainly, a committee of management may fulfil a useful purpose, but only as advisory to the head of the administration, and as a representative body for the proper adjustment of those works activities which concern more than one function. A committee can criticize and can approve, but it cannot of itself construct. What is most needed at the top of every organization is a single mind which can devote itself wholly to the regulation of inter-functional activities, to the moulding of the form of the organization, and to the business of thinking constructively. Such a mind could view the whole of the administration, from the buying of materials and reception of customers' orders to the sale of the product, and, at the same time, accumulate information upon the best theoretical and actual methods of industrial management, with a view to their application to the particular business. Such work, such viewing of a business as a whole, presents different problems from the direction of a single function. It is a study not of perpendicular management only—that is, management from top to bottom, from manager to worker, through various grades of executives— but also of horizontal management—that is, management as it concerns cross-relationships; and cumulative management—that is, management as it concerns the welding together of several separate parts.

Below this central administrative control, the two main

aspects of the business divide ; on the one hand, the functional groups, on the other, the manufacturing groups. As functionalization develops, the relations between the two become a problem of pressing importance. The duties of the manufacturing manager have already been stated to be—co-ordination of functional activities in so far as they affect his department ; responsibility for producing the planned output with the maximum of efficiency ; responsibility for the effective workmanship and team spirit of his workers, and responsibility for the quality of the product. His duties may, therefore, be summarized as co-ordination of functions, output, leadership, work efficiency. Intermingled with these duties, are the duties of functional departments, which may be described as the efficient execution of the work involved in carrying out the functions. The difficulty arises in that such functions necessarily operate through the work of manufacturing. Planning is not a self-supporting function ; it is planning of manufacturing. Clearly, therefore, the relations of the function and the manufacturing require careful definition—relations, not only in the human sense of the relations between the functional head and staff and the manufacturing manager and staff, but also in the " work " sense of the relations between the work of the function and the work of manufacturing.

In the British interpretation of functionalization, there can be no other principle than that the functions are supplementary to, not in control of, the manufacturing, and that no manufacturing manager shall be compelled to adopt any recommendations of the functional staff against his judgment. Only so can the cohesion of a factory be maintained. For this reason, in the main, arises the urgent need that our managers should be men of mature judgment and large vision, and that their duties should be studied and defined. The manager is called upon to deal, in a co-ordinating capacity, with every function from Labour to Comparison. He will be expected to determine with equal ease questions of the education of the workers, the time-study of his processes, the costing of his products and the planning of his operations. Intimate knowledge of how each function operates is hardly to be expected, nor would it be necessary ; but knowledge of what to expect from the activities of a function, and of how to utilize the services each function provides, is a primary qualification in the manager of a functionalized concern. All the more necessary is this capacity on account of the tendency, which is apparently inevitable in every business, for one function to rise superior to the rest. This may often largely result from the personality of the head of the function. In one factory it may be the Labour manager who tends to advance the interests of his function at the expense of others ; in another, the head of the Comparison function ; in another, the Equipment manager. This tendency is more than likely to warp both the form of the organization and the balance of the management. If the British inter-pretation of functional organizing and management is to stand the test of efficiency, there can be little doubt that the outstanding personalities in the factory must be the manufacturing managers. In other words, if specialization is allowed to over-ride co-ordination, chaotic results must ensue. Just as functionalization makes co-ordination necessary at the supreme head of any business, equally does it entail co-ordination at other points in the organiza-tion. Those points can only be where the functions cross the path of the manufacturing departments. Co-ordination of functions is, therefore, the prime duty of the manufacturing manager.

We may perhaps be justified here in taking an example of how this co-ordination and relationship between function and manufacturing may operate in practice. Take one department of a factory which is engaged in the manufac-ture of some edible product, and in which functionalization has been worked out to a considerable extent. We may imagine that the functions of Labour and Comparison have special dealings with this particular department. From the work of these two functions, we may abstract three activities affecting the department, e.g. the engagement of workers for the department by the Labour function, the assessment of labour turnover by the Comparison function, and the research into productive methods by the Comparison function. What are the relations between the manufacturing manager and the functional heads in these three aspects of functional work?

Working upon the principles already suggested, namely, that a manager shall be compelled to do nothing against his judgment, and that his main duty is the co-ordination of functions, we may briefly sketch the procedure with regard to these three activities.

(a) The engagement of personnel will be carried out by the Labour function, at the request of the manager of the manufacturing department. The Labour function will select those men whom it considers the most suitable for the work involved. It will take all the necessary steps to introduce the new employees to the factory and the department. It will make a complete record of the individuals. The manufacturing manager has the right to reject the persons suggested to him, but may only do so on grounds other than Labour grounds. For instance, he may object to them because the wage payable disproportionately increases his costs, or because the men are unsuitable for a job which is to be time-studied. Settlement of any differences between the Labour function and the manufacturing manager must be effected by the co-ordinating body—either a Works Manager, or a Labour Committee on which the manufacturing manager sits.

(b) In assessing a departmental Labour Turnover, the business of the Comparison function will be to point out the special features of the turnover to the manufacturing manager. Should the turnover be too high, it is then the duty of the manager to take all the necessary steps to reduce it, in conjunction with the Labour function. If the successive figures still reveal a high turnover, it is again the duty of the Comparison function to point it out, and, if no reduction in it is achieved by the manager, to point out the figures to the co-ordinating body.

(c) In the operations of the research side of the function of Comparison, it will naturally be necessary for the persons engaged in such research constantly to be in the manufacturing department, making tests and experiments. Ultimately, the function will suggest a standard method of operation. The manager will doubtless have been in constant touch with the work of the research experts, and will be well aware of the reasons for their recommendations. Nevertheless he may accept or reject them. Rejection will naturally involve the matter being referred for decision to the co-ordinating body between Comparison and Manufacturing. So long as the manager is responsible for the quality of the product, he must hold the last word in the methods of manufacture, except when a superior authority intervenes. Similarly, if he accepts the recommendations, he also accepts responsibility for their correctness. The subsequent carrying out of the standard method of operation is the responsibility of the manager alone.

It will be clear from the above briefly reviewed instances of functionalization in operation that the relation of the manufacturing to the functional staff is roughly comparable with that relation referred to by Sidney Webb when he describes the concern of the London County Council in the erection of a new bridge. [1] " Out of our deep wisdom," he says, " we decided to build a bridge over the Thames. But we could proceed no further without calling in an engineer. . . . We found we could discuss little more than the colour the bridge was to be painted. Even on that point we consulted artists. . . . After all, in nearly every case, in the last resort, it is the facts that decide, and they can be interpreted only by the men who know the facts."

[1] " The New Spirit in Industry." A lecture by Sidney Webb, LL.B., at Oxford. (April, 1920.)

The London County Council here is comparable to the manufacturing manager ; the engineer and the artist to the functional heads. The manager, like the London County Council, takes the final decision and accepts the responsibility ; the functional heads, like the engineer and artist, put forward schemes based upon the necessary knowledge of the facts. Alike in running the administration of an urban community or of an industrial community, there must be both an ultimate authority and an expert staff. The facts alone, as presented by the experts and considered by the ultimate authority, finally decide the policy.

Yet, it is important to note, in this incident referred to by Mr. Webb, exactly where the London County Council came into the picture. "When I was on the London County Council," he says, "we of the Progressive Party took ourselves very seriously," so apparently they felt that their functions were not merely nominal. On the other hand, if the facts decide, and if only those who interpret them know them, it might be legitimate to ask what exactly the London County Council had to do in the matter. The point is fundamental. It is simply this—that the engineer knew his facts, the artist knew his facts, but neither knew all the facts, whereas the London County Council could gather all the facts from all concerned. The manufacturing manager in an industrial concern is in a similar position. He cannot be an expert in engineering, research, costing, purchasing, labour, planning and selling, but he can obtain the essential facts about each, and marshal those various facts to indicate a successful policy. The engineer will present the engineering facts, the cost accountant the costing facts, the labour manager the labour facts, but none of these has the opportunity of balancing one set of facts against another except the manager for whom each function collects its own facts. We may, therefore, agree with Sidney Webb that exact scientific measurement will transform industry, but we may also add that such measurement will tend to upset what we may call " the administrative balance " unless it be also co-ordinated measurement. Measurement of machine capacity may be scientific within its own sphere, but valueless unless co-ordinated with measurement of human capacity.

Functional management, therefore, holds no guarantee that, without the co-ordination provided by the manufacturing manager, the activities of the various functions will not be mutually conflicting. Only with such co-ordination will they be mutually complementary. Such co-ordination, however, is not an end in itself, but is the necessary basis for that leadership, responsibility for output, and work efficiency which constitute the remaining duties of the manufacturing manager. The two are indeed interdependent ; for efficient leadership, when coupled with efficient co-ordination of efficiently executed functions, is a guarantee of efficient work.

Departmental leadership demands a departmental head. Just as so many functions cannot collectively produce the desired corporate result without co-ordination, so a group of men cannot collectively apply their labour to the common task without leadership. The leadership of a departmental manager is of the same genus as the leadership of the foremen—though of a different order (*vide* Chapter VIII). The one is concerned in immediate supervision, the other in indirect supervision. In speaking of leadership, the terms " manager " and " foreman " are often considered interchangeable. This is clearly erroneous, for, if the proper co-ordination of functions is to be effectively carried out by the manager, it is obvious that his relation to the workers in his department cannot be so immediate or intimate as that of his foremen, who form the direct link between himself and the workers. Functionalization may certainly claim to relieve the foreman, considered as the immediate leader of the workers, from all duties except leadership, but it cannot claim to do this for the departmental manufacturing manager. Any such claim rests upon a lack of definition of the respective spheres of manager and foreman. Certainly, the manager is or should be relieved of a vast amount of detailed work, but in so far as that work is done by others, there is a special call upon him to ensure its effective correlation. This is not leadership in the sense in which a foreman may be said to lead. It is co-ordination of external activities for constructive internal application ; it is correlation of subsidiary activities for leadership in main activities.

The manager then must rely, firstly, upon his own leadership of the foremen and their efficiency as leaders in the shops ; secondly, upon adequate methods for keeping in touch with facts ; thirdly, upon personality. These are the three elements of managerial leadership in a department.

The leadership of foremen differs from the leadership of workers. In the latter case, leadership is largely a question of stimulating interest ; in the former, it is rather a matter of directing interest. The average foreman, in so far as responsibility is given to him, already has an interest in his work. Leadership is necessary to direct that interest into profitable channels. A great deal can be achieved by conferences. " Hermits don't learn leadership," says Mr. Denning. " Employers are, perhaps," writes Mr. B. S. Rowntree, [1] " a little apt to forget the few opportunities a foreman gets of enlarging his ideas on industrial matters. . . . If we do not give him the opportunity to enlarge his ideas, we cannot blame him if he gets into a rut. Nor can we blame him if he fails to grasp the changes which are so rapidly coming over industry." To meet this, he suggests conferences between foremen of different factories. Important as this is, of even greater importance are regular conferences with the manager. The manager must not only stimulate the initiative and broadmindedness of his foremen, but must also win their loyalty, and direct their leadership of the workers in accordance with the ideals of

[1] *The Human Factor in Business.* By B. Seebohm Rowntree. (Longmans, Green & Co., 1921.)

the business. Regular and constant conference upon departmental matters is a *sine qua non* of management. It is the only way in which personal relationships can blossom into mutual respect and friendship.

But the manager must also display the utmost discernment in the selection of his subordinates and in the assessment of their capacities, bestowing praise and blame, encouragement and advice where merited. An essential ingredient of managerial leadership is that rare appreciation of subordinates which tempers praise with judgment, and criticism with inspiration. Important, too, is the capacity for business-like treatment of problems, the giving of judicial and prompt decisions, and the grip of the facts involved in putting that decision into operation. A manager should never ask a foreman to do what he would not do himself ; but if his decision is not only right, but clear and prompt, he should see that its execution is equally effective.

Leadership of foremen, however, does not alone depend upon the relations of foremen and manager. Much may be achieved by a proper organization of the department, and by an open disclosure to the foremen of those facts which concern their work. The foreman whose task is clearly defined, whose duties are succinctly stated, whose field is concisely limited, and whose men are definitely allotted to him, is likely to succeed better than one whose duties are vague, whose scope is uncharted, and whose men are liable to be transferred to other work. It is a maxim of leadership that a leader must have a clearly defined job and be left to do it. But apart from this, the proper grouping of work is stimulating because it introduces a competitive element. Rivalry between foremen, each endeavouring to make his own group the most efficient, is a healthy outcome of sound organizing. It is sound policy, further, to put the foreman in touch with the records of his own and other foremen's work. He should be informed of his section's daily and weekly output, the sectional timekeeping, the waste time on his machines, the sales of his products, etc. These facts should always be available to him in the manager's office, being supplied to it by the various functional departments. The use of graphic charts for this is thoroughly to be recommended.

This combination of conference with the manager, proper organization and adequate information for foremen, will result in effective and inspiring leadership, both of the foremen by the manager and of the workers by the foremen.

The manager, however, must not only direct his foremen, but keep in touch with the essential facts of his department. Naturally, the primary method of achieving this is through d rect contact with the workers and the work. It is impossible for the manager to be in the workrooms from morning to night like his foremen, but he should be there as often as possible. There is a tendency for managers to surround themselves with the sanctity of offices, and live perpetually in them. Functionalization removes nine-tenths of the need for this. Under a functional organization, the manufacturing manager should be free to spend the greater part of his working day actually with his own foremen and the workers, seeing to their training, workmanship, conditions, and morale. There is little hope of a real, throbbing shop-spirit, the spirit of the " team," without personal and constant intimacy between workers, foremen, and manager. Such intimacy, however, should be supplemented by standard machinery for the regular presentation of facts. In this respect, the manager should especially avail himself of the services of the Comparison function. He should be always cognizant of the facts— his output, his costs, his overhead charges, his waste time, the product per worker, the proportion of day-work and piece-work, wages, the amount of material wastage, the proportion of occupied to unoccupied floorspace, the degree of " broken " time, etc. It is the business of the manager to ensure that such facts are forthcoming. He may obtain them either in graphic form, or in the shape of statistical reports. Without them he has no basis for judgment or for the institution of new administrative methods ; he cannot accurately assess whether efficiency is 100 per cent or whether it is only 75 per cent ; he cannot trace leakage or suggest improvements. Facts alone determine what is to be done and how it shall be done ; and constantly to be faced with the facts is the royal road to efficiency. Acquaintance with such facts, together with his own personal observations as he goes round the shop, and his own intimacy with the calibre of his workers and the technique of their work, will place the manager in an unassailable position.

Finally, the manager needs personality. Without it, his leadership of the foremen, and his intimacy with the workers cannot create the enthusiasm, confidence, vigour, and cheerfulness which form the basis of smooth-running production. The personality of the manager should be one which foremen will aspire to emulate. We select our foremen largely to make of them managers ; and the manager's characteristics are those of the successful foreman—initiative and broadmindedness. This point is elaborated in Chapter VIII, in discussing the qualifications for foremanship. Perhaps that which becomes increasingly essential, as the foreman rises to be manager, is the capacity for working with, over, and under other men. Functionalization presumes good managers, and especially managers with tact. It takes for granted that there are no rough corners or sharp edges. Under the " departmental " form of organization, the manager works by himself ; under the functional form, in conjunction with others. It is the difference between autocratic and bureaucratic working. The danger of all bureaucracies is that its members may fall out among themselves. That is the danger of functionalization. It is therefore supremely necessary that both functional heads and manufacturing managers shall be men of no petty personal prejudices. " They must be

' big ' men—not only ' big ' to command, but ' big ' to
understand, ' big ' to study the science of their management,
' big ' to grip and kindle the spirit of their men, ' big ' to
inspire by the sheer leadership of personality and by the
possession of a trained understanding of all conditions
and movements in the industrial world." [1]   Perhaps this
chapter will have revealed something of what the manager
is called upon to grasp and to do, and something of the
qualities which he will need in contributing his quota to
the business of producing the best goods under the best
conditions in the best way.

[1] " The Immediate Future of Industrial Management."   By
Oliver Sheldon, in *Business Organisation and Management*.
(September, 1920.)

CHAPTER VII

TRAINING FOR INDUSTRIAL MANAGEMENT

SUMMARY

(a) The higher status of Management emphasizes the need for training ; the science grows in the teaching ; the urgent need for more thinking and study ; intricacy of Management has necessitated the formulation of a managerial technique ; the relative values of theory and experience ; functional organizing impossible without training ; need for pooling of knowledge to elaborate a science.

(b) The training of higher executive officers ; their new position in industry ; training by study, the value of University training ; the subjects of training—general education, industrial history, trade technique, economics, scientific management, and ethics.

(c) The training of foremen ; change in foremanship due to functional organizing ; old " Departmental " foremanship is passing ; definition of a foreman ; his primary duty of leadership ; his training, by environment and schooling ; the subjects for training.

(d) The new position of clerical work under the functional form of organization, no longer synonymous with routine ; specialization growing with the development of the Facilitative functions ; new relation to management ; impossibility of " the offices " idea ; importance of selection and training.

WITH the development of every science comes a necessarily higher standard of training in that science. The elaboration of the science of Mechanics raised the standard of training for engineers ; of Medicine, for doctors ; of War, for soldiers. The wider our knowledge, the more difficult is it to acquire. The science of industrial management is developing before our eyes. As it develops, correspondingly higher qualifications are required in those who practise it. A science, further, grows in the teaching. It develops with the dispersion of its data through an increasing number of minds, each of which may contribute fresh data to the common stock. Science is the correlation of proven facts ; it is organized truth. The facts have always existed, but science has converted what is true into what is known. The elements of scientific management have always been present in industry, but we have not known them.   Modern progress is bringing these elements into some ordered and definite form.   Truth is being assimilated, is becoming knowledge.

The amazing diversity of methods of management, and the insularity of the average business render the co-ordination and sifting of the facts a matter of extreme difficulty. Nevertheless, if indeed a science of management is to be evolved, it is essential, firstly, that all concerned in practising management should contribute to the common pool of knowledge, and, secondly, that what is known and established should be widely disseminated.   Only by the more widespread teaching, learning and application of the facts of which we are assured can management eventually come to be practised according to commonly accepted scientific principles.   We cannot continue for ever to drive the vehicle of management in the ruts left in the track of our forefathers.

Mechanical appliances have improved ; the factory has probably grown; the mentality of Labour has advanced. Can we also claim that our practice of management has progressed to the same degree ?   Can we say that the direction of industry has developed in proportion to the responsibility laid upon its leaders ?   If not, is it possible to assess the waste incurred ?   One may deny the possibility that a complete science of management can ever be formulated ; but at least one cannot deny that there is infinite room for study.   The very intricacy of management is the justification for the scientific analysis of its composition. In the past, scientific management has not been so clearly essential ; perseverance, decisive control, and an example of hard work were of more importance.   Later came the stage when the capacity for choosing men was the most vital element in management.   To-day, with the growth in the size and complexity of the average business, the outstanding need has come to be that of a profound knowledge of the principles and practice of what is scientifically the best in management.   " Though it is true," says Professor

Marshall, [1] " that the industrial evolution caused by the advance of technique during the last few decades has been much more rapid than at any other time, yet the leading characteristic of modern advance is its increasing dependence on faculties and aptitudes that need to be developed by patient study, if not by some sort of academic discipline."

This is the new note in management—the need for patient study. The manager is no longer the man with the greatest " drive " ; no longer the bully with the hardest fist ; no longer the opportunist with the keenest intu'tion ; no longer the skilled picker of other men's brains. Such characteristics may serve a purpose, but the prime qualification of the manager of the future will be knowledge, won by study, and applied by that natural ability which study quickens. Management is no longer the simple control of simple processes. We may note but a few modern developments—costing, planning, time-study, psychological selection, scientific research. Knowledge of what each of these involves is essential to management in all its ranks. Ignorance is not only the cause of some of the misguided actions of Labour, but of much managerial inefficiency. It is useless for management to accuse Labour of ignorance of economics whilst it is itself ignorant of its own science. There is, let us be clear, no lack of effort on the part of management in the performance of its tasks, according to its lights, but is management keeping its lamps trimmed and full ?

The present need is for a scientific training of management. No one embarks on a professional career without study and training. The medical man does not pick up his knowledge as he goes along, learning by his mistakes. He does not rely on his experience so much as on the knowledge born of his training and study. He does not ridicule the writers who discuss his science, who publish the results

[1] *Industry and Trade.* By Alfred Marshall. (Macmillan & Co., 1919.)

of their researches, who lead his thoughts into new channels. He does not reject the learning of the Universities. He does not condemn all theorists. He does not operate on the human body without first diagnosing the disease and founding his diagnosis on a knowledge of the facts of medicine and physiology. He is, rather, proud of his learning and of the scientific status of his profession. If management is indeed a science, and if its practice is an art, we must not only elaborate the science, but also provide training in the art. Experience in management, as in every profession, is much, but by no means all—and, indeed, it counts for little, if it has not been marshalled into some form whereby it acts as both a guide for practice and a sponge for the absorption of new ideas. Experience quickly atrophies, unless it is constantly subjected to analysis and to the challenge of what is new. A little experience is apt to act as a bolt on the door of knowledge, closing it fast against the incursions of the novel and the unknown. Even the best of experience—an experience which has collected the gold and rejected the dross, which has gone out of its way to assimilate new facts, which has arranged its knowledge in a serviceable form and has never succumbed to the blight of finality—even this is inadequate. Experience of war has not removed the need for the study of military strategy. Experience and learning indeed travel together, helping each other. New facts not only add to experience, but also to what must in future be studied. Trench warfare has added fresh fields to military science, as costing and industrial psychology have added fresh fields to industrial science. Our soldiers are now studying the one ; are our managers studying the other ? Satisfaction with past experience led our army in 1914 to the brink of ruin. Management is confronted with its industrial Gallipoli to-day.

There are two necessary preliminaries to training— definition of those to be taught, and definition of what they are to learn. We must, in fact, define exactly what constitutes management, and what management is called upon to do.

Management may be said to be composed of those officers in a business whose duties involve the control of others or assistance in such control. This certainly includes all grades of foremen. There is an inclination to regard the foremen as distinct from the management. The distinction is invidious—as we shall see later. As regards the definition of what management is called upon to do, it is clearly of little avail to train management or expect management to train itself, if its functions are not determined. Yet the elaboration of the science and the training in that science may advance together. Sound factory organizing must accompany scientific training. Training for management is, in part, general, but it is also largely concerned in the particular branch of management for which the individual under training is destined or in which he is occupied. It is, therefore, clearly useless to train individuals for particular positions which will not be perpetuated. Indeed the training of the next generation of managers is of greater importance than that of the present generation. It is vital, therefore, that such training should be devoted to preparing individuals for the positions which they will actually be called upon to fill, not the positions which the illogical groupings of to-day have brought about. "What we are looking for," said Mr. F. W. Taylor, "is the ready-made, competent man whom someone else has trained. It is only when we fully realize that our duty, as well as our opportunity, lies in systematically co-operating to train and make this competent man, instead of hunting for a man whom somebody else has trained, that we shall be on the road to national efficiency."

Functional management is, indeed, almost impossible without training of both a general and a vocational character. We have already seen the new demand it makes upon executive officers. The functional officers require a highly specialized and technical ability which cannot be picked up by the haphazard methods of the past. The manufacturing executives become the focus of many functional converging activities, which must be fully appreciated if their work is to run smoothly. Functional management makes a great demand upon technique of an administrative nature, and upon co-operation between executives. Two men cannot work together unless they have a common objective and each knows what the other is trying to accomplish. This knowledge is largely to be acquired by training.

Finally, having determined what constitutes the management, and having so perfected organization that the end of the more specialized training is clearly in view, it remains only to ensure that the knowledge acquired by training is true, and is so presented that it can be easily assimilated. The science of management has at present none of the definite features of Medicine or Law. It is chaotic ; it has no accepted text-books or principles. It has no accepted ideals, no proven methods. Every factory makes its own stumbling experiments in management and, often enough, endeavours to keep its methods secret. If industrial management is to be raised to a standing more appropriate to its responsibilities, we must share our knowledge, publish our discoveries, and co-operate in our researches. Industry is at present too insular to allow of the formation of a science based on comprehensive data. Training, therefore, must for the present largely remain the endeavour of each separate concern, and must inculcate what that concern, after due research and study, considers to be the best knowledge. It might even be wise, therefore, to appoint some officer, whose business it would be to see that administrative officers study along the right lines. He would maintain a library of managerial literature, sift the constant output of pamphlets and books, obtain detailed statements from the present staff of any developments in their work, organize conferences, lectures, and study-circles, and ensure that the best information was made available for executive officers. America is ahead of us in this respect ; the training of staff there is a matter of primary importance.

America also leads us in the sharing of knowledge. The Institute of Mechanical Engineers, the Harvard School of Business Practice, and the Taylor Society, together with the American Universities responsible for courses of instruction in Business Administration, and other bodies, are rapidly collecting in a convenient form the data upon which a concrete science may be erected. Over here, we are making a beginning. Such bodies as the Institute of Industrial Administration, the London School of Economics, the Manchester College of Technology, and various trade federations, are contributing to the common end. Such efforts merit support. We should encourage students to attend the classes ; we should study their publications, and assist in their efforts to arrive at standards. We should also pool our experiences. In framing a science of management there is no room for competition. The competition should mainly come in the art of applying that science.

The training of different grades of executive officers is bound to be somewhat different. We may therefore divide our remarks into two main sections, the first dealing with the training of higher executive officers, the second with training for foremanship.

The problems which to-day confront managing directors, works managers, and heads of departments, are vastly different from those of even a decade ago. Labour, the war, science, foreign competition, and developments in government have combined to alter the whole position of the higher managerial staff. Where formerly each factory was a practically self-contained unit, there are now constant relations with trade unions, trade boards, industrial councils, employers' federations, government offices, scientific societies, local municipal bodies, and other comparable firms even in other industries. Where formerly

British industry stood pre-eminent, it is now challenged
on every side.   Where formerly the public knew next to
nothing of industry, there is now a general eagerness to
know and to criticize.   Where once the workers were but
poorly organized, now the vast majority are in strong,
national organizations.   " The negotiations an industrial
administrator has to carry out," said Mr. B. S. Rowntree
recently, " are, I imagine, on a larger scale than those which
are carried out by the Government of Luxembourg, and
almost on as large a scale as if he were administering a
country like Belgium or Holland."   Clumsy administration, where such responsibility is involved, is hardly to be
tolerated.   We certainly cannot tolerate administration
which has not developed with at least the same rapidity
and to a similar extent as the labour it controls and the
sciences it employs.   Management, in its higher grades,
has frankly to ask itself whether it is fit for the job.   It
must honestly question its ideals, its aims, its methods and
its capacity.   It must compare in all honesty the growth
of its responsibility with the growth of its ability.   Has it
attempted, viewed broadly as a governing body in industry,
to lift itself to a higher degree of efficiency, to define its
ideals and aims, to acquire the necessary equipment in
character, mentality and knowledge to meet adequately
the problems of this present stage of industrial evolution ?
We grumble much about the faulty workmanship and small
output of the worker.   Is such waste comparable with the
waste due to inadequate costing, slipshod organizing, lack
of technical research, unimaginative leadership, poor
salesmanship, and absence of ideas and ideals ?   Would
not a portrayal of the management of to-day too often
give us a picture of a management feverishly endeavouring
to circumvent the manoeuvres of Labour ;   desperately
rallying round the earth-works of prehistoric methods ;
nervously trying this and that palliative ;   hysterically,
in Press and on platform, imploring the community to view
in horror the painful features of its dilemma ;   stubbornly

clinging to formulae and catchwords, as if salvation lay in a dogma ; longingly casting eyes across the Atlantic, and finding little relief ?   Does not this show that, though awaking from its sleep, it has yet to develop its capacity and formulate its faith, knowledge and ideals ?

As members of the higher ranks of management, what steps can we take to win knowledge and apply it, and to give to the next generation the incentive to improve upon our legacy ?   For many of us, study is a thing of the past. If we can keep abreast with the newspapers, we are satisfied.   We have almost lost the habit of concentrated study.   We cannot start again at Universities.   What can we do ?   We must read.   We must attend lectures, and organize them in our own factories.   We must mix with other executives in other establishments, and with the increasing number of individuals who, both from a theoretical and from a practical point of view, are bringing high intelligence to bear upon industry from outside.   We must visit other factories, note their methods, exchange experiences, and discuss mutual problems.   We must have conferences with the more intelligent of our workers, discuss difficulties with our foremen, listen to the views of thinkers on the future of industry, particularly when those views may appear wholly opposed to our own.   We must, first, appreciate our needs and the penalties of incapacity ; then, cultivate the inquiring and the acquisitive mind. We must never rest content that we know enough.   We need less unconsidered action, more truly constructive thought.   We are too fettered with the shackles of routine. We must break away and devote a part of each day to studying and theorizing.   We have filled our diaries too full ; we must get away from the factory and view ourselves from outside.   We must allow for thought in our form of organization.   We must make more room for research and inquiry, and allow ourselves more time to digest the results of research.   So long as the horizon of our world is the job of to-morrow, so long will our progress be spasmodic, beset with strife and unillumined by vision. Our ignorance has been the result rather of lack of opportunity than of willingness to learn. We must make that opportunity for ourselves.

For those who are likely to follow us, we must provide for and insist upon the finest possible training. The old prejudice against the University man—often not without some justification—must go. We must realize that both the Universities and their graduates have changed. An increasing number of University men are finding their way into and making their way in industry.[1] A still larger number are studying industrial problems from outside. Is it not a significant criticism of management that so many of them are identified with the cause of Labour? Most of our Universities are beginning to cater for students of industrial management. The ideal training is probably a combination of practical experience and theoretical study. Two years of University training should immediately follow school life : a third year should be occupied in practical working experience in the factory ; a fourth year should be a final course at the University again. Older individuals would do well, if possible, to secure one year of concentrated University training. It is to be hoped that all our Universities will soon make provision for such students to study in what time they can.[2]

What are the subjects to be learnt—whether at the University or by one's own study and choice of opportunities ?

It is impossible, in the first instance, to overstate the value of a general education, not so much for the knowledge which it gives the student, as for the " open mind " which it engenders. Naturally, training depends

---

[1] In 1920, 108 business firms were supplied with graduates of Cambridge University by the University Appointments Board, says *Business Organisation and Management* for January, 1922.

[2] This idea is advocated by the late Mr. St. John Heath in a lecture at the Manchester College of Technology. (*Lectures on Industrial Administration*, 1919.)

on the individual.   " Training will always have the greatest effect upon the more or less average man, who has some capacity for his subjects, but who can, by training, learn how to use this capacity to its fullest effect." [1]

General capacity is primarily enlarged by general education. The method of such education is of more importance than the subject. The important point is that the student should be enabled to use his brain more fully in observation, in reasoning, in drawing conclusions from given facts, in balancing the pros and cons of an argument, and in seizing on the vital points of strength or weakness in any situation.   It is relatively of little importance whether a man has studied languages or mathematics. What matters is that he should strengthen his adaptability, resource, mental balance and initiative, in the course of his studies.

Upon the basis of general education should be established a course of training in the subjects immediately concerned with management.   Some technical training, according to the character of the factory product, is necessary for those managers directly in charge of manufacturing ; but such technique becomes of less moment the further the individual is removed from the actual control of processes, and, simultaneously, the greater becomes the need for managerial technique.   It is only of secondary importance for the Employment Manager or the Transport Manager to know the technique of biscuit-making, for instance, but it is of primary importance to know respectively the technique of labour management and traffic management. The more the science of management is elaborated, the clearer does it become that its technique is wholly distinguishable from the technique of any particular factory. It is important, therefore, that in our training of executive officers, we should realize that the peculiar processes of our particular factory are among the less important things that they should study.

[1] The late Mr. St. John Heath.

Four subjects are suggested as being essential parts of any curriculum, whether undertaken by the voluntary effort of individuals, or as part of a standard course. These subjects are: (a) Industrial History, (b) Economics, (c) Business Ethics, (d) The Science of Management. Industrial History, especially that of the last century, is necessary to place the present in the right focus. History can never act as an infallible guide for the present. Historical analogy is no proof. Every problem has peculiar features which demand that it shall be treated on its merits. But history gives the necessary background and places events in their true perspective. It gives proportion and a sense of relative values. It shows the forces which have fostered the growth of what to-day are problems. Trade Unionism, for instance, is not a phenomenon of this generation to be regarded as a singular excrescence of the times. Only by a study of its past can its present position be comprehended. The history of the building trade, again, is the key to that trade's attitude to-day. Management, without a broad knowledge of industrial history, is apt to be impressed only by the vivid colours of the present.

The study of Economics is, again, essential both in the abstract and as applied in the activities of modern industry and commerce. Every day of every week the directors and managers of factories are discussing problems, singularly reminiscent of lecture-rooms and colleges. Questions of demand, of price, of wages are discussed in the same way as in the text-books. Indirectly, economic principles are everywhere being considered in connection with welfare work, Whitley Councils, wage systems, questions of output and cost. Adam Smith on the division of labour, Malthus on population, Ricardo on rent, Mill on value, and Jevons on statistics, all find their modern and often unconscious exponents in the council rooms and offices of any modern factory. Every discussion of markets, cost of production, price, demand, marginal utility, which precedes every selling campaign, could be lifted to a higher level, were all those concerned in the formation of policy fully grounded in the principles of Economics.

Then, it is very necessary that those engaged in the control and direction of industry should grasp the significance of what we have termed Business Ethics, or, as the late Mr. St. John Heath defines it " the relation of business to human well-being." No better statement of what this subject involves has been written than in the words of the same writer. " In its broadest sense," he says, " it means a study of the relation of wealth and material things to man's spiritual nature, or the question of well-being as contrasted with wealth, and a study of the spiritual aims and ideals of business. It would involve a study of the claim put forward so widely at the present time that the fundamental aim of business is service to the community in supplying those material goods which are necessary for the spiritual life of the nation. It would involve, too, an inquiry into the distinction sometimes drawn between necessary expenditure and luxurious expenditure, and into the relationship of luxury to spiritual well-being. It involves an inquiry into the spiritual ideals put forward in modern times on behalf of Labour, and into the part played by leisure and by education in this spiritual ideal. It would involve a consideration of the question as to whether a business career can be regarded as a vocation in the spiritual sense, and what changes are needed in business structure to enable the sense of vocation to have free play. If by philosophy we mean a persistent and obstinate attempt to understand the meaning of things, then this last subject of study is a branch of philosophy; and if by religion we mean an inquiry into the spiritual value of life, then it may be truly called a branch of religion."

" And in this sense," he continues, " the present writer agrees with those who hold that the study of economics, apart from philosophy, is fraught with danger, and that there can be no real study of the production of wealth without a study of what are the truly valuable things in life." [1]

This is indeed a study of fundamentals—of the philosophy upon which our practice of management is founded. But for those who are engaged in industry seriously to consider its ethical significance is not a mere academic pursuit. It means the formulation of a clear judgment as to the place of industry in the social structure. It means, too, the questioning of the individual purpose, the searching of heart, the weighing of the material against the spiritual, the immediate against the ultimate, which are inevitable for a man who is resolved to justify his own attitude towards industry from the ethical standpoint. As in all fields of human activity, the question arises as to our purpose and end, and the answer lies hidden in our philosophy of life entire. In the framing of that philosophy, however, we are not to be guided by personal inclination or prejudice, but rather by as deep a knowledge as we can attain by dint of wide but yet intensive reading, hard thinking, and honest acceptance of the teaching of experience. Ethics is as essential to management as economics. Together, they furnish it with a coherent philosophy. As our knowledge and thought extend, the clearer becomes the object towards which we, as a body of administrators, must guide industry ; the clearer, too, does it become that the purpose of industry is something infinitely nobler than the mere production of commodities—a purpose so noble as to inform our daily tasks with a new spirit and our efforts with a new zest.

Finally, the manager must apply himself to the study of management itself—the technique of his profession. He must study the theory and practice of Organization ; of Commercial and Industrial Law ; of Banking, Finance and Insurance ; of Costing, Research and Statistics ; of Standards and their application ; of Planning Systems ;

[1] " Training for Industrial Administration." A lecture to the Manchester College of Technology, 1919.

of Factory Lay-out and Location ; of Sales Promotion and Advertising ; of Office Routine ; of Traffic Management ; of Applied Psychology ; of Personnel Management. Naturally, he will specialize upon that branch of management in which he is immediately concerned, but the wider his knowledge of other branches, the more effective will be his service.　Perhaps, more particularly, he will concentrate upon the human factors, since the higher administration of industry is increasingly concerned with relationships, leadership, and co-operation.　He will study wage-systems and profit-sharing schemes, welfare work, the incidence of fatigue and monotony.　He will study the principles governing the relations of Industry and State, Industry and Trade Unionism, and Industry and the Consumer. He will study the problem of hours, the possibilities of democratic control, and the questions of unemployment and of productivity.

Speaking generally, every function of management must be studied, if we are to realize the extent of our responsibility. There is much American thought and experience to be sifted and assimilated.　We must not allow any prejudice against " efficiency " to discourage such study.　We must understand before we criticize, and absorb before we construct, and this implies detailed, impartial, and eager study of all that is best in the practice and theory of management on both sides of the Atlantic.

We may now consider the training necessary for that part of management known as foremanship.

Organizing on functional lines involves a recasting of the duties of a foreman.　As it alters his duties, so it alters his qualifications.　The Taylorian conception of eight foremen of equal status in charge of the shops we may discard as impracticable in British workshops, but the traditional idea of the foreman as the autocrat of his shop must also pass.　We have to find a working compromise between these two conceptions.　Certainly, where the body of management is in constant and daily contact with the workers, that contact must be through the medium of one individual—the foreman. To the workers, the foreman must be the synthesis of management. Yet it is no longer possible to regard him as a pure autocrat. The processes of manufacture have become so technical; the planning of the work is necessarily so detailed; the control of labour is so much a concern of others beside himself that these and other developments make it essential that the foreman should be assisted by qualified experts in the different fields of management. The essence of his new position, therefore, like that of the manager, is co-ordination of functional activities in so far as they affect the rank and file of the shop or department. But where the manager co-ordinates functional activities with a view to the best management of the department, the foreman on the other hand co-ordinates those activities to preserve the single leadership of his workers. His business is to maintain a true balance between the functions, and between them and his leadership, and to act as the representative of all the functions in those activities which directly affect his men. Thus, while his primary duty remains the control of the workers as in the past, it now comes about that to preserve that control he must act as the intermediary between many functions and the workers.

Industrial administration in the past has given far too little thought to the problem of foremanship. It has not attempted to define the actual duties and qualifications of a foreman under the new circumstances of modern management, or to determine the mode of his training and selection, and his relation to the rest of the management. It has not apparently been realized that the old-time foremanship, quite apart from changes in the mentality of the workers, is no longer adequate to interpret the policies and composition of the higher management. Thus, little attempt has been made to train up a differently qualified foremanship to cope with the new conditions.

Every advance in organization involves a reconsideration of what is implied in foremanship. If we introduce a Planning system, a Research organization or a revised Costing or Storekeeping system, for instance, we must consider, as a vital part of the new scheme, what adjustment will be necessary in the duties and position of the foreman. Too often such schemes are initiated without any such consideration, with the result that the foreman is placed in the unenviable position of not knowing where he stands, and the scheme, in consequence, works with difficulty. If in the past too much has been thrust upon the foreman, with the result that the scientific conduct of management has been impossible, it is not clear that new developments, even those of such a character as are intended ultimately to relieve the foreman, will be productive of harmonious management, unless the duties and relations of the foreman are wisely and promptly adjusted to the new developments. It is clearly dangerous for what are called, technically speaking, the higher grades of management, to advance towards scientific efficiency unless foremanship is proceeding at the same pace in the same direction. We are often apt to blame our foremen for acting as stumbling-blocks in the way of the introduction of new methods, when we ourselves are to blame for introducing a fresh scheme without first explaining it to them, gaining their support, and defining their new duties and relationships. One cannot alter the track of a railroad without also altering the points.

That the old foremanship was inadequate requires little demonstration. Mr. H. N. Casson[1] has outlined a foreman's duties under the old form of organization—responsibility for output, discipline, fitting men to jobs, fixing rates, paying his men, discharging the inefficient, giving out work, obtaining materials, setting up jobs, teaching new workers, preventing "soldiering," arranging for

[1] *Factory Efficiency.* By H. N. Casson. (Efficiency Magazine Co.)

repairs, keeping records and statistics, etc., etc. It is the job of an industrial Hercules. The result was that much went undone, while what was done was done unscientifically, much was glossed over and skimped, and much was " camouflaged " for the easy satisfaction of the manager. The most prominent result was, however, that the foreman became three-parts a clerk. He was given an office in which he spent much time at work for which his experience and training had not qualified him, and at which he was often less competent than a junior clerk. He was expected to be a teacher, statistician, psychologist, engineer, technical expert, clerk, and amidst it all, a leader of men. When industry was a matter of sheer effort, tempered neither by science or theory, the best a foreman could do to cope with this medley of duties was probably adequate. But to-day it is quite impossible to carry out such a medley of duties in accordance with the standard of a scientific age. We have all known foremen who have made gallant attempts to fulfil such duties. They were held to be irreplaceable, as indeed they were, for few were the men who could follow in their steps. The British foremen, as a class, are probably the sturdiest element in industry to-day, but they are facing a hopeless future if they continue in the way they have come.

Whilst foremanship continues in the main to be what it always has been, it will fail, because it is the donkey on which management loads all its lumber. The exponents of " Scientific Management " insist that the fallacy in the present methods of management is that everything is " up to the worker," whilst management shirks its true duties. It is at least equally true that too much is " up to the foreman," whilst the remainder of management " travels light." We have expected the finger-tips of management, where contact is made with the workers, to bear both the brains and the body of management. We have seen with delight that our overhead costs, other than oversight, were low, omitting to note that this was possible because our foremen were performing much clerical and administrative work, to the detriment of management, leadership, training, and the shop morale. We viewed with concern the difficulties inherent in the leadership of labour, little realizing that the assumption by the higher management of its legitimate and scientific duties, to the relief of the foremen, would go far to render the task easier. Labour, indeed, is not led from the Board Room. But so long as the foreman is tied to duties which deprive him of the opportunity of real shop leadership, we can only blame ourselves if suspicion and dissatisfaction grow among his men. Loyalty is the fruit of intimacy, and intimacy does not bloom when the foreman is preparing statistics in his office and the workers are left to do as much or as little as they choose.

Just as management is being changed, so foremanship must correspondingly change. It is essential that the changes should be made in a harmonious progression.

We should, therefore, be clear as to the particular grades of the management we mean when speaking of " foremen." As a generic title, the word " foremen " conveys no precise significance. In one factory the foreman may be in immediate charge of a process ; in another, in charge of several processes with other foremen under him ; in another, he may be appointed for certain technical skill, having under him but one or two men ; in another, he may control what is, to all intents and purposes, a department. Here, as throughout all factory activities, we need a standard nomenclature. The root of the trouble lies in unscientific organizing. Because we have not determined duties we cannot determine titles. Despite changes in duties, men are still called " foremen," because they have not the necessary status vaguely attributed to the title of " manager." Such indefiniteness in titles is a visible sign of a chaotic organization. Because " it works " we are satisfied ; but it can only be said to " work," either because our standard of achievement is low, or because our staffs display a capacity for adapting themselves, after long experience, to the needs of a particular business. In the average concern, the newcomer is completely lost ; he takes months to find out exactly who is responsible for certain duties. In fact, it is no exaggeration to say that a considerable part of every official's time is taken up with making discoveries or remedying his own errors with regard to the distribution of duties between individuals. Instead of carrying out his duties, he wastes his time finding out what are the duties of other people, so that he may fit in with them.

The distinguishing feature of the foreman, however, is that he is immediately in charge of the workers. Naturally there are grades of foremen, according to the number of men controlled or the complexity of the work performed, but a very clear distinction can always be drawn between foremen and those other officials who do not exercise direct supervision of the workers. For instance, a store-keeper, an examiner, an inspector or a wage clerk, although his duties may involve his presence in the workroom, is not, in this strict sense, a " foreman."

The duties of a foreman, then, may be summarized as the supervision and leadership of the workers at their work, and the creation of the right atmosphere in the shop. A foreman, however, cannot lead on behalf of an organization which has not the spirit of leadership. The whole management, in one sense, forms a body of leaders, although the foreman alone actually takes the workers in hand and directs them day by day. Too often foremen are engaged in rendering returns, planning work, drawing up specifications, and interviewing applicants for work. This is not foremanship. Foremanship is the supervision of work and the creation of a shop spirit as a result of an invigorating and compelling leadership. Too often these are regarded as incidental to the general business of " running " a shop, section, or workroom. We must, however, convince ourselves that such work is not incidental, but primary.

All the machinery in the world, all the wage incentives that ingenuity can devise, all the working arrangements which efficiency experts can install will not produce that keen, steady and industrious working force which makes a factory alive. Leadership is that great incentive to work and loyalty, which makes men put forth their best endeavour for the sake of something indefinable, which creates a team out of a miscellany of ability, which builds up a collective shop spirit in place of dissatisfaction and suspicion.

Leaders of men come to light as a result of a combination of natural ability and the subsequent development of that ability. The " born leader " has normally contributed more than native genius to his own success. We have our " village Hampdens " in industry, but they remain obscure through lack of effort, opportunity, or training. The gift of leadership requires development in the sphere in which it is to be exercised. Every man born with a spark of leadership will not necessarily make a good foreman. We must determine, therefore, the basic qualities which a foreman should possess.

Technique in the processes of manufacture has tended to occupy too large a place in our estimate of the qualifications for foremanship. The time is passing when the foreman could himself be both a technician and a leader. Industry is becoming daily more technical. The processes of manufacture are becoming the province of engineers and chemists. The foreman, if he is to remain a foreman, cannot compete with the growing complexity and intricacy of technical processes. Mr. T. Gorst, of the Ford Motor Company, has said : " Under the specialized methods of production of this surprising Company it is not vitally necessary that the chargehand should be a skilled exponent of any particular trade in the usually accepted sense of the term."[1] Technical skill is no guarantee of leadership.

[1] " The Selection and Training of Chargehands "—a paper read before the Association for the Scientific Development of Industry, January, 1919, by the Vice-Chairman of the Association, Mr. T. Gorst, of the Ford Motor Company.

The best worker is not by any means necessarily the best leader or the best teacher. In this connection, an intelligent understanding of what is to be done and how it is done is normally adequate.

Prime among the capacities requisite in the foreman is that subtle attribute termed initiative or enterprise—the mind which is always alert, keen and intelligent, eager and contemptuous of difficulties, full of the impetus which " gets things done." It combines self-confidence, dependableness, courage, intelligence, grit, personality and common sense, and welds them all into a compelling, forceful whole. Second to this comes what, for lack of a better word, may be called " broad mindedness "—that capacity which embraces a sense of justice, teachableness, tact, sympathy, understanding of human nature and moral motives, openness of mind and demeanour, and the capacity for working with, over, and under other men. Thirdly, comes the knowledge of administrative technique—the knowledge of economics, of scientific methods of management, of functional organizing and its implications, and of labour management. Lastly, comes practical technical ability, in the form of either manual dexterity or specialized trade knowledge.

Obviously, we are postulating something of a divinity. But it is essential to formulate some ideal to guide us in our selection of foremen. It is important to consider, further, how far the individuals selected are capable of being trained to be more than foremen, and how far we are providing facilities for them to advance.

Where, then, are we to find our ideal foreman ? We may wait for him to come, or we may manufacture him. Unless we adopt the latter alternative, we may wait in vain. In other words, we must train men who possess sufficient general ability and a certain degree of natural aptitude for leadership. The selection of the right men for training is therefore the first step. The manager should note the conspicuous workers in his shop, those who stand out above the rest in intelligence, initiative, reliability, and character. In this, the employment manager should assist.

The actual training of foremen will differ little in essentials from that of higher officials in the management. If our choice of foremen has been wise, we may expect at any rate a proportion of them ultimately to qualify for posts as managers. Their training should, therefore, form a natural stepping-stone to that training we have suggested for the higher officers. First, it should include all those subjects which are conducive to what has been termed broadmindedness. The education of the higher official has normally been such as to induce a broad view of things. The normal education of the foreman has not. His sphere has been limited, and his opportunities have been restricted. Whereas, therefore, training in the technique of management is the first essential for the higher officer, a general widening of outlook is the first essential in the training of foremen. This involves a certain proportion of the training being spent upon general education. But the widening of outlook may be achieved as much by the broad treatment of technical subjects as by the study of subjects in themselves broad. Industrial history is necessary to give an adequate background. History is by far the best subject, properly taught, for the development of judgment, mental balance, and a wide human outlook. Economics again is essential, since ignorance of its main theories is an impassable barrier to a broad industrial viewpoint. Its study, moreover, develops those powers of reasoning, impartial judgment and balancing of arguments, which are the foundation of justice. Psychology must also be taught—not the deeper psychology of the scientist so much as the everyday psychology of factory relationships. We have yet to realize that the mind of the individual, as also the collective mind of many individuals engaged in a common enterprise, presents a profound problem, an abyss upon which little light has as yet been shed. We have far to travel before we can win an understanding of those elements in men which lead them to adopt certain attitudes in certain circumstances, which almost compel them to combine in an unconscious unanimity of sentiment or belief, which provoke their imitative tendencies, which occasion in them certain reactions in response to certain modes of treatment, or which direct their inexplicable movements of temper and emotion. This shop psychology must form the study of the foreman. The mentality of the individual or of the group will respond more surely to the leadership of the foreman gifted with understanding, insight, sympathy, and knowledge, than to the devices of the scientist, the engineer, or the economist. Such foremanship is only to be attained by the fullest comprehension of the " make-up " of individual men and women.

Foremen, further, need to be trained in the spirit of the business. As the representatives in the shop of the whole body of management, it is essential that they should present to the workers the very heart of that for which the whole organization stands. It is vain for directors to be animated by motives which find no reflection in the workrooms. The foremen should know the history of the firm ; be intimate with its products, its methods, and its repute. They should be enabled to take a wider survey than the circumscribed view possible from their own immediate niches in the organization. They should be schooled and encouraged in the pursuit of the ideals and methods which imbue those who direct the business policy. Where the heads of the business are distinguished in their policy by enterprise, by high ethical standards, by a spirit of goodwill, or by an ideal of service, the same qualities should animate the foremen. The atmosphere of the Board Room should be the atmosphere of the shops.

Equally, the foreman needs training in the actual technique of management, both personal and impersonal— the significance of costs, standards and records ; the necessity for planning and control, and their machinery ;

the function of process research ; the principles of rate-setting ; the methods of engaging, maintaining and discharging labour ; the psychology of selection and training ; the importance of health and safety ; and the place of works councils and committees generally.   These are the subjects which will emerge in his dealings with the various functional officials.   These, too, are the subjects, a knowledge of which forms the roadway to high positions of responsibility.

Finally, the foreman must formulate a philosophy of his task.   He must determine whether to regard it as a generous effort in the service of his fellows, or as a self-seeking domination.   He must consider his motives, and question himself as to how far he carries them into effect in the daily round of business.   He must, for the fundamental satisfaction of his best self, find an ethical basis for his work.   Every foreman should be encouraged to regard his foremanship as a great piece of public service. The workers under him are committed to his charge as a public trustee.   Each worker is a mine of infinite potentiality, the exploration of which has been entrusted to him. He stands in the midst of his fellows, charged with the direction of their well-being and the application of their efforts.   If foremanship is to be great, it must rise above the petty difficulties and advantages of power, and devote itself wholeheartedly to leading manfully and controlling strongly in the spirit of a great responsibility.

The development of an ideal foreman, however, is not entirely in his own hands.   It requires some consideration on the part of the higher grades of management.   Management, as a body, has been slow in treating foremen as members of its own corporation.   Many a conscientious firm has pursued an admirable labour policy, but has neglected its foremen.   It has not offered them the advantages of the workers, nor has it incorporated them clearly in the ranks of management.   The foreman is an integral part of the management, and the full recognition of this fact is the first step in his development. Every opportunity should be taken to hold conferences with the foremen on matters of departmental policy, and they in turn should be encouraged to hold periodical conferences amongst themselves. The free intercourse which social functions permit should be fostered. We constantly need to meet our foremen at clubs and meetings, to join with them in sports, pursuits and hobbies. We should help them to speak out at meetings with the workers, discuss the agenda of works councils with them, and, in general, formulate a managerial attitude, in which they concur, to such problems as arise.

Then, we should institute specific courses of training. The expenditure will be well repaid of appointing a broadminded and well-educated man to assist foremen in training. He would institute study and discussion clubs, lectures, debates and public meetings. He would arrange classes in the subjects already suggested—both in and out of factory hours, teaching himself and obtaining assistance from qualified members of the staff. He would encourage each foreman to speak upon his own subject to his fellows. He would set up a friendly rivalry between the classes. He would arrange visits for classes to other firms, to exhibitions or places of interest. He would foster self-expression by writing and speaking. He would circulate summaries of lectures, lists of books to read, and extracts from current industrial and economic journals. He would institute classes both for men qualifying to be foremen and for those who have already been appointed. He would make recommendations as to the most suitable candidates, and report upon their individual capacities. In his training, he would divide the men into " study-groups," according to grades, departments, interests, temperaments, or abilities. He would limit his groups to, perhaps, a dozen, and arrange for " group-leaders." Each group would conduct its own studies under his direction ; it would go its own outings and trips ; it would meet regularly and discuss its subject in a friendly circle ;

it would read books aloud or arrange for members to read books between meetings.   Such an intimate form of training is more necessary for foremen already appointed than for candidates for foremanship.   Most of the former will be men past their youth, with a natural antipathy to a revival of schooling.   They will only respond to friendliness and " fire-side " education ;   stereotyped classes, in an atmosphere of the schoolroom, will not succeed.   It is important, also, that it should be widely known that such training has the support of the higher management.   This will be ensured if it is related to selection and promotion—not by examinations, but by the foreman's own interest, keenness and initiative as displayed in the course of the training.[1]

It is clear that modern industry cannot be conducted efficiently without enlightened foremanship.   However efficient our higher administration may be, the results must be largely negatived unless, at those points where management comes into immediate and constant touch with the workers, the foreman, representing it as a whole, is conversant both with the policy and methods of the higher management and with the mentality of the workers. The proper training of foremen and the establishment of foremanship in its proper place in the factory organization are essential parts of any efforts to render industry both more efficient and more stable.

Together with the training of higher administrative officers and of foremen, it will be well to consider the

[1] The reader is referred to the following examples of training schemes for foremen—

(a) *Personnel Administration*.   By Ordway Tead and H. C. Metcalf, Ph.D. ;   Chapter XII.   (McGraw Hill Book Co., 1920.)

(b) Federal Board for Vocational Education.   Foremen Training Courses.   Bulletin 36.   Trade and Industrial Series.   No. 7. (Washington, Gov't. Print. Off., 1920.)

(c) " The Foreman and His Development."   By C. W. Clark. (*Industrial Management*, August, 1920.)   Also " Qualifications for Foremanship."   By C. W. Clark.   (*Industrial Management*, March, 1920.)

(d) " A Plan for a Foremen's Development Course."   Adopted by the International Harvester Company.   (Chicago, 1920.)

training and position of the clerk in industry.[1] Industry
has always had a suspicion of the clerk. To the factory
worker, he is always something of a parasite ; to the
administrator, something of an inevitable nuisance.
Clinging to the skirts of management, yet shackled with
the bonds of labour, the routine clerk is neglected by both.
He falls between two stools and is trodden upon by those
who sit on them. For a thousand books and articles dealing
with labour in the factory there are but one or two treating
of labour in the offices. Yet a rough estimate would suggest that in industries engaged in the production of small
goods such as articles of food, 10 per cent of the personnel
are engaged on clerical work, exclusive of managers,
secretaries, etc., and that, even in concerns manufacturing
large goods such as locomotives and motors, the percentage
of clerical labour is from 4 to 6 per cent. We cannot
longer afford to disregard this partner in industry.

This subject is naturally appended to a chapter dealing
with the training and qualifications necessary for industrial
management, since it is tolerably certain that efficiency in
management in the future is bound to entail not only more
clerical work but clerical work of a higher order. We shall
be compelled to revise our views as to the proportion of
clerical to manual work. Mr. F. E. Cardullo wrote some
years ago : " A new attitude in regard to the employment
of indirect labour is a pre-requisite to greater efficiency in
many of our shops." There is no virtue in a low indirect
labour cost if the shop efficiency is thereby impaired, nor
in boasting of a low clerical cost if our foremen and managers are withheld from their true functions by devoting
themselves to clerical work outside their province. The
development of functional forms of organization is already
proving the need for both a greater volume and a higher

[1] The notes which follow upon the position of the clerk in
industry are based upon, and, in places, repeat the wording of a
series of articles by the present author, published in *The Organiser*
(March to September, 1920), to which journal the author now
wishes to make his acknowledgments.

standard of clerical work. The functions of Planning and Comparison are largely clerical in character, whilst those of Design, Equipment, Labour and Transport involve a greater proportion of clerical work than we have previously imagined. To realize the truth of this statement, we need only consider the increasing use of statistics, records and charts, and the increasing complexity of wage calculations, data for planning, records for employment work, standard practices for manufacturing, and calculations for costing.

It is obvious, therefore, that, in view of new developments, a fresh significance must be given to the terms " clerk," and " clerical work," and the generic title of " the offices." Routine clerical work is becoming to a growing extent a matter for machines and women—for women, not because of any inherent inferiority in capacity, but rather because their normal term of service to industry ends about the age of 24 or 25. The work which the male clerk is now being called upon to cover is on a higher plane. The day of the so-called " desk-hand " is passing, as his work becomes more specialized and even professional. The Costing and Planning clerks are clearly engaged in occupations calling for more than routine ability. With the development of the Facilitative functions, clerical work is rapidly becoming the stepping-stone to positions in the management—not the management of the manufacturing departments, but of the functional activities supplementary to manufacturing. Modern developments indeed indicate that, at a guess, some 50 per cent of the managerial positions in the industry of the future will need to be filled by men trained and qualified in various branches —statistical, analytical, investigational, and co-ordinative —of clerical work. This tendency places clerical work in a new light. It involves for the clerk the obligation to regard his work as professional, and to make those sacrifices for study which every professional man in his youth must make, in order to equip himself for his task. It involves for the employer, the obligation to furnish the means, the opportunity and the incentive for such equipment, and, later, to provide the positions, responsibility, and remuneration for those clerks, who, by their sacrifices and assiduity, have qualified themselves to undertake this new managerial type of work.

We are still somewhat hide-bound by the old idea conveyed in the term " the offices." It is now misleading. The distinction between offices and factory is false, since the two, in the light of recent progress, are clearly intertwined. There is no common bond between clerks engaged in costing, planning or statistical work, and clerks engaged upon ledger work, order correspondence and invoicing. In terms of work they are poles apart. We must, therefore, look to the functionalization of office work—the Planning clerks under the Planning function, the Costing clerks under the Comparison function, the Ledger clerks under the Selling function, the Cash clerks under the Finance function, the Wages clerks under the Labour function, the Purchasing clerks under the Design function. The old conception of Office Manager cannot much longer persist. Each function will come to be responsible for its own clerical work ; otherwise, functionalization falls to the ground, since clearly some of the functions are almost wholly clerical in character. The future of the clerk lies in the direction of the more recent functional developments. The commercial clerk will find his work increasingly encroached upon by mechanical devices and female clerks. The majority of the male clerks of the future will be found in the Costing Department, the Employment Department, the Planning Department, the Traffic Department, etc.

We must realize, therefore, that the selection and training of clerks is intimately related to the success of our management methods. The future personnel of management, apart from the direct management of the manufacturing departments, will be drawn from two main sources—firstly, the technical universities, for the more technical functional activities such as research, and, secondly, from the new type of clerical staff, for the more statistical and co-ordinative sides of functional work such as planning and comparison. Selection in the future should, therefore, include some form of examination relative, as in the Civil Service, to the standards of education normally achieved at the various ages of leaving school and university—not alone the stereotyped examination in history, geography, English and mathematics, but a thorough survey of the candidate's business capacity, sense of orderly work, initiative, and power of application of practical ideas. It is conceivable even that, were the clerks highly organized in a professional association with a high conception and intelligent prevision of what clerical work should be, they themselves might institute a qualifying test for their own profession.

The training of the clerk, again, assumes a new aspect under modern conditions. We need an apprenticeship system for clerical work based upon some definite grading of clerks. We must make provision not only for allowing and encouraging clerks to take the courses in Costing and other subjects which are provided by several Universities and Correspondence Colleges, but also for training them in the factory itself. The emphasis laid upon training in the Civil Service is well worthy of note. The grading arranged by the Joint Committee in 1920[1] allows for a Training Grade, prior to the taking of positions in the Executive Class, for which it is laid down that officers " during the term of their employment in this grade should be given the widest possible training in all branches of the work of the department or branch to which they are assigned." The Administrative Class, again, is preceded by what is known as the Cadet Corps, from the personnel of which, after training, selection is made for the higher administrative posts. In industry, we need some similar system. If our clerks are to occupy

[1] Civil Service National Whitley Council : Report of the Joint Committee on the Organization, etc., of the Civil Service, 1920. (H.M. Stationery Office.)

important functional positions in the future, we must give them opportunity, not only of qualifying themselves generally, but also of gaining experience in many branches of the work. We may well apply to industrial purposes the " central pooling arrangement " advocated in this same Civil Service Report. The object of this " pool " is to make provision for those members of the Clerical Class who, though fit for admission to the Executive Class, can find no opening within their own department. This fluidity between departments is as necessary in industry as in the Government service.

In this connection, both for training and for the movement of personnel, the existence at the head of the educational system of the factory of an enlightened and far-seeing administrator, who realizes the extent to which his system of training can affect the whole management of the business in the future, is an invaluable asset. Next to the training of foremen, the training of clerks of the new order will be his most important task. The training of the clerk, indeed, so that he may take his legitimate position in the ranks of the highly developed system of management which is growing before our eyes, is a necessary and practical recognition of tendencies in industry which promise to make a highly trained and broadly educated staff indispensable to efficient administration.

CHAPTER VIII

IN a book of this character, it is not intended to analyse and weigh up the various schemes promulgated for the moulding of industry, either by means revolutionary or evolutionary, into a form fundamentally different from the shape it assumes at present. In any event, all such schemes must necessarily be largely manufactured of the tissue of dreams, since, though in some cases they may be based squarely enough upon the facts of to-day, they cannot by any conceivable means take adequately into account the circumstances and the influences which will affect our kaleidoscopic society as it moves forward towards the dawns of days to come. He who sets himself either to design a future form of industry or to conjure up a vision of what industry may yet become, faces a problem not of logical construction or of scientific planning, but of continual adjustment and adaptation to circumstances which cannot be foretold. The value of such schemes is rather that they may trace the outline of our ideals, and thus mayhap can guide our progress. But that our progress will lead us to any prefigured land of promise is as improbable as the existence of Utopia itself.

Therefore, though the thoughts of the more daring and speculative may fare ahead of the times, to set before us social systems wherein our present ills have vanished, the thoughts of others, who offer gifts of no less value to future generations, may well, whilst accepting the criticism of being opportunistic, take only into consideration the immediate tendencies in the area where forecasts bear some chance of realization. For such as these, the analysis of the present provides as large a scope as the uncharted future offers to others.

The present form of industry is determined, in a broad sense, by the interplay of forces and tendencies, both within and without industry. The main forces, outside industry, which to-day appear to be exercising the greatest effect upon the evolution of the industrial structure, may be summarized as, firstly, the action of the State, viewed not as the whole of organized society, but as one of several forms of social organization ; secondly, the attitude of the general public in the capacity of consumers and critics ; thirdly, education ; fourthly, foreign competition and foreign trade conditions ; and fifthly, finance. The main forces affecting industry from within are, firstly, the position and progress of Labour ; secondly, the progress of science in management, organization and manufacturing technique.

With none of these are we immediately concerned, save one—the progress of science in management and organization. In management we have the one stable element in our process of evolution. Whether the State continues increasingly to circumscribe the activities of industry, or leaves it to shoulder its own way into the future ; whether foreign competition overwhelms us or compels us radically to reconstruct the form of our industry ; whether the consciousness, on the part of society, of its responsibility for those who toil for it develops, as education proceeds, or becomes less insistent as industry grows more complex ; whether, indeed, the means of production come to be owned by the State or continue in the hands of private Capital— no matter what the changes, management as a function remains constant. There is no conceivable structure of industry—whether we take the self-governing and self-ownership conception of Syndicalism, the State ownership and Government management of State Socialism, the Guild management and State ownership of Guild Socialism, or the Soviet system as exemplified in Russia to-day—there is no structure where management does not fulfil approximately the same functions as under the present system in this country. Every scheme for the reconstruction of industry is concerned primarily with the ownership of the means of production and, only as incidental to that, with the management of industry.   Whether the managers of the factories are appointed, as on the Soviet model, by the Minister or local representative of the " Supreme Council of Political Economy "; or, as visualized by the Guild Socialists, by a National Guild composed of representatives of all those engaged, whether on manual, technical or intellectual work, in the particular industry; or, as under our present system, by the acting representatives of the private capitalistic owners, will not materially affect the duties they have to perform.   Each system will, of course, occasion different relations between management and labour, management and ownership, management and State, management and the organized consumers, but the functions of management will remain much the same under each régime.   Efficiency engineers will still be necessary, whether State, Guild or Syndicalist Committee is in supreme command.   Management is as inherent in the composition of industry as Labour.   By virtue of its functions, moreover, it is that element in industry which, whatever changes may come, will be charged with the piloting of the ship through the waters of change. A firmly established body of management, therefore, is the greatest safeguard against disruptive change.

Looking immediately ahead, the two major forces making for change, with which management has to deal, are Labour and Science.   The greater the changes these forces portend, the greater the responsibility of management for the safe pilotage of the vessel.   The activities of these two forces indicate most surely that the sea which has to be traversed in the years ahead will be far from placid.   Labour, viewed either as an organized entity or as a heaving, throbbing movement of the times, is wedded to progress. Chafing at the restrictions of economic logic, it grounds its faith upon a profound moral reconstruction of society. It steps forward into the future, deeply assured that, despite the abstractions of economists, statisticians and politicians, the days to come will witness a revision of the ethical principles of our social order. It is convinced by neither argument nor experience. It clings to its faith in a new world of justice ; it thinks upon the moral plane. It trusts to progress, primarily and fundamentally, not because progress means more material advantages and a wider and higher field for human intelligence, but rather because it promises a state of society in which the principles governing the form and conduct of society shall be founded upon neither expediency nor force but upon what is morally right. Amid the whirling of widely divergent movements and manifold philosophies, its ultimate goal is clearly established. Its discontent is neither of mind nor of body, but of spirit. It demands a constant impulse to go forward, it resents every setback and hindrance.

Science is similarly imbued with the forward-looking mind. It subjects every established precedent to dispassionate research. It is continually amending our methods both of manufacture and of management. It impels us to a higher and still higher standard of efficiency. It installs method in the place of chaos, laws in the place of " rule-of-thumb," knowledge in the place of ignorance. It sifts our experience, analyses our practices, and puts to new purpose our energies. It devises machines for our manual work, new methods for our procedure in management, new forms of our organization. It experiments, compares, tests, standardizes, organizes and re-builds. It regards no standard as final, no method as ideal, no sphere as sacred. It applies its analytical process to both the things and the men of production. Without partiality, it marshals facts, discovers principles, and unhesitatingly applies them. It improves quality, decreases cost, designs products, and effects economies. It holds efficiency to be not the negative virtue of eliminating what is wasteful, but the positive virtue of building up what is the best. In its own sphere, it spells as great an era of change and progress as does the restless mentality of Labour in the sphere of human relations. Neither is content with the *status quo* ; both insist upon growth and renovation.

As for the forces outside industry, a greater exercise of regulatory activity by the State, a greater concern on the part of all grades of the community in the conduct of industry, a steady uplift of the general intelligence, a more menacing assault upon our industrial supremacy as a nation, and a greater complication, or, alternatively, prodigious disruption of the powers of finance—these, in their effect upon industry, promise at least no stagnation, no respite from the strain of progressive change.

Amid the waters, blown stormy by the blast of all these forces, management stands at the helm of industry. Labour may bring about a change in its composition and relations ; Science in its methods and materials, but neither can change its functions. The man at the wheel may be replaced, may be put under a new authority, may be regarded differently by the crew, and may work with different instruments in a different way, but the functions performed remain constant, essential under every conceivable circumstance. It is important, therefore, that we should devise a philosophy of management, a code of principles, scientifically determined and generally accepted, to act as a guide, by reason of its foundation upon ultimate things, for the daily practice of the profession. The adoption of this or that principle in this or that plant will avail but little. Management must link up all its practitioners into one body, pursuing a common end, conscious of a common purpose, actuated by a common motive, adhering to a corporate creed, governed by common laws of practice, sharing a common fund of knowledge. Without this not only have we no guarantee of efficiency, no hope of concerted effort, but also no assurance of stability.

It may be a fitting conclusion, therefore, to state as concisely as possible a suggested codification of such a philosophy, not with any hope that it will be adopted as it stands, but rather that it may form a concrete beginning, in the criticism and explanation, elaboration and amendment of which some acceptable creed may be ultimately arrived at which shall govern the practice of management in the future.

A PHILOSOPHY OF INDUSTRIAL MANAGEMENT

I

Industry exists to provide the commodities and services which are necessary for the good life of the community, in whatever volume they are required. These commodities and services must be furnished at the lowest prices compatible with an adequate standard of quality, and distributed in such a way as directly or indirectly to promote the highest ends of the community.

II

Industrial management, in a broad sense, is the function, practised by whatever persons or classes, responsible for the direction of industry to the above end. It must, therefore, be governed by certain principles inherent in the motive of service to the community.

Such principles are—

Firstly, that the policies, conditions, and methods of industry shall conduce to communal well-being. It is therefore part of the task of management to value such policies, conditions, and methods, by an ethical measure.

Secondly, that, in this ethical valuation, management shall endeavour to interpret the highest moral sanction of the community as a whole, as distinct from any sanction resting upon group or class interests, or, in other words, shall attempt to give practical effect to those ideals of social justice which would generally be accepted by the most unbiased portion of communal opinion.

Thirdly, that, though the community, expressing itself through some representative organization, is, consequently, the ultimate authority in the determination of such matters as legitimate wages and profits, it is for management, as an integral and a highly trained part of the community, to take the initiative, so far as possible within its own sphere, in raising the general ethical standard and conception of social justice.

III

Management, as a comprehensive division of industry, is to be distinguished on the one hand from Capital, and, on the other hand, from Labour. It is divisible into three main parts—

ADMINISTRATION, which is concerned in the determination of corporate policy, the co-ordination of finance, production and distribution, the settlement of the compass of the organization, and the ultimate control ofthe executive;

MANAGEMENT proper, which is concerned in the execution of policy, within the limits set up by Administration, and the employment of the organization for the particular objects set before it ; and

ORGANIZATION, which is the process of so combining the work which individuals or groups have to perform with the faculties necessary for its execution that the duties, so formed, provide the best channels for the efficient, systematic, positive and co-ordinated application of effort.

IV

It is for Management, while maintaining industry upon an economic basis, to achieve the object for which it exists by the development of efficiency—both personal or human efficiency, in the workers, in the managerial staff, and in the relations between the two, and impersonal efficiency, in the methods and material conditions of the factory.

V

Such efficiency is, in general, to be developed by Management—

Firstly, through the treatment of all features in every

field of industry by the scientific method of analysis and the synthetical use of established knowledge, with the object of determining standards of operative and managerial practice ; the application of the accepted sciences to those features of industry to which they are applicable ; and the gradual formation and subsequent elaboration of a science of management, as distinct from those accepted sciences which, in practice, it employs ; and

Secondly, through the development of the human potentialities of all those who serve industry, in a co-operation consequent upon the common acceptance of a definite motive and ideal in industry, and through the pursuit of that policy, as affecting the human agent in production, which a social responsibility to the community imposes.

VI

Efficiency in management by these general means is, in the first instance, dependent upon a structure of organization, based upon a detailed analysis of the work to be done and the faculties requisite for doing it, and built up on the principle of combining related activities in such a way as to allow for the economical practice, progressive development, and constant co-ordination of all such activities.

VII

Apart from Finance, which is primarily concerned in the provision and usage of Capital, and Administration which determines the field and ultimately controls and co-ordinates the activities of Management proper, the various activities of Management proper are divisible, on the above principle, into the following functions—

Firstly, those functions essential to the inception of manufacture—

DESIGN (Purchasing), or that group of activities which determines the final character of the product and specifies and provides the material for its manufacture ; and

EQUIPMENT, or that group of activities which provides and maintains the necessary means of production.

Secondly, the function dealing with the actual production, i.e. with all those activities whereby skill and effort are applied to the transformation of the material into the finished product. This function may broadly be described as MANUFACTURE.

Thirdly, those functions comprising the work necessary to facilitate the manufacture of the product—

TRANSPORT, or that group of activities which connects up the various units of production, stores or moves the material between the processes of manufacture, and provides the means of transportation for each function;

PLANNING, or that group of activities which determines the volume and progress of work;

COMPARISON, or that group of activities which analyses the work of each function and compares the records of its activities with the scientific standards set up for each function;

LABOUR, or that group of activities concerned in the application and maintenance of the human agent in production, and the promotion of co-operation between all engaged in production.

Fourthly, those functions comprising the work necessary for the distribution of the product—

SALES PLANNING, or that group of activities which determines, according to the data available, the policy and methods of distribution; and

SALES EXECUTION, or that group of activities which disposes of and actually distributes the product.

VIII

The use of the scientific method to ensure the most economical utilization of the impersonal factors—or, of the personal factors regarded purely as productive units—in industry, involves in particular—

Firstly, the development of research and accurate

measurement in each branch of activity which management undertakes or controls, followed by experiments upon or deductions from the data established by such research ;

Secondly, the preparation and use of precise definitions and statements of what actually constitutes each item of work in each function ;

Thirdly, the determination, after the analysis of the constituent parts of any activity and their synthetical reconstruction, of reference and working standards, both for manufacture and for management, representing, for the present, a justifiable and precise appraisement of desirable achievement ; and

Fourthly, the institution of the necessary supervision, authority, and machinery to ensure the application of, adherence to, and improvement upon such standards, the measurement of actual practice by such standards, and their utilization for planning the most economical mode of production and management.

IX

The application of that policy, which responsibility to the community imposes, involves certain practices as regards the human agent in production, whether by hand or by brain. These may be enumerated as follows—

Firstly, in the relation of such human agent to the community—(*a*) the recognition of and co-operation with such forms of association as may be founded for the further-ance of the ends of those engaged in industry, provided such ends are not held, by the community, to be deleterious to communal well-being ; and (*b*) the facilitation, within the necessary economic limits of the conduct of industry, of the exercise by the individual, in his own self-develop-ment, of his higher faculties for the better service of the community.

Secondly, in the relation of such human agent to his industrial work—the promotion of individual and corporate effectiveness of effort, by the stimulus of a compelling leadership and an equitable discipline, in turn developing a corporate spirit of loyalty and high endeavour ; by the provision of such training as will qualify the individual effectively to carry out his work, whilst at the same time furthering his general mental capacity ; by the provision for each individual of work as far as possible calling for the exercise of his best ability, and in any event suited to his type of mentality ; by the provision of conditions, both material and spiritual, conducive to the highest working efficiency ; by the provision of legitimate and equitable incentives to and opportunities for the exercise of interest, both in the particular task of the individual and the general policy and progress of the business ; and, by the cultivation of co-operation, as a working principle, among all concerned in the activities of production.

Thirdly, in the relation of such human agent to his life as an individual—(*a*) the provision of means whereby all concerned may share in the determination and maintenance of the conditions under which work is to be conducted ; (*b*) the provision of the means requisite to furnish a standard of living appropriate to a civilized community ; (*c*) an allowance of leisure adequate for the maintenance of bodily and mental health and the development of individual capacity both as workers and as citizens ; (*d*) the provision of security for efficient workers from the hardships incidental to involuntary unemployment due to trade conditions or other unfavourable circumstances ; (*e*) the provision of a share in industrial prosperity proportionate to the share taken in the promotion of such prosperity ; and (*f*) the conduct of the relations arising in the course of industrial activities in a strict spirit of equity.

X

By the elaboration of Standards, on the impersonal side of industry, through the analytical and synthetical methods of Science, and by the deductive determination of the principles and methods of management on the personal or human side, it is the aim of those practising management to evolve, by a sharing of knowledge and experience, irrespective of trade and business divisions, a SCIENCE OF INDUSTRIAL MANAGEMENT, distinct alike from the sciences it employs and the technique of any particular industry, for the several purposes of forming a code to govern the general conduct of industry, of raising the general level and providing a standard measure of managerial efficiency, of formulating the basis for further development and improvement, and of instituting a standard as a necessary qualification for the practice of the profession.

INDEX

PRINTED IN GREAT BRITAIN AT THE PITMAN PRESS, BATH
z—(1896)

HISTORY OF MANAGEMENT THOUGHT

An Arno Press Collection

Arnold, Horace Lucian. **The Complete Cost-Keeper.** 1901

Austin, Bertram and W. Francis Lloyd. **The Secret of High Wages.** 1926

Berriman, A. E., et al. **Industrial Administration.** 1920

Cadbury, Edward. **Experiments In Industrial Organization.** 1912

Carlson, Sune. **Executive Behaviour.** 1951

Carney, Edward M. et al. **The American Business Manual.** 1914

Casson, Herbert N. **Factory Efficiency.** 1917

Chandler, Alfred D., editor. **The Application of Modern Systematic Management.** 1979

Chandler, Alfred D., editor. **Management Thought in Great Britain.** 1979

Chandler, Alfred D., editor. **Managerial Innovation at General Motors.** 1979

Chandler, Alfred D., editor. **Pioneers in Modern Factory Management.** 1979

Chandler, Alfred D., editor. **Precursors of Modern Management.** 1979

Chandler, Alfred D., editor. **The Railroads.** 1979

Church, A. Hamilton. **The Proper Distribution Of Expense Burden.** 1908

Davis, Ralph Currier. **The Fundamentals Of Top Management.** 1951

Devinat, Paul. **Scientific Management In Europe.** 1927

Diemer, Hugo. **Factory Organization and Administration.** 1910 and 1935

Elbourne, Edward T. **Factory Administration and Accounts.** 1919

Elbourne, Edward T. **Fundamentals of Industrial Administration.** 1934

Emerson, Harrington. **Efficiency as a Basis for Operation and Wages.** 1909

Kirkman, Marshall M[onroe]. **Railway Revenue.** 1879

Kirkman, Marshall M[onroe]. **Railway Expenditures.** 1880

Laurence, Edward. **The Duty and Office of a Land Steward.** 1731

Lee, John. **Management.** 1921

Lee, John, editor. **Pitman's Dictionary of Industrial Administration.** 1928

McKinsey, James O. **Managerial Accounting.** 1924

Rowntree, B. Seebohm. **The Human Factor in Business.** 1921

Schell, Erwin Haskell. **The Technique of Executive Control.** 1924

Sheldon, Oliver. **The Philosophy of Management.** 1923

Tead, Ordway and Henry C. Metcalfe. **Personnel Administration.** 1926

Urwick, L[yndall]. **The Golden Book of Management.** 1956

Urwick, L[yndall]. **Management of Tomorrow.** 1933